SOUTHERN ALPS

ALISON BALLANCE

SOUTHERN ALPS

NATURE & HISTORY OF NEW ZEALAND'S MOUNTAIN WORLD

RANDOM HOUSE
NEW ZEALAND

Front jacket: Aoraki Mount Cook (3754 metres), the highest mountain in New Zealand, stands head and shoulders above all other peaks in the Southern Alps.

Back jacket and this page: Mountaineering party at the Hochstetter Bivouac (6977 feet, 2126 metres), May 1905. Chief guide Peter Graham stands with ice axe at right. Photograph by Thomas Pringle.

Cover illustration: Arthur's Pass was the first major crossing between the east and west coasts to be fully developed as a road, rather than a rough track. Wallace's Point in the Otira Gorge, on the western side of Arthur's Pass, in 1876; from the *Illustrated New Zealand Herald*.

End papers: Mount Cook series, alpine flora from Mount Cook and its surrounds. Mixed media 2006, by Jo Ogier.

Title page: Mount Aspiring is a glacial horn, created by a number of glaciers cutting back to a common point. The steep ridges of Mount Aspiring are classic arêtes, created between two cirque glaciers.

Page 8–9: South face of Aoraki Mount Cook viewed from Sealy Tarns, in late summer.

A catalogue record for this book is available from the National Library of New Zealand

A RANDOM HOUSE BOOK
published by
Random House New Zealand
18 Poland Road, Glenfield, Auckland, New Zealand
www.randomhouse.co.nz

First published 2007

© 2007 text Alison Ballance; images as shown on page 313

The moral rights of the author have been asserted

ISBN 978 1 86941 875 5

Design: Trevor Newman
Jacket photography: Arno Gasteiger
Cover illustration: Alexander Turnbull Library
Endpapers: Jo Ogier
Printed in China by Everbest Printing Co Ltd

Hochstetter Bivouac, 8,977ft.

For my parents, Queenie and Peter, with all my love

CONTENTS

FOREWORD

The land's heart

New Zealand's Southern Alps are the rugged, mountainous backbone of the South Island, but they are much more than just a physical spine. Beyond giving the land itself shape and form, they help to create the weather that is such a defining feature of the South Island, and their slopes have allowed unique and varied communities of plants and animals to evolve. Their impact goes far beyond their immediate footprint: they are the source of great glaciers and rivers which shape faraway coasts, and whose cast-offs have built the great glacial outwash plains in the east.

Although they define the character of the South Island, for such a large and striking geographical feature the Southern Alps themselves are surprisingly hard to define. Everybody knows what the Southern Alps are, but nowhere does it say exactly where they start and stop. National parks and the old provinces have boundaries marked on maps; it's possible to locate a single peak or even an entire mountain range, or to precisely follow the course of a river from its highest headwaters; but nowhere is the area of the Southern Alps precisely delineated. Mapmakers loosely thread the words Southern Alps Ka Tiritiri o te Moana along the axial mountain chain where it passes between Canterbury and Westland, and that's about as defined as it gets.

In researching this book, I found definitions varied by occupation. The broadest definition came from a glaciologist, who thought that it included all the high, glaciated mountains in the South Island, giving a broad sweep from southern Fiordland to the Seaward Kaikouras. Another scientist proffered the thought it was the mountains which belonged to the recognisable Main Divide, and that it probably didn't include Fiordland and northwest Nelson, as their rocks were quite different. The tightest definition came from a geologist, who suggested that perhaps the Southern Alps was the area of greatest uplift along the Alpine Fault, essentially the core of mountains between Haast Pass and Arthur's Pass.

Aerial view of the northwest ridge of Mount Aspiring, with the upper Volta Glacier in the background.

The universally agreed compromise is that the Alpine Fault neatly determines both the western and the southern boundaries of the mountains known as the Southern Alps. The Alpine Fault provides a clear boundary between the flatlands and the mountains on the West Coast, while the Hollyford River more or less marks both the departure of the Alpine Fault offshore and the separation between distinctively Fiordland rocks and different rocks to the north.

The eastern and northern boundaries are more difficult and diffuse. In the east the Southern Alps dip their toes in the southern lakes, and hold hands with much lower foothills that aren't really deserving of the title 'alps'. In the north, where the Alpine Fault splinters into many branches, the Nelson Lakes area seems a reasonable inclusion, while the Wairau River basin and the Kaikoura Ranges have their own independent identities.

The Alpine Fault is one of New Zealand's most striking geological features: from just north of Milford Sound it runs roughly parallel to the west coast and the Southern Alps for more than 600 kilometres as far as the Spenser Mountains at Nelson Lakes.

It is often called the Alpine Fault System, because it splinters into a number of branches at its northern end, including the Wairau, Awatere and Hope faults. By virtue of its size and strength it has spawned a number of other fault systems, such as the Main Divide faults, which have fractured at an angle to the Alpine Fault.

The Alpine Fault wasn't 'discovered' or recognised until 1941. On a field trip to the West Coast in 1941, geologists Harold Wellman and R.W. (Dick) Willett travelled on foot to trace the Alpine Fault south from Ross as far as Lake McKerrow. (North of Ross, it had already been identified as a large fault by geologist P.G. Morgan, who named it the Gregory Valley.) Following Wellman and Willett's publication in late 1941 of evidence for the presence of a single large fault, there was general acceptance of the Alpine Fault, and it appeared on a new geological map of New Zealand published in 1947.

In 1948, when Wellman made the startling suggestion that the rocks of northwest Nelson and Fiordland, now lying 480 kilometres apart, had once been joined, many of his colleagues initially rejected the idea. Wellman believed the Alpine Fault provided the mechanism by which the two areas had slid apart, but it wouldn't be until the late 1960s and early 1970s that the theory of plate tectonics became widely accepted, and provided the support that Wellman's idea required for general acceptance.

As Wellman had discovered, there are many places where one can see parts of the fault at ground level, and aerial photographs taken from aircraft since the late 1940s had given new perspectives on it, but its's seen from space that the ruler-straight length of the fault is truly breathtaking.

The name Southern Alps was bestowed by Captain James Cook. Cook was commander on board HMB *Endeavour* which, between 17 and 20 March, 1770, was sailing up the west coast of the South Island completing the first circumnavigation of New Zealand. Sea and wind conditions were rough and not to Cook's liking, and the ship sailed up the coast without attempting any landings. It's highly probable that the highest peaks of the alps were hidden by cloud, as they frequently are, as neither Cook nor ship's naturalist Joseph Banks mention seeing the striking peaks of what would later be called Mount Cook and Mount Tasman. As Cook hints in his diary entry, late March is also the time of year when the alps carry the least amount of snow, and the greatest amount of rock is exposed:

What are alps?

The name 'alps' goes back to the Latin of the Romans, possibly even earlier. The exact meaning of the word is unknown, but it has hints of *albus*, meaning white, or perhaps *altus* or high. Including the Japanese and Australian alps there are four mountain ranges in the world which have inherited the name alps.

Close behind these hills lies a ridge of mountains of prodigious height, which appear to consist of nothing but barren rocks, covered in many places with large patches of snow which appear to have been there since creation. No country upon earth can appear with a more rugged and barren aspect than this doth for as far as the eye can reach nothing is to be seen but the summits of these rocky mountains which seem to lay so near to one another as not to admit any Vallies between them.

But Cook did see enough to believe that '. . . there is great reason to believe that the same ridge of mountains extends nearly the whole length of the island'. On his map of New Zealand he drew a line of mountains up the western side of the South Island and labelled them the Southern Alps.

Cook's expedition may have failed to prove the existence of the fabled Great Southern Continent, but it could at least continue the tradition of naming places and features after northern hemisphere equivalents. Following Abel Tasman's earlier 'discovery', New Zealand had already been named Staten Land and then renamed after Zeeland, one of two maritime provinces in the Netherlands. Cook, in his turn, named the Southern Alps after the great European alps, which neither he nor the well-travelled Banks had ever seen, but which they would have known by reputation.

At the time of Cook's naming, the alps were already known to local Maori as Ka Tiritiri o te Moana, literally 'the frothing waters of the ocean', or perhaps 'a haziness or mirage above the ocean'. Voyaging Maori may have first seen the snowy peaks of the Southern Alps from the west; from a distance at sea they can appear as an unworldly apparition floating above the water, especially when they are entwined in cloud. For a people unused to snow and ice they may have seemed like enormous foam-capped waves. This original name has now been formally recognised, and the official name for the South Island's mountainous spine is Southern Alps/Ka Tiritiri o te Moana.

The first Maori and European inhabitants of this country kept their distance from the snow-covered mountains; there was no food to be found there, no grazing to be had. The alps were merely a barrier to be crossed to get to the other side; it wasn't until later that people began seeking ways up the mountains, rather than around them.

The desire to find routes between the east and west coasts for people and stock fuelled many of the early European forays in the 1850s and 1860s, following trans-alpine routes long established by Maori trading pounamu, or greenstone. The employment of surveyors to map the mountains was initially driven by no more than the need to provide reliable maps of the provinces so that their boundaries could be ascertained, and grazing claims reliably documented. The search for gold and coal prompted geologists and explorers to continue to fill in blanks on the maps, a job that was finally finished by amateur trampers and mountaineers well into the first half of the twentieth century.

Today there are three sealed road routes and a rail route across the Southern Alps. Journeys that once took weeks or even months on foot or horse now take just hours in a car, or mere minutes by plane or helicopter. All of the mountain peaks have been climbed, although it is still easy to find unclimbed routes.

Although we've mapped the mountains, walked and flown over them, and photographed every square centimetre of them from space, we have in no way tamed them. Their weather continues to be fierce and unpredictable, and they remain as dangerous to human visitors as ever. Apart from small villages at Arthur's Pass and Aoraki Mount Cook, they are for the most part as remote and wild as they have always been. But they've also become integral to us as a nation — our great national hero, Sir Edmund Hillary, cut his mountaineering teeth in the Southern Alps before conquering Mount Everest. Our mountains might not rank among the tallest in the world, but they are damned challenging, largely as a result of the weather; considering the small size of the country our mountains punch above their height. The Southern Alps are much more than the backbone of the country — these young mountains are the land's heart.

Being in the mountains challenges all one's senses. Mountains are big, dramatic and confronting, and although they can inspire us to greatness, they are equally capable of putting us firmly in our place. They can offer new perspectives on the world, and sometimes on ourselves. Such insights are as likely to come from meditative contemplation while enjoying the view as from overcoming physical and mental challenges while climbing a difficult mountain.

Being in the Southern Alps

Mountains inspire different things in different people; the peak that one person wants to climb drives another person to poetry, motivates another to take a photograph, and in someone else creates a desire to discover new knowledge. Others are content just knowing that the mountains exist, and are out there. This exploration of the unique mountain world of the Southern Alps begins on a perfect day in late spring. I'm not struggling up the final few feet of an adrenalin-raising climb to the summit of a high peak; rather, after a steep but straightforward walk from the river flats below, I am sitting on a rocky ridge below Mueller Hut in the Sealy Range, in Aoraki Mount Cook National Park, and admiring the panorama of snow-covered mountains. Looking across towards Aoraki Mount Cook I notice a snake of cloud fingering over from the West Coast, at bellybutton height on New Zealand's highest mountain. Otherwise there is not a cloud in the sky, and only an occasional breeze. Below me a helicopter flies self-

importantly across the broad grassy valley flats in front of Aoraki Mount Cook village, two kea call occasionally in the distance, and on the far side of the Mueller Glacier the line of glaciers hanging off the Main Divide below Mount Sefton settle, occasionally dumping a dramatic rumble of ice down an icefall. As I enjoy the view I begin to consider where I am, and what these mountains are.

The Southern Alps are a classic 'dividing range'; they have an extraordinarily well-defined Main Divide, which can be plotted as a single line along the alps, separating river catchments that flow east from those that flow west. Where I am sitting, on the eastern side of the Main Divide, everything flows east, and will eventually make its way to the Pacific Ocean, more than 120 kilometres away beyond the wide plains and rolling foothills. The summit of Mount Sefton lies directly on the Main Divide; the glaciers I can see are all eastward-bound. Out of sight on the western side, everything flows west, travelling

Right: The south ridge leading up to the summit of Aoraki Mount Cook.
Over page: Hanging glaciers and icefalls, on the east side of the Main Divide below Mount Sefton, viewed from Sealy Tarns.

a much shorter distance, just 20 or so kilometres, to the Tasman Sea.

As I look ahead to Aoraki Mount Cook rising solidly behind the rocky foreground of the Mount Cook Range it's easy to see that it lies just east of the Main Divide, yet I reflect on how long it took for the early explorers and surveyors to note this. It wasn't until 1875 that two geologists, S. Herbert Cox and Alex MacKay, made this discovery from the west. Although they weren't great mountaineers they had thought they might be able to be the first people to climb the fabled Aoraki Mount Cook. However, as soon as they actually laid eyes on the peak, which rises impressively above Gillespies Beach on the West Coast, they realised that it was beyond their ability. Nevertheless, they did manage to climb the Fox Range, and looking across from there realised for the first time that Aoraki Mount Cook is not, in fact, on the divide.

Things are often different than they appear at first glance. Everything around me seems so solid, so permanent, but as I watch ice noisily cascading down a rock funnel onto a huge fan of avalanche debris below a glacier perching atop a steep cliff, I reflect how the opposite is true. Although New Zealand as a whole is often referred to as 'ancient islands', these mountains are geological babies, little more than five million years old, and they are still actively growing, being pushed up by the meeting of two great tectonic plates. Their very presence creates the weather — intercepting wind and generating rain and snow — that constantly gnaws away at their peaks, battering them down, turning solid rock to sliding, unreliable scree. A network of faults tears the mountains, the land fretting and straining along these mobile joints. The faultlines stretch like unhealed wounds, large enough to stand on, and filled with shattered rock that is the visible sign of the enormous subterranean forces at work. The biggest fault of all — the Alpine Fault — lies to the west of me, a tectonic boundary separating these mountains on the Pacific Plate from the strip of lowlands that marks the eastern edge of the Australian Plate.

Alpine cousins

A comparison with the European alps gives different perspectives on the Southern Alps, and is both an acknowledgement of the universal features that New Zealand mountains share with other alpine environments, and also a recognition of their distinctness. Although different in many respects — age, rock type, flora and fauna, human history — the European and Southern alps are also recognisably similar. They share a topography of steep, snow-capped, rocky mountains, glaciers and U-shaped valleys that bear the distinctive imprint of earlier, larger glaciations, all of which combine to give them a feeling of familiarity.

The European alps curve for more than 800 kilometres from the Riviera on the Mediterranean coast into the northwest part of the Balkan Peninsula, spanning France, Italy, Switzerland, Germany, Austria and the Balkans. The Southern Alps are a simpler and smaller range of mountains, which stretch for about 500 kilometres in a straight line.

Both sets of alps were born from collision. The European alps are much older than the five-million-year-old Southern Alps and have a complicated geological history, which at its simplest involved the collision of the African Plate with the European Plate. There have been several periods of mountain building, one beginning 80–90 million years ago, with the main one starting 30 million years ago. The collision was strongest in the western alps, which as a result are narrower and taller than the eastern alps, which are up to 250 kilometres wide.

Both mountain ranges are continuing to rise, although the rate of uplift of just 1–2 millimetres a year for the European alps is less than a quarter of the rate of the rapidly rising Southern Alps; yet in both cases the amount of erosion balances the uplift, so they remain the same height. The European alps are in general much higher than the Southern Alps, with the very highest peaks reaching 4810 metres (Mont Blanc) compared with 3754 metres (Aoraki Mount Cook). In the European alps the permanent snowline lies between 2400 and 2900 metres above sea level. New Zealand's Southern Alps may be much lower than their European counterparts, but their permanent snowlines also reach much lower altitudes: 1600 metres in the west, where annual precipitation is high, rising to 2200 metres in drier areas to the east. New Zealand glaciers also reach much lower altitudes than European glaciers, coming as low as 300 metres above sea level on the West Coast, and 700 metres on the eastern side of the Main Divide.

Both sets of alps experience hot, dry winds on the sheltered side of the mountains: New Zealand has its nor'wester, and Europe has the föhn wind.

The highest mountains are concentrated in the Mount Cook region; this is the area of greatest uplift in an ongoing collision between the two mighty tectonic plates, and the mountains here are being pushed skywards at about ten millimetres a year. But the movement isn't all upwards — the same sideways wrenching and sliding that has moved northwest Nelson apart from Fiordland is continuing, and in the relatively near geological future, although not for many lifetimes, the familiar and comforting shape of the South Island will distort into something quite unrecognisable. It doesn't take many lifetimes for significant change to accumulate, however; since Abel Tasman glimpsed the Southern Alps in 1642 and presciently described New Zealand as this 'large land, uplifted high', the mountains are already higher, the west coast has shifted eight kilometres further northeast, and a mind-boggling 30 million cubic metres of continental crust has been lifted above sea level, while a similar quantity has washed down rivers and out to sea.

It's possible to find many mind-bending figures and concepts in these mountains. Consider rainfall. The average annual rainfall for New Zealand as a whole is comparatively high, for the most part lying between 600 and 1500 millimetres — which put another way is between 0.6 and 1.5 metres of rain a year. It's common to see a figure of 12 to 15 metres of average rainfall a year quoted as the highest rainfall for the mountains on the western side of the alps, which is an extraordinary amount by any standard. Here are my favourite extreme rainfall statistics: 473 millimetres, which is nearly half a metre of rain, fell in a single 12-hour period in January 1994 at Colliers Creek, which flows into the Hokitika River. For the calendar year 1998, MetService reports that 16.6 metres of rainfall was recorded on the Cropp River, a tributary of the Whitcombe River that also ultimately flows into the Hokitika River. But for the year between the end of October 1997 and the end of October 1998, the rainfall in the Cropp clocked in at a staggering 18.44 metres.

The Cropp River is not unique in the amount of rainfall it receives; it just happens to have automatic rain gauges installed and good rainfall records. The very high rainfall zone stretches the length of the alps, a ten kilometre-wide band that lies parallel to, and between five and 15 kilometres inland from, the Alpine Fault, to the west of the Main Divide.

The South Island's backbone of snow-covered alps is clearly marked in this true-colour image taken by NASA's Terra satellite on 23 October 2002.

Along the alps, which emerge more steeply from the sea than any other mountain range on earth, a graph of rainfall plotted up the western slopes is as steep as the mountainsides themselves. Each hundred metres you ascend, a further metre of rain falls per annum. Yet the clouds eventually begin to run out of water, and as soon as the Main Divide is crossed rainfall drops away just as precipitously. A short kea flight to the east of the Cropp River, in the eastern rainshadow of the alps, many parts of the Rakaia River catchment are lucky to receive much more than half a metre of rain a year. Thus rainfall in all its variety creates the three distinctive zones which characterise the alps: the wet west slopes, the snowy peaks and the dry eastern ranges.

Up to a quarter of the precipitation in New Zealand's mountains falls as snow, mostly during winter. This snow accumulates on the high slopes and basins of the mountains and nourishes great glaciers, which in the case of the Fox and Franz Josef glaciers race down steep valleys to just 300 metres above sea level. Glacier accumulation aside, most of the precipitation rushes down the mountain slopes as water; very little rain evaporates, the ground is always saturated and almost all the water pours into streams and rivers. Little wonder there are so many rivers on the wet West Coast, all carving short, straight channels directly from the mountains to the coast by the shortest route possible. High rainfall is very erosive, and this severe erosion is in large part the reason why the western slopes of the alps are extremely steep. Vast amounts of rock and rubble are washed off the mountains each year; this pours into the rivers, along with all the water and together they make their way out to sea in frequent floods. These fill rivers bank to bank and beyond with churning torrents of water that are capable of moving tonnes of debris. When you see a West Coast river in full flood, you begin to understand how easily 30 million cubic metres of continental crust has disappeared in the last 350 or so years. As described by geologist Dave Craw:

. . . the mountains are not just going vertically upwards they are also being forced horizontally towards the Alpine Fault by the same plate tectonic forces. This means that the river valleys near the Main Divide in the drier eastern ranges are being driven westwards, at the same time as the steep Westland rivers are cutting back into the divide ridges. The effect is very much like pushing a piece of timber into a circular saw.

Yet just as quickly as the rivers flood, so they subside. Once the rains stop it is as if someone flicked a switch. The rivers

Previous page: View from Sealy Tarns across snout and terminal lake of Mueller Glacier (foreground), terminal moraine and lake of Hooker Glacier (middle of shot), and Mount Cook Range leading to Mount Cook (obscured in cloud, top left).

Fools think that Knowledge can be got only from books and men, and call me a Fool for wasting my life in mountain Solitudes, but if in so doing I have found nothing new in Thought or worth giving to the World, I have at least gathered glimmerings of Truth as to how nature works.

Charlie Douglas 1891

Across the alps

A walk east to west across Copland Pass in the central Southern Alps is a geological journey to the centre of the earth. Here, the 40 kilometre-thick layer of rocks that lies beneath the surface of the Pacific Plate has been tilted up into a narrow cross-section that spans the western flanks of the alps. On the eastern side of the pass the surface layer of Torlesse greywacke is visible. Beyond the pass, on the descent to the West Coast, lies a narrow band of the first, shallowest layer of chlorite schist. That's quickly followed by a deeper layer of biotite schist and finally, in the zone of greatest uplift, the deepest layer of garnet schist, lying alongside the Alpine Fault. Step across the fault, and you've left the Pacific Plate behind and are standing on the Australian Plate.

retreat into their usual channels unless, as occasionally happens, they've switched course during the flood. But a river moving a few tens or hundreds of metres is just a minor misdemeanour considering that even a river as large and permanent-seeming as the Landsborough is a temporary phenomenon when viewed in terms of geological time.

The remote and dramatic Landsborough River has its beginnings not far south of my vantage point in the Sealy Range. Although technically on the western side of the Main Divide it takes a more circuitous route to the sea than many west coast rivers, heading southwest for 50 kilometres before it joins the Haast River and takes a sharp dogleg to the west. I discovered why the Landsborough River has this unusual configuration when I rafted it recently, discovering along the way that hitching a ride on one of the largest rivers in the area is a very pleasant way of traversing a largely inaccessible and rarely travelled section of the Southern Alps.

We began within sight of the striking meringue-capped ice dome of Mount Dechen, and were swept southwest on a steady grey surge of glacier-fed water that easily carried a raft-load of people along at more than 20 kilometres an hour. Where the river channelled through the deep-cut Upper Gates Gorge, which the rafting guides affectionately referred to as The Squeeze, we were entertained by a succession of turbulent rapids. Ahead of us as we approached the top end of the gorge, but partially obscured in wraith-like skeins of mist that delicately draped the beech forest-covered slopes, was a steep two kilometre-long ridge separating the Landsborough River from the Hunter River. It appeared unbreachable, but little more than two million years ago it didn't even exist, and the Landsborough didn't flow where we were about to go; instead, it went to the left of the ridge, joining the Hunter and flowing south all the way to Southland. Suddenly it all made sense: why the Landsborough trended to the south in a long, broad valley, parallel to the Main Divide like all the rivers east of the divide, rather than plunging at steep

right-angles away from the divide out to sea. Less than three million years ago this had been an east coast river, which had then been 'captured' in a stately dance that was motivated partly by hydrology and partly by geology.

This dance began when what was then a much smaller Haast River cut through a ridge, allowing it to 'capture' the Clarke River. The Haast continued to cut back into its neighbouring mountain range, eventually breaching it and allowing it to gather up the Landsborough River, which changed course and began to cut its way west through what became the exhilarating Upper Gates Gorge. Meanwhile, what would become the high ridge separating it from the Hunter River began to be pushed up, ensuring that the Landsborough could never change its mind and return to its previous dance partner.

The Landsborough and Haast rivers weren't alone in forming alliances with new rivers. They are just part of an ongoing cascade of events which has seen many rivers in the southern part of the alps reverse their direction of flow, break through mountain ridges and radically influence the topography. And that was before nature's earth-moving machines, the glaciers, got seriously involved about two million years ago.

A significant result of all of this has been that the Main Divide is continually stepping to the east; each time a river diverts to flow west the line of the divide must be reconfigured. Back on the Sealy Range ridge I look across at Aoraki Mount Cook and wonder how long it will be before it gets to straddle the Main Divide, and how long it will hold onto that honour before it, too, is chewed up by the circular saw of the west coast rivers. As to what will happen behind me in the Landsborough — well, I've read speculation that it wouldn't take much, just one glaciation lasting 10,000 years, for the Landsborough to 'capture' the North Huxley. The eventual consequence of that might be the Main Divide moving as far east as the eastern rim of the Mackenzie Basin, which is a staggering thought.

The Haast River in full flood thunders through the Gates of Haast after an overnight storm.

After time-travelling forward to imagine a future in which all the familiar peaks and valleys and rivers have either disappeared or been monumentally rearranged, another rumble of falling ice reminds me that the past is almost as inconceivable. All around are glaciers: small, clean, white alpine and cirque glaciers clinging tenaciously to near-vertical rock faces, and below me the final few hundred metres of enormous valley glaciers such as the Hooker and the Mueller, and largest of all, the Tasman, out of sight from this vantage point. They are grimy, their surfaces mostly hidden by the loads of rock and grit they carry on the final part of their journey. Their snouts have melted into uninviting silty lakes that are the beasts which will ultimately consume the glaciers. These mighty but dwindling ice rivers are slowly sinking between growing moraine walls, which stand as testament to where the glaciers reached a hundred years earlier. But if the moraine walls give a scale on which to imagine that sight, I have to look further afield to glimpse where the glaciers have been over millions of years.

There are signs of glaciers past written all across the landscape. Like the rivers, they have been involved in their own dance over the last two million years. Over the last quarter of a million years alone, at least five great synchronised advances and retreats of ice have swept back and forth, from the mountains out to the plains and back. Their moves are choreographed by temperature; when it drops between 4°C and 6°C below today's average, a greater proportion of precipitation falls as snow, and the glaciers come rushing forth from their mountain lairs. As temperatures rise during the interglacial periods they melt and slink back to their cooler hideouts. Glaciologists and geologists have pieced together the evidence for the last five glaciations from what they left behind, but as each subsequent glacial advance removes previous evidence, what happened in the preceding 1.75 million years remains a wonderful mystery.

As I spread out a map and calculate that my eyrie on the ridge is about 1500 metres above sea level, and that I have climbed about 670 or so metres on my day-trip from the base of the mountain, I suddenly realise that where I am sitting would have been buried under ice 18,000 years ago, at the height of the last glaciation. All the valleys I can see would have been filled with ice to this altitude, and the Hooker, Mueller, Murchison and Tasman would have coalesced into a single mighty glacier. This uber-glacier stretched for 85 kilometres, finishing beyond the southern end of the present-day Lake Pukaki. It was up to 13 kilometres wide, and was at least 1000 metres deep, possibly up to 1500 metres. This figure perplexes me until I remember that what we perceive to be the floor of the Tasman Valley today is not bedrock, but a thick layer of gravels left behind after the glaciers receded. The great glaciers ground the true floor of the valley down to sea level or below, which shows what efficient excavators they are.

At the height of the Otira glaciation, as the last big glaciation was known, the Tasman Glacier was one in a series of large piedmont glaciers that joined to form an enormous ice sheet which covered the Southern Alps and Fiordland. All of the big southern lakes, from Tekapo in the north to Wakatipu in the south, were gripped by an enormous sheet of ice more than 700 kilometres long and 100 kilometres wide. The whole world was gripped in the same ice age, and so much water was locked up in ice that world sea levels were about 130 metres lower than they are today. The New Zealand coastline was tens of kilometres further out than it is today (it would have been possible to walk between the North and South islands), and on the west coast the great glaciers extended well beyond today's coastline. The southernmost of these glaciers were carving what are today Fiordland's enormous deep-sided fiords.

Like all good dance moves, the recognisable glaciations have been given names, and in some cases sub-names; a smaller glaciation about 8–10,000 years ago is known as Birch Hill, while the Otira glaciation which lasted the preceding 60,000 years is divided into Tekapo, Mount John

Ice avalanche falling from the Douglas névé onto the Douglas Glacier, Westland.

and Balmoral 2. The Waimea glaciation lasted between 128–186,000 years ago, while the earliest known glaciation was the Waimaungu, 246–303,000 years ago. Before that everything is hazy.

There is plenty of evidence of this glaciation. The strikingly eroded pinnacles of the clay cliffs near Omarama are remnants of the oldest known glacial deposits, which have since been pushed up by the nearby Ostler Fault. Like the other glacial lakes, Lake Pukaki was formed when the terminus of the glacier melted rapidly after the last glaciation. There are steps and terraces carved across the sides of valleys, and piles of moraine, all of which I drove past on my way to Aoraki Mount Cook village. Glaciers have smoothed the valleys into distinctive U shapes, so different from the V-shaped valleys that rivers create; on the high valley sides there are the cirques or hanging basins created by smaller glaciers. And of course the wide valley floor across which the Tasman River weaves a complicated braid is also a pile of glacial rubble.

A slight wind teases the edges of the map, and the spill of cloud from the west coast is becoming thicker, faster, and more urgent. The peaks remain clear, and I wonder how many people stood on their summits this morning, timing their climbs in this window of perfect weather. Many people have made the journey to Aoraki Mount Cook village today, because mountains are places of pilgrimage. People come for many different reasons: some come to climb, some come to walk in the great outdoors, while others come just to admire the scenery, to say they've been there. Many people come here and never see the mountains at all, but today is a day which will disappoint no one.

A man appears above me, his walking poles waving like demented insect antennae as he clambers down the rocky ridge. He sits beside me to rest his knees and enjoy the view, and he is exuberant, having achieved a long-held personal ambition: to get to Mueller Hut. After a few minutes he says he's off, knowing his sore knees will make his descent a slow, painful one. Others today may have had more ambitious plans, but this man has achieved what he set out to do in the mountains, and because of that he's happy, which in the end is what matters most.

View looking west across the Main Divide, and the West Coast valleys filled with cloud.

Tame mountains

The European alps have a well-worn patina of human history, and small villages dot the landscape. Climb a mountain in Europe and the houses crawl up the mountainside with you, as high it seems as the summer snowline. Turn a corner on a long-trodden path and you are as likely to meet another person, as you are a stone building, perhaps shuttered and closed for now but nonetheless used every summer when sheep and cows are taken to the high alpine meadows for grazing, and the metallic sound of bells is part of the mountain soundscape.

Europeans were living in the mountains and threading a vast network of trails from valley to valley, and from farmhouse to alpine pasture, several thousand or more years before Polynesian explorers first set foot in Aotearoa New Zealand. Even so, the high mountains remained 'landscapes of fear' to most lowland people. When the Italian Francesco Petrarca wrote of his experience climbing Mount Ventoux in Provence in 1336, he was very much a man ahead of his time. It would be another 300 years before the mountains were discovered for recreation, by which time people had begun writing about them and portraying them in paintings and prints. Published in 1732, Swiss physician and botanist Albrecht von Haller's famous — and lengthy — poem 'The Alps' celebrated the idyllic lifestyle of the mountain dwellers and introduced the idea of mountain beauty to the literary world, and by the mid-nineteenth century painters such as John Rudkin were encouraging an appreciation of mountain glory.

In 1760 the Swiss aristocrat and scientist Horace-Bénédict de Saussure visited Chamonix in France, and offered a reward to the first person to reach the summit of Mont Blanc. The reward was claimed in 1786, an occasion which is generally considered to be the birth of modern mountaineering. By 1850, when European settlement was well underway in New Zealand, the English seriously discovered mountaineering, achieving many first ascents in the playground of Europe's peaks, leading to the formation of the English Alpine Club in 1857.

Around the same time, the development of railways and the building of cable cars and funicular railways to the summits of many peaks opened up the European alps for the growth of mass tourism. Mountains have become big business. More than 120 million tourists a year are now estimated to visit the European alps. Mont Blanc has a cable car to within 1000 metres of its summit, and is climbed by more than 20,000 people a year. By comparison, New Zealand as a whole is visited by nearly two and a half million tourists a year, and the majority of these include Aoraki Mount Cook, the West Coast glaciers or a southern skifield in their visit.

Hugging the ground to avoid the extremes of mountain weather, miniature plants and lichens cover a high apline ridge in a textured tapestry.

The snow on the slope below me is soft and slushy, melting quickly in the warm sun. On the lower flanks of the valley, large sprays of satin-white Mount Cook buttercup flowers poke up exuberantly among the hebes and other bushes, but up here newly uncovered snow tussocks, speargrasses and mountain daisies are still flattened from lying beneath snow for more than six months.

We think of the alpine zone as a place of extreme cold, but for a plant these are mild mountains compared to many of the world's continental mountain ranges. Close proximity to the sea ensures that temperatures never drop very low. Although New Zealand lies in the temperate mid-latitudes, botanically and ecologically the Southern Alps are more similar to tropical alpine environments such as Ecuador's Andes than they are to the European alps, which lie at equivalent latitudes in the northern hemisphere but are subject to the greater extremes of a continental climate.

Snow tussocks are one of the defining features of the New Zealand alpine environment, and although they seem limp and lifeless after their snowy internment they will soon reclaim their place as the king of plants here, a role that is theirs by virtue of the moderate maritime climate. The fact that snow tussocks and so many other New Zealand alpine plants keep their leaves year-round is a distinctive feature of both the alpine zone and the forests; on colder continents many plants must resort to more extreme tactics, growing leaves only during summer and shedding them during the long icy winter.

During the previous summer the *Chionochloa* snow tussocks had turned on an impressive spectacle across the Southern Alps: high temperatures the summer before had induced the many species of snow tussock into one of their periodic mass flowerings, and whole mountainsides were covered in tall, graceful flower-heads rippling in the wind like tawny alpine wheatfields. This year the snow tussocks were resting, and recovering from their prodigious effort. I wonder how many overseas visitors noted and appreciated the subtle wonder of that natural flowering phenomenon, and decide that instead most of them would have been more bewitched by the colourful banks of introduced lupins that line the roads leading to the mountains. Plants move in quickly when opportunity presents; first planted in the 1930s, lupins are now so widespread in the Mackenzie Basin as to be ubiquitous. Native plants can be fast movers, too — it's staggering to think that less than 10,000 years ago there were no plants in this ice-filled valley, but when the glaciers retreated plants were hot on their heels.

The striking Mount Cook buttercup (*Ranunculus lyalli*) has leaves that can be as large as dinner plates, and flower spikes that can reach nearly a metre tall. Arthur's Pass National Park.

The highest plants — and animals

The record for the highest altitude plant in New Zealand is awarded to the lichen *Rhizocarpon geographicum*, which lives on the summit rocks of Aoraki Mount Cook. Lichens do well at altitude because they have in-built filters that minimise damage from the high levels of ultraviolet radiation there, and they can grow on bare, inhospitable rock by fixing the carbon and nitrogen they need for growth from the atmosphere.

For higher or vascular plants the record goes jointly to two hardy little shrubs, *Parahebe birleyi* and *Hebe haastii*. *Parahebe birleyi* is a high-altitude specialist which has been recorded as high as 2930 metres. Its altitudinal range begins where most plants stop, at 2000 metres. In appearance there is nothing to suggest *Parahebe birleyi*'s remarkable ability to live at altitude; it is a straggling white-flowered 'sub-shrub', with dark, almost fleshy leaves, which may reach ten centimetres in height and form a loose plant about 20 centimetres across, that grows either in loose debris or tucked in rock clefts in stable boulder fields.

Hebe haastii has leaves which sit tightly against its twisting branches in four distinctive rows in a protective braid, and it has small white flowers on its branch tips.

Reaching to just 100 metres below these two plants, at an altitude of 2830 metres, the large yellow flowers of *Ranunculus grahamii* poke out of clefts and ledges as early as November, when winter snows have barely begun to melt. This striking plant grows only as low as 2400 metres, so in some ways it is even more of a high-altitude specialist than the *Parahebe*.

The highest resident animals appear to be the larvae of a recently dis-covered flightless moth in the genus *Dichromodes*. They live by browsing lichens from rock surfaces on the summits of peaks such as Malte Brun, more than 3000 metres above sea level.

The jewel gecko (*Naultinus gemmeus*), seen here amongst *Corokia* berries, often feeds on the fruit of alpine plants such as the snow totara, and can survive up to altitudes of 1600 metres.

It's hard to make out natural vegetation patterns in the Tasman Valley and on the surrounding mountains, as frequent burn-offs by early European settlers to encourage grass growth, and occasional recent accidental conflagrations, have destroyed much of the original plant cover. Irish climber William Spotswood Green wrote about an early fire in his book describing the first unsuccessful attempt to climb Aoraki Mount Cook in 1882:

All day long the shepherds on the left bank of the Tasman had been mustering the sheep on the range of hills — marked on the map as the Liebig Range. To carry out this manoeuvre the shepherds mount the highest slopes, and then by shouting, setting fire to the grass, and encouraging their dogs to bark, drive the sheep downwards where they are easily collected into inclosures [sic] on the flat. The fires still burnt brightly on the mountain sides, circling the rugged peaks with a cordon of ruddy light, *and forming the most wonderful contrast to the dark blue gloom which shrouded the valley.*

A small patch of silver beech forest still grows across the hillside behind the village, but that only survived the general pyromania at the special request of then Governor George Bowen, who was one of the first visitors to the valley in 1873. He asked the runholder of Birch Hill Station to preserve the forest remnant; in his honour it's been known since as Governor's Bush.

Elsewhere in the Southern Alps the mountains are marked in clear vertical bands as plants respond to cooler temperatures at greater heights, a situation I've always thought of as the mountains wearing the appropriate clothes. Their lower slopes are dressed in a broad skirt of rainforest, which stops suddenly at the clearly defined treeline. Above the dark green of the forest skirt, the mountain slopes wear a golden top of low-growing alpine vegetation which

View from Green, Boss and Kaufmann's base camp, looking across the Tasman Glacier to fires lit by the Birch Hill Station shepherds to drive sheep down from the high slopes of the Liebig Range. Painting by William Spotswood Green, 1882.

often, at a distance, seems to have the texture and colour of a rich, tawny velvet. In places, between the green skirt and the tussock top, there is a decorative belt of subalpine scrub. Above the zone of velvet alpine plants rise the bare rocky shoulders of the mountain, often topped with a hat of permanent ice and snow, and draped each winter in a white snowy shawl.

Around much of the Southern Alps the forest skirt is southern beech, comprising various combinations of four species of *Nothofagus*. But much of the Tasman Sea side of the Main Divide is home a very different kind of forest. For 150 kilometres down the west coast, spreading more than a degree of latitude from just below Greymouth to as far south as the Paringa River, the rich, wet rainforest is formed from hardwood trees such as kamahi and rata, and podocarps such as rimu and kahikatea. There has been much speculation about the absence of beech trees from this so-called 'Westland gap', which is also much poorer in insects and land snails than forests to the north and south. Is it a result of glaciations, perhaps, or is it a consequence of mountain building? Whatever the cause, the lush hardwood-podocarp forests give the western side of the Southern Alps a very different feel to the eastern. The contrast is greatest in the rainshadow area east of the Main Divide, where mountain beech and hard beech are the mainstays of dry, open forests with very little undergrowth.

The beech forest floor and even the lower trunks of the dominant silver beech trees are swaddled in a thick layer of mosses and ferns. Haast Pass.

The origins of alpine plants and animals

The origins of New Zealand's rich alpine biota is an intriguing and ongoing biological debate. More than 600 species of vascular plants occur in the alpine zone, and 93 percent of this alpine flora is described as endemic, meaning it's found nowhere else, yet the alpine zone here didn't exist until the mountains became high enough to exceed the limits of where trees could grow. It's significant that it is only plant species that are endemic; most of the genera and families are found elsewhere, either in New Zealand or overseas. Only one strictly high-alpine plant, a cushion plant called *Hectorella*, is endemic at a family level, which botanists recognise as meaning that *Hectorella* has probably been isolated in New Zealand for a very long time. Geologically speaking, the mountains are so young and New Zealand so isolated from other land masses that it's hard to conceive where such a great diversity of specialised plants and animals could have come from.

There is no single tidy answer, and various theories have been proposed to explain where our alpine plants have come from: that they are descended from New Zealand lowland plants that evolved to live in the mountains; that they are ancient mountain species which managed to survive in New Zealand for tens of millions of years when it was a warmer, lower-lying country; that they are alpine plants that dispersed here more recently from the northern hemisphere, using southeast Asian, New Guinean and Australian mountain tops as stepping stones; or perhaps they came from Antarctica, when it was free of ice and closer to New Zealand and Australia.

Recent molecular research has begun to show that the truth may be a combination of these theories. Some of our plant groups, such as *Myosotis*, a genus of forget-me-nots, the *Hebe* group, and *Ranunculus* buttercups, do indeed seem to hail from the northern hemisphere. But rather than being ancestors along the stepping-stone route, their relatives in New Guinea and Australia seem to be descendants of the New Zealand plants, which have somehow managed to travel against the prevailing wind. In the same way, some of our alpine plants such as the first-flowering *Psychrophila* and pretty *Ourisias* dispersed here from South America, possibly via Antarctica. Antarctica itself may have been the ancestral home of the unique endemic *Hectorella*. There is also evidence that some members of lowland groups of plants have recently evolved to live in alpine habitats, especially those that are already adapted to living in dry, harsh environments.

Regardless of where it came from, it is clear that New Zealand's alpine flora has evolved rapidly in the last few million years, coinciding with the period of mountain building and also with great climatic change during the glaciations. Often one species has radiated into many; for example, most of the

nearly 40 species of *Aciphylla*, or speargrass, are alpine species. One of the results of such rapid, and ongoing, evolution of new species is that boundaries between many species are a little blurred, and there are many examples of hybrids created when two closely related species interbreed. There are even a few examples of hybrids formed between two plants classified in different genera, such as *Phyllachne* and *Forstera*; internationally inter-specific hybrids are rare, while inter-generic hybrids are considered impossible!

The story is a little more clear-cut for animals; it seems that groups such as the geckos, weta, cicadas and grasshoppers were already well established in New Zealand, then, like the plants, they evolved rapidly over the last five million years to take advantage of opportunities in the new mountains, and to become cold-adapted alpine specialists.

Mountain Daisy (*Celmisia semicordata*)

This immense variety of landscapes and environ-ments in close proximity to each other is one of the charms of New Zealand in general, and the Southern Alps in particular. Capricious weather, which is largely responsible for the variety, adds to the kaleidoscope of experience, ensuring that day by day, and sometimes even hour by hour, the world around us is changing. As I've been sitting on the Sealy Range ridge the wind has begun to pick up, lifting flattened tussock stems and playfully threatening my cap. The cloud oozing over the ridge from the West Coast alternately pulses forward and shrinks back like white-capped waves at the beach. Out of nowhere a single cloud has appeared high above Aoraki Mount Cook, a fat, unexpected cottonwool puffball that hangs like a blimp.

Suddenly, on an updraft forced up the side of the ridge by the rising wind, a kea appears, wings stretched in taut concentration. Buffeted and barely in control it slips sideways to land, slightly clumsily, on a rock a few metres in front of me, a mountain parrot posing in front of Aoraki Mount Cook. A second bird whistles above me, orange underwings vivid against the immeasurably blue sky, flexing its wings as with feet outstretched it comes in to land on another nearby rock. A sharp call behind me announces a third bird that has landed unseen.

We watch each other with shared curiosity, and as I sit in still quietness they begin to sidle closer in big awkward hops with turned-in toes and tilted heads, keeping a close eye on me to gauge my response. One bird is an adult female, her bill, nostrils and eye-rings dark with age, her upper bill smaller than that of a male kea but a vicious scimitar nonetheless. The second bird is perhaps a year or a year and a half old, still retaining some yellow around the base of its bill and eyes, but clearly older and more experienced than the third bird, which is a youngster new out of the nest and only recently fledged. The young bird has bright yellow eye rings, and very yellow nostrils

New Zealand's mountain parrot, the kea (*Nestor notabilis*), takes advantage of a turbulent updraft to effortlessly ride the breeze high in the Southern Alps.

and base to its bill. Its feathers are softer and fluffier than the smooth glossy feathers of the bird I suspect is its mother. I wonder if the adolescent bird is her chick from last year, and wonder also where the female's mate might be.

The female chooses a sheltered spot under a small rock overhang, less than a metre from where I sit, while the adolescent hops clumsily on top of a small bush. Facing away from me, it begins to preen, spreading one wing at a time across the leaves and turning its head to smooth each feather into place with its bill. I talk quietly to them and the female begins to respond with a gentle chawing that is quite unlike the raucous *kea* these birds make in flight. The youngster gathers courage and approaches slowly. Casually it hops to my backpack and leans forward to investigate, but the female rushes forward as if to scold its boldness, and it flaps off a way. The adolescent moves to where the female had sat, and the female trades places for a while before assertively hustling the younger bird away and reclaiming the rock shelter.

The youngster sidles in closer and, facing me, begins to slide its lower bill back and forth inside the longer top one, pushing its tongue around and uttering an unusual chatter, like a human toddler trying to speak. Staring at me intently and keeping up a constant stream of noise it raises one leg and clenches its foot in an odd salute. It looks both absurd and endearing. It's as if they find my calmness and quiet talk reassuring, and feel able to confide in me. Kea have a likeable intelligence and a curiosity that is very engaging. But I know from long experience not to trust their beguiling air of innocence: if I was to move away they would be down like a flash to tug and pull at everything on my pack, looking for something loose to play with.

Two walkers arrive on the ridge for a cursory look at the view, and the kea depart quickly. Within a few seconds they could be anywhere: checking out people snacking at Mueller Hut or eyeing people's lunches and tents in the campground below. Kea congregate in this valley, attracted by the handouts and entertained by the paraphernalia of human existence. They are a very familiar sight, but I wonder how much many visitors know of them and the parallel private lives that they lead away from the village.

All around me, plants and animals are leading astonishing secret lives, interconnected in complex ways that we are only just beginning to fathom. Even the big inanimate objects around me have their own life stories, all of which run over very different time scales. The tiny hoverflies I saw crowding the bright yellow centres of the Mount Cook buttercup flowers on my way up the mountain probably live as adults for just a few weeks, but the rocks which form the mountain beneath them have spent hundreds of millions of years getting to this point in their existence.

And I realise this is how I want to explore the nature of this mountain world: to climb inside the life stories of the Southern Alps; to track the journey of a single grain of sand, to follow the path of a snowflake; to unravel the complexity of an alpine community from the perspective of a single snow tussock; to be part of the birth and death of a southern beech tree; to soar above the mountains with the kea. I want to weave together a kind of literary walk through place and time, the written equivalent of 'being' in the mountains.

Mountaineer and prolific writer John Pascoe once wrote: 'My concept of New Zealand mountains is a whole one . . . Thus my examination is indeed a wide one.' These stories of the Southern Alps will also be wide ranging, encompassing the mountains from head to toe, shedding light on ecological patterns and processes by focusing on the intimacy of detail, and offering a new way of seeing them.

The great mountain, or Mount Cook, buttercup flowers in late spring and early summer, and relies on small flying insects such as hoverflies for pollination.

Geologically the Southern Alps are young — about five million years old — but they are made from old rocks. To understand the history of these rocks, and to discover how they came to be part of some of the youngest and fastest growing mountains on earth, we must step back in time.

A land uplifted high

This is the story of the Southern Alps, told through the journey of a single grain of sand. This grain of sand has already been bound in a granite rock for perhaps a hundred million years when it reaches the summit of a long-ago mountain. It is as if the grain of sand is the rock of Sisyphus, doomed to get to the top of a mountain, only to roll down and have to get to the top again. This isn't the first mountain the grain of sand has ascended, nor will it be the last. The mountain is on the edge of an enormous landmass, the great southern continent of Gondwana; perhaps what European explorers in the 1600s and 1700s had in mind when they sailed south looking for Terra Australis Incognita. But they were 55 million years too late — because 55 million years ago is when Gondwana finally tore completely apart. When the explorers went looking it existed only in fragments. However, 300 million years ago, when this story begins, there was indeed a great southern continent, which

together with its giant northern counterpart Laurasia comprised most of the world's dry land.

Back then, from space, Earth would have looked nothing like it does today — the land was arranged differently, and was in different places. Nonetheless, all the ingredients were there, and would eventually be recombined into the geography we recognise today. Between then and now, an enormous geological conveyor belt has been in action, creating land and pushing it up as mountains, then, knocking them down and washing them away before beginning again to build new land and uplift new mountains. We might not be aware of it, but we live in an ever-changing world. The ground that feels so solid under our feet is moving all the time, albeit extremely slowly. Our present familiar Earth is just a snapshot in geological time — right now is the only time it will only ever look exactly like this.

The grain of sand is about to discover the truth of this

The Southern Alps are part of an enormous geological conveyor belt which has been at work for hundreds of millions of years, constantly recycling sand and mud from the ocean floor into mountains and then back to sand and mud.

for itself. Its coarse granite boulder doesn't last long on the top of its mountain, just a few thousand years. It's shoved from below by more rock being pushed upwards, helped on its way by a big storm, and with the inevitable aid of gravity falls down the mountain, eventually ending up in a river. It arrives in an enormous debris fan, settled along the edge of a river, and remains stable for so long that lichens, mosses and ferns establish on it.

This would have been a strangely unfamiliar world to us, as many of the plants and animals we take for granted today had not yet evolved; back then there were no birds, no mammals and no flowering plants, although there were tree ferns, insects and early reptiles. Then one day it begins to rain and rain, and the high slopes above the fan begin to collapse into the valley. Rock, mud and water begin to surge and pour out from the top of the fan in a thick slurry that washes over the lower fan, digging a deep channel and scouring enormous quantities of debris into the river. In the midst of this debris flow is the boulder containing the sand grain.

Over the next few hundred years the boulder spends long periods of time at the bottom of the river. At other times it is tossed ashore and marooned on boulder banks, to be moved downstream by the occasional torrential flood which fills the canyon from bank to bank and moves everything in its path, including the very largest boulders. As it's jostled and rolled, bumped and rubbed on its journey down the long, winding river, the boulder becomes smaller as grains of sand wear off and begin their own separate journeys.

So, in fits and starts, the boulder makes its way to the sea, where what remains is worked in the washing machine of waves and tides until it dissolves completely, and the grain of sand is liberated. The grain becomes part of a great outwash of river sand that slowly builds up on the shallow continental shelf skirting the landmass.

Rivers remove enormous amounts of water and rock from the Southern Alps each year, and on the western side of the Main Divide they tend to be short and steep, and run directly out to sea. Fish River, Haast Pass.

Further out, in much deeper water past the continental shelf, a thin layer of very fine mud is slowly accumulating on the sea floor, in water so deep it's barely disturbed by any movement. (Mud is quite different from sand, with its own character and behaviour; officially, mud is a fine rock particle less than 0.06 of a millimetre across, while sand is a coarser rock particle, larger than 0.06 of a millimetre, but less than two millimetres across, and clearly visible to the human eye.)

The sand on the edge of the continental shelf builds up until, like a wind-blown sand dune on dry land, it becomes steep and unstable and begins to slide down a canyon leading to the deep sea floor beyond. The sand grain is caught in an underwater avalanche which pours with increasing speed down the steep canyon side, mixing with sea water to create a churning mass called a turbidity current. Like a river in flood or a snow avalanche, the turbidity current tears at mud on the sides and bottom of the canyon and gathers it into the flow. At last the avalanche reaches the deep ocean floor and slows, spreading out a blanket of sand across the thin sheet of mud. The two layers of sediments settle and compact, and very slowly more fine mud begins to drift down on top of the sand. More sand accumulates on the continental shelf until eventually another turbidity current is sparked, rapidly throwing a new thick sand blanket across everything.

For two hundred million years alternating strata of sand and mud build up like layers in a liquorice allsort. Pressed by the weight of sediment and water above, the water is squeezed out of them, and they become mudstone and sandstone, a group of sedimentary rocks which geologists now recognise as Torlesse rocks. The sand grain is now firmly embedded in the matrix of a new rock at the bottom of the sea. This rock will ultimately become one of the building blocks of the Southern Alps, but before then it will be subjected to more dramatic changes.

Geologists believe this granite mountain and river were on the eastern seaboard of Gondwana, in the area that would eventually become northeastern Australia. Further south, in what would later be Antarctica, a thousand kilometre-long chain of volcanoes was erupting ash which washed into the sea along with volcanic rocks and sediment, forming a pile of sedimentary rocks that would become known as the Arc rocks, making up much of the rocks of Southland. Enormous quantities of sedimentary rocks accumulated, but they remained merely a surface feature; it was what was happening to the crust of the planet itself that would define the future of the new rocks.

The crust of the earth is a tightly fitting jigsaw of rigid plates, riding like ships on semi-molten magma in the earth's mantle, and carrying the continents like passengers. During the mid-twentieth century geologists came to accept that the plates are in constant motion, sliding past, colliding with, and being sucked under or over each other, inexorably rearranging the earth's surface. The Torlesse sediments containing the grain of sand have fallen onto a plate that 250 million years ago began being pushed away from a distant, expanding mid-ocean ridge, where magma is erupting onto the sea floor. As if on a giant conveyor belt the sediments are moved towards a collision zone where the plate on which they are travelling rams into the plate carrying the Gondwana continent. The point of collision becomes a subduction zone, a deep ocean trench where the heavier ocean crust is forced beneath the lighter continental crust. But the sediments sitting on top of each plate like icing on a cake are too buoyant to follow, and are scraped off to the sides. For 50 million years a great crumpled mass of sediments piles up as more and more sediment continues to arrive on the conveyor belt.

All the time the grain of sand is buried at sea great evolutionary events are taking place on land. Tuatara evolve, followed by dinosaurs, crocodiles and soon mammals, although it's still too soon for birds and flowering plants.

Heat, cold and water are powerful forces which have the power to shatter rock and bring down mountains.

It is a time of tumult for the grain of sand as the tidy layers of mudstone and sandstone are squeezed and crushed as they're scraped off at the subduction zone. In places the sedimentary layers are mixed, forming a hard, dirty-grey rock known as greywacke, with sand grains embedded in a matrix of silt and mud; this is the fate of the grain of sand. In other places the rocks hold onto their distinct layers, which are folded and tilted into convoluted curves. Fractures between the layers fill with new minerals such as quartz, which give the rock distinctive white veins. Eventually the rocks become tens of kilometres thick, and as well as buckling the earth's crust downwards, they also rumple up above sea level, creating new land. As the compression and uplift continues the grain of sand is pushed up to become part of a new mountain range, during a period of mountain building known as the first Rangitata Orogeny.

Some of the Torlesse greywacke buried deeply at the bottom of the sedimentary rock stack that has become the mountains of the first Rangitata Orogeny is pushed into the deep region of the Earth's crust. Between 200 to 160 million years ago intense heat, reaching at least 300°C, and pressure from being buried at least ten kilometres beneath the earth's surface metamorphoses, or changes, the original sedimentary rock into a new type of metamorphic rock known as schist. The original sand grains recrystallise completely, while the pale-coloured minerals quartz and feldspar, and darker coloured biotite, develop into thin layers, giving the resulting schist its characteristic finely striped appearance.

Between 200 and 160 million years ago the ocean floor conveyor belt slows, and stops. Then it begins again, pulling in more Torlesse sediments and piling them up alongside the original mountains during a new phase of mountain building, the second Rangitata Orogeny. For 150 million years collision and accumulation have been adding to the edge of Gondwana the rocks of what will later become New Zealand; 105 million years ago the conveyor belt finally grinds to a complete halt. By now ancestral New Zealand is a large mountainous area, and since the period of the original Rangitata Orogeny the sand grain has remained on the high slopes of a grey, rocky peak. But mountain building has come to an end, and now a period of mountain destruction begins, as water and wind start to erode the mountains away; this is a much warmer time, and ice is not yet involved in shaping the land. Great quantities of Torlesse sediments are washed out to sea, building a wide continental shelf out to the east. The mountains disappear, and the grain of sand now becomes part of a low hill in the midst of a wide fertile plain, covered in lush, swampy vegetation which is destined to form the South Island's enormous coal deposits.

Old Gondwana rocks

Not all of New Zealand is made from reconstituted Gondwana rocks. Some intact remnants of the original Gondwana supercontinent can be found in New Zealand today, in Fiordland, the West Coast and northwest Nelson. Some of these basement rocks date back 600 million years, making them well and truly the oldest rocks in New Zealand.

Meanwhile, ancestral New Zealand is on the move. Magma begins to well up along a rift separating the Rangitata mountains from the rest of Gondwana, forming new oceanic crust and pushing New Zealand away. By 85 million years ago the mini-continent of Zealandia is on a journey out into the Pacific, while behind it the Tasman Sea is being born. By 55 million years ago, when the Tasman Sea stops widening, the newly formed and separated New Zealand landmass is slowly disappearing under the sea. Now well away from any subduction or spreading zone, the crust begins to cool; it becomes denser and heavier, and slowly sinks.

By 35 million years ago, only the drowned remnants of the Rangitata mountains remain above water as numerous small islands. The grain of sand has journeyed back to the coast, which in turn has come to meet it. The entire country seems in imminent danger of disappearing beneath the waves completely when circumstances change once more. New Zealand has ended up straddling an evolving boundary between two tectonic plates, the Pacific and the Australian.

Around 25 million years ago the Pacific and Australian plates begin to push into one another across the New Zealand region, setting in motion a train of events that will eventually see the grain of sand pushed to the summit of a new mountain range.

At first all the action is in the sea, in oceanic crust to the north of the New Zealand crust. Over 15 million years the crust of New Zealand itself gradually begins to compress and fracture, and is raised out of the sea. Slowly the Alpine Fault develops, tearing the crust apart. The Pacific Plate is moving southwest, and as it begins to significantly compress New Zealand the Torlesse rocks are pushed upwards. A new phase of mountain building, the Kaikoura Orogeny, has begun.

By five million years ago the mountains are growing rapidly. As the plates slide past each other at about 37 millimetres a year the continental crust on the Pacific Plate, east of the Alpine Fault, is being rammed over the granite rocks of the Australian Plate, and being rotated and shoved upwards.

The bands of schist lying beneath the thick layer of Torlesse rocks are also being pushed upwards. The deepest, and therefore most greatly metamorphosed, garnet schists have been steeply bent up directly against the Alpine Fault, the middle layer of biotite schist has been pushed up to the east of the garnet schists, while the top layer of chlorite schist lies further east again, closest to the wide band of Torlesse rocks, which are the most common rock in the mountains and cover the greatest area. The interaction between these two plates is complex.

Today, far to the north of New Zealand in the Kermadec Trench, slightly heavier oceanic crust on the Pacific Plate is sucked under lighter oceanic crust on the Australian Plate. Between East Cape in the North Island and Kaikoura in the South, the Pacific Plate's oceanic crust meets the continental crust of New Zealand on the Australian Plate, and continues to be forced underneath; molten rock resulting from this subduction feeds the volcanoes of the central North Island.

At Kaikoura the interaction between the two plates changes, because both are now carrying continental crust. One piece of continental crust can't slip under another piece, so instead there is a sliding side-on collision. The most well-known part of this sideswipe is the Alpine Fault, along which the Pacific Plate is being shunted; its softer crust is being pushed up against the harder, unyielding Australian Plate to form mountains.

The plate boundary leaves mainland New Zealand at Milford Sound, and from here south the situation is the reverse of what happens north of New Zealand. The crust of the Australian Plate is now oceanic, and is being forced under the continental crust of the Pacific Plate along the Puysegur Trench.

So from north to south along this one plate boundary the motion changes from right under left, to right past left, to left under right. Not only that, but the Pacific Plate is moving at varying speeds in varying directions, which adds a twist to the collisions. In the north it pushes west at more or less 50 millimetres a year, in the middle west-southwest at 40 millimetres a year, and in the south it moves southwest at 30 millimetres a year.

Like an iceberg, the height and bulk of the Southern Alps pale into insignificance in relation to the thickness and mass of rocks lying beneath them. If one were to drill straight down from the summit of Aoraki Mount Cook, the drill would leave the Torlesse rock that makes up the mountain just below sea level. Beneath lies the first layer of schist, coloured by the pale green mineral chlorite. After ten kilometres or so the schist changes to darker, more shiny biotite, which is more strongly layered as it has been metamorphosed at greater depths than the chlorite layer. After a further ten kilometres the third and deepest layer of hard schist containing red garnets is reached.

At about thirty kilometres' depth the drill bit would encounter the Alpine Fault, which dips east beneath the Pacific Plate at an angle of about 55°. Below that lie rocks belonging to the Australian Plate, until finally, more than 40 kilometres below the surface, is the zone where oceanic crust from the Pacific Plate is sucked into the molten magma of the Earth's mantle.

The layers of rocks are much thicker directly under the alps than they are to either side; they form a root of crust, as if the Southern Alps were the visible tip of an enormous buried iceberg of rock. Geophysicists use gravity measurements to determine the thickness of subterranean rocks, and on gravity maps of the South Island the alps and their crustal root are clearly visible as the area with the lowest gravity. This 'negative gravity anomaly' occurs because much of this crustal rock is less dense than the rock surrounding it. In fact, this measurable effect extends more than 200 kilometres below the earth's surface.

The rate of mountain building has continued unabated for the last five million years at about ten millimetres per year. During that time more than 20 vertical kilometres of rock has been uplifted, but at its highest point less than 3.8 kilometres remains, for the rate of uplift has been evenly matched by erosion, which has conspired to wear down the mountains almost as fast as they grow. For the last million years the Southern Alps have been more or less the height they are today, maintaining a steady equilibrium between growth and wear. Without the might of erosion, the Southern Alps would be six times taller than they are today.

In all this movement, the rocks containing the grain of sand end up near the middle of the South Island, having been slowly carried into the mountain chain as rocks to the west of them were pushed up. The sand grain arrives below the mountains about a million years ago, buried beneath a ten kilometre-thick layer of rock. The rock begins to be pushed up, and by about 380,000 years ago it has reached sea level. Buried deep in the heart of the mountain, the grain of sand is able to resist the water and ice that constantly strive to send rocks on the flanks of the mountain back down to the valley below.

The surface of the mountain is under continuous attack: it is forced to expand and contract on a daily basis, as it is heated by the sun during the day and then cooled at night. Water penetrates the hairline cracks and begins to lever them apart as it freezes and thaws. Water expands by four percent as it freezes, and the resulting ice is a subtle but persistent wedge. Gradually solid rock is turned into shattered piles of rock pieces that resemble heaps of broken pottery. Slowly, over time, fragments of rock fall off and accumulate as the great scree fans that are such a feature of the Torlesse rock mountains to the east of the Main Divide.

Scree slopes are one of the most distinctive mountain landscapes in New Zealand, especially in the dry rain-shadow of the Southern Alps, where they are home to a small but very distinctive group of plants. The word scree comes from an old Norse word 'skritha', which described any landslide on a mountainside, and scree slopes are also sometimes referred to as shingle slides. Their presence has

Over long periods of time, fragments of rock loosened by alternating cycles of freezing and thawing fall and accumulate into the enormous scree fans which typify the dry eastern alps, such as these on the Torlesse Range.

caused more than one tramper to refer to Canterbury's mountains as piles of rubble.

Scree, or talus, slopes form from a thick layer of shattered greywacke rock, and often occur on steep slopes below gullies and bluffs as widening fans or cones. The fans accumulate as long as slopes are no steeper than 32°, which is the 'angle of repose' for rocks; on flatter slopes rocks are more likely to form into stable boulder or fellfields, while any steeper and the rocks either slide to the bottom, or are highly unstable. Scree slopes are notoriously mobile; the surface debris is always incrementally rolling and sliding, often as a result of alternate freezing and thawing, and new material is constantly being added to the top of the fan from the surrounding rock faces. As well as being continually on the move, scree slopes can get extremely hot during summer days — up to 50°C — and extremely cold during winter.

Frost and ice shape the scree slopes wherever silt or soil accumulates. As damp soil freezes, ice crystals grow vertically, creating frost heave that can lift small rock flakes and stones. When the ice melts the soil slumps, and gradually the rock flakes and stones are shifted downhill. Rain washes material off the mountain, especially during heavy falls, when even large boulders are set in motion.

The whole time the sand grain is on its journey upwards, the surface of the land is being overcome by the advance and retreat of enormous glaciers that grind rock to dust, make their way downhill carrying heavy loads of sediment, and finally deliver it to a river to carry to the sea. But deep inside the mountain the grain of sand is immune to this . . . for now. It is inching its way up, entombed in a mass of grey rock, on an infinitesimally slow elevator ride to the top. But the mountain is not as solid as it seems: it is crossed with small fault lines, tension cracks that have splintered off the main Alpine Fault. Within these cracks the rock is being crushed and ground to the consistency of broken concrete.

The base and sides of glaciers pluck rocks and boulders from their valley floors to become giant grinding machines, which wear away the rock bed below. Schist rock sculpted by the Franz Josef Glacier.

Scree plants

In his 1864 Report on the Geological Survey of the Province of Canterbury, Julius Haast wrote:

The reputation which NZ had obtained of being very deficient in flowering plants is undeserved, as far as concerns the Southern Alps, which have proved to be wonderfully rich; during the right seasons the mountains and valleys are covered with flowers and blossoms, and even the crumbling mountain, the surface of which consists almost entirely of detritus, gives life and offers ample nourishment to a great many of the most curious and marvellous plants in existence.

At first glance scree slopes often seem barren and lifeless, and it requires a closer look to find the widely scattered and well-camouflaged plants, all of which share the same cryptic blue-grey or bronze colouration, even though they come from widely differing plant groups. No one knows why the scree plants need to be so camouflaged, although one idea is that it makes it harder for grasshoppers to find them. When they flower, however, it's a different story, and their often large yellow and white flowers are conspicuous against the grey or reddish rocks, serving as a strong advertisement to potential pollinating insects that would otherwise have difficulty finding them on the barren mountainside. Penwiper flowers are strongly scented for the same reason. Unlike the crowded snow tussock fields, there is plenty of space for seeds on the scree slopes — the question is whether they can put down their roots quickly and deeply enough before they are destroyed by moving rocks.

Around 25 scree-specialist plants have all evolved similar solutions to enable them to survive in this harsh environment. They are able to do this because the surface layer of mobile rocks is usually only 10–20 centimetres

Tufted haastia (*Haastia sinclairii*) occurs on stable scree slopes, and its young leaves are covered in thick white hairs. Although it is related to vegetable sheep it has a very different growth form. Nelson Lakes National Park.

thick. Below these rocks is a crust of fine sand, silt and small pebbles about eight centimetres thick, and beneath that a stable, permanently moist sandy layer. This moist layer is the secret to the scree plants' survival, as they anchor their extensive roots in it. A plant's thick perennial underground stem sits within the drier crust above, and it's only the leaves from each growing season that brave the sliding debris layer. If the slope moves the leaves shear off, but the stem and roots survive and can regrow.

The leaves are usually small, fleshy and divided into many lobes; they contain lots of water and not much solid matter, so if they are destroyed it is not a major loss of energy or nutrients to the plant. The leaves have no ability to conserve water; in fact, they transpire rapidly. Although this seems counterintuitive in a hot, dry and windy environment it is in fact a cunning cooling mechanism. Each winter the plants die back, leaving the underground tuber to regrow the following spring.

Some of New Zealand's most unusual mountains plants occur on more stable dry scree slopes. In his classic book *New Zealand Plants and their Story*, which was deservedly reprinted four times between 1907 and 1967, botanist Leonard Cockayne gives a wonderful description of cushion plants:

Perhaps the most striking denizens of the rocks are the various kinds of vegetable sheep (species of Raoulia*), which form hard cushions, mostly white but occasionally green . . . The* Raoulia *cushions are all constructed on the same plan. Above, the stems branch again and again, and towards their extremities are covered with small woolly leaves, packed as tightly as possible. Finally, stems, leaves and all are pressed into a dense, hard, convex mass, making in the case of* Raoulia eximia *an excellent and appropriate seat for a wearied botanist . . . The vegetable sheep are not inaptly named, for at a distance an inexperienced shepherd might perhaps be misled.*

Top left: A typical plant of dry eastern greywacke mountains, the black daisy (*Cotula dendryi*) has hairy feather-like leaves which sprout from branching underground stems.
Bottom left: Plants in the large genus *Raoulia* are a distinctive feature of the New Zealand alpine zone, where they grow either as tight cushions or as loose shaggy mats.

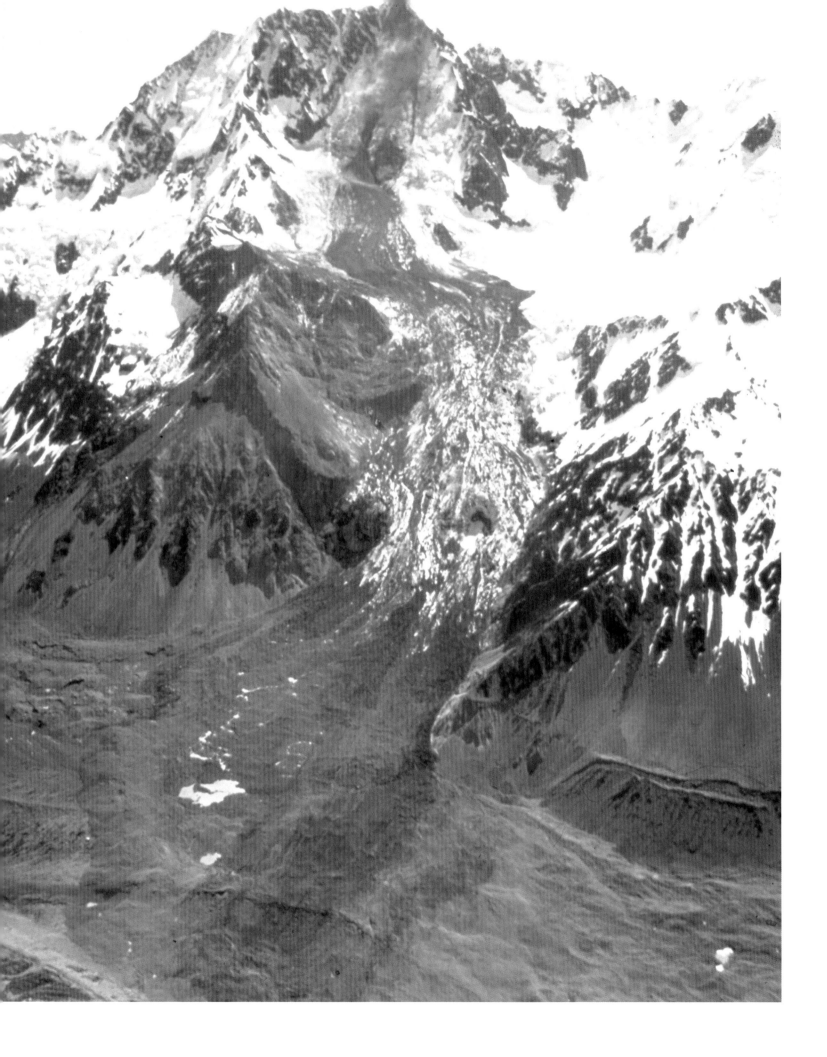

By the time the first humans discover and settle in New Zealand the grain of sand has summited. It has reached 3764 metres, in the narrow taper at the top of the highest mountain in the Southern Alps. Most of the other grains with which it began the journey didn't reach the summit, having fallen along the way.

Then, in a geological blink, the grain of sand suffers a monumental fall from grace. Just after midnight on the still, calm night of 14 December 1991, 14 million cubic metres of rock and ice on the summit of Aoraki Mount Cook gives way and plummets onto the Tasman Glacier below. The rock avalanche gathers up a further 40 million cubic metres of rock and ice as it hurtles down the mountain at 300 kilometres per hour, throwing off orange sparks in the darkness as rocks collide, and gaining so much momentum in its minute of descent that it spreads debris across to the far side of the glacier. The impact shaves ten metres off the height of the mountain, and registers as an earthquake on local seismographs.

Ice and water slice continual tiny increments off mountains, but it is intermittent catastrophes like this which are the true demolition machines. It took the grain of sand 300,000 years to ascend Aoraki Mount Cook; its descent took 30 or so seconds. Now it lies in a shattered fragment of rock, in a pile of rubble on the surface of the Tasman Glacier, surrounded by clouds of settling dust. From here it is all downhill to the sea again.

Ahead lies a journey of nearly 400 years to travel the 13 or so kilometres to the bottom of the glacier, although this could conceivably be faster if the glacier begins to shrink in response to global warming. Once it falls into the lake at the glacier's terminus the mode of transport changes from ice to water, and the shattered rock fragment will become at first smoothed, then slowly worn away, until all the sand grains that have been bound together for 200 million years as a hunk of Torlesse rock break apart.

The fragment begins its journey by negotiating the braided channels of the Tasman River as far as the milky turquoise waters of Lake Pukaki. Beyond the lake, and into the Pukaki River, it would have once followed a braided river all the way to the sea; now the grain of sand has to negotiate the hydro lakes of Benmore and Aviemore, before reaching what remains of the wide braid of the Waitaki River.

Depending on how many delays the grain of sand faces en route, how many back eddies it washes into compared with how many floods speed it along, the journey to the sea may take hundreds or thousands of years, probably much longer. It will eventually arrive at the beach, but even there will be only a temporary halt. Its destiny is to keep moving, to continually cycle between deep ocean and mountain top. Beyond the beach lies an enormous submarine canyon, down which the sand grain and many more will one day pour in the churning flurry of an underwater avalanche.

The canyon joins others, taking the sediments far out to the Bounty Fan, a thousand kilometres east, where everything settles gently on the deep ocean floor. It is a grain of sand for now, but one day it will be rock again. And who knows how long it will take to reach the next mountain top, or what the surface of the earth will look like by the time it gets there.

In December 1991, the summit of Aoraki Mount Cook was lowered by ten metres when an enormous rockfall collapsed down the East Face, spreading debris six kilometres down the Hochstetter icefall and across the Tasman Glacier.

Braided rivers

Braided rivers are one of the Southern Alps' most distinctive legacies, especially on the wide plains of Canterbury and North Otago. Braided rivers flow on a wide, flat riverbed in a continually changing network of interconnecting shallow channels, separated by low, temporary gravel bars or islands. They often occur downstream from glaciers, where they flow across deep beds of gravels and silt which fill great U-shaped valleys carved out in earlier glaciations. Globally, braided rivers are a very unusual type of river, found in only a few places with glaciers and rapidly eroding mountains.

Frequent floods move the channels and bars, and scour vegetation. A particular suite of plants and animals has adapted to this distinctive unpredictable environment, resting and breeding on the gravel islands, and feeding in the river channels and associated wetlands. Notable nesting birds include endangered black stilts, black-fronted terns and wrybills whose beaks bend to the right. Specialist braided river plants and invertebrates tend to have cryptic colouration for camouflage.

Major braided rivers include the Waimakariri, Rakaia, Rangitata, Godley, Ahuriri, Waitaki and Tasman, which at five kilometres across is the widest of the braided rivers.

Braided rivers such as the Rangitata River are a distinctive feature of New Zealand's rapidly eroding eastern glacial valleys, and their shallow channels are very mobile especially during floods.

LA NUOVA
ZELANDA
trascorsa nel 1769. e 1770.
DAL COOK COMANDANTE.
DELL'ENDEAVOUR
Vascello di S. M. Britannica

VENEZIA 1778
Presso Antonio Zatta
Con Privilegio dell'Ecc̃mo Senato.

C. Ma

Var. 12.°26.° E.

C.
(del m

in

50
33
P.ª delle Cascate   B. Aperta

50

B. Trompeuse
(Ingannatrice)

MERIDION

Var. 13.°31.° E.
51
P. Dubbioso

ALPI

AI

NAMING THE ALPS

Today's maps of the South Island are covered in names. Most peaks, streams, rivers, lakes and glaciers bear names, because naming a landscape helps us make sense of it, and allows us to locate ourselves in it. Names also give parts of that landscape an identity; they create an individual history for it, because each name has been bestowed by someone, for a reason, at a particular point in time.

Naming the land

When Maori first arrived in New Zealand 800 or so years ago they were faced with an unknown country, a terra incognita. Relying on an oral rather than written tradition, they began to use geographical names to help them memorise mental maps of the country, to guide them on their many journeys.

Captain James Cook used pen and paper to map the outlines of the country on his charts and to measure and record distances and locations, yet while many explorers and surveyors carried on this task more than 150 years later many parts of the Southern Alps were still unnamed and remained empty spaces on the map. Mountaineers then began to take on the challenge of filling in the blanks; climbing in the Mount Aspiring area during the 1940s and 1950s Paul Powell wrote:

. . . the first thing mountaineers do when they've climbed a virgin peak is to think of a suitable name; it's one of the perks of climbing and gives them a justifiable feeling of importance in an environment which is uncaring of their existence.

Not every name lasts. Many early Europeans were unaware of, or often had little regard for, the Maori place-names that already graced the land. As well as explaining their understanding of how the land came into being, many of the Maori names and associated myths paid tribute to gods and to ancestors. Aoraki, named Mount Cook by the Europeans, represents the most sacred ancestor of Ngai Tahu Maori, and is a link between the supernatural and the natural world, as their story of its creation explains:

In the beginning there was no land, and the waters of Kiwa rolled over the place now occupied by the South Island, the North Island and Stewart Island.

Captain James Cook's Chart of Newzeland or the Islands of Aeheinomouwe and Tovpoenammu was completed after his first voyage in 1769–70, and includes the first appearance of the name Southern Alps on a map of New Zealand.

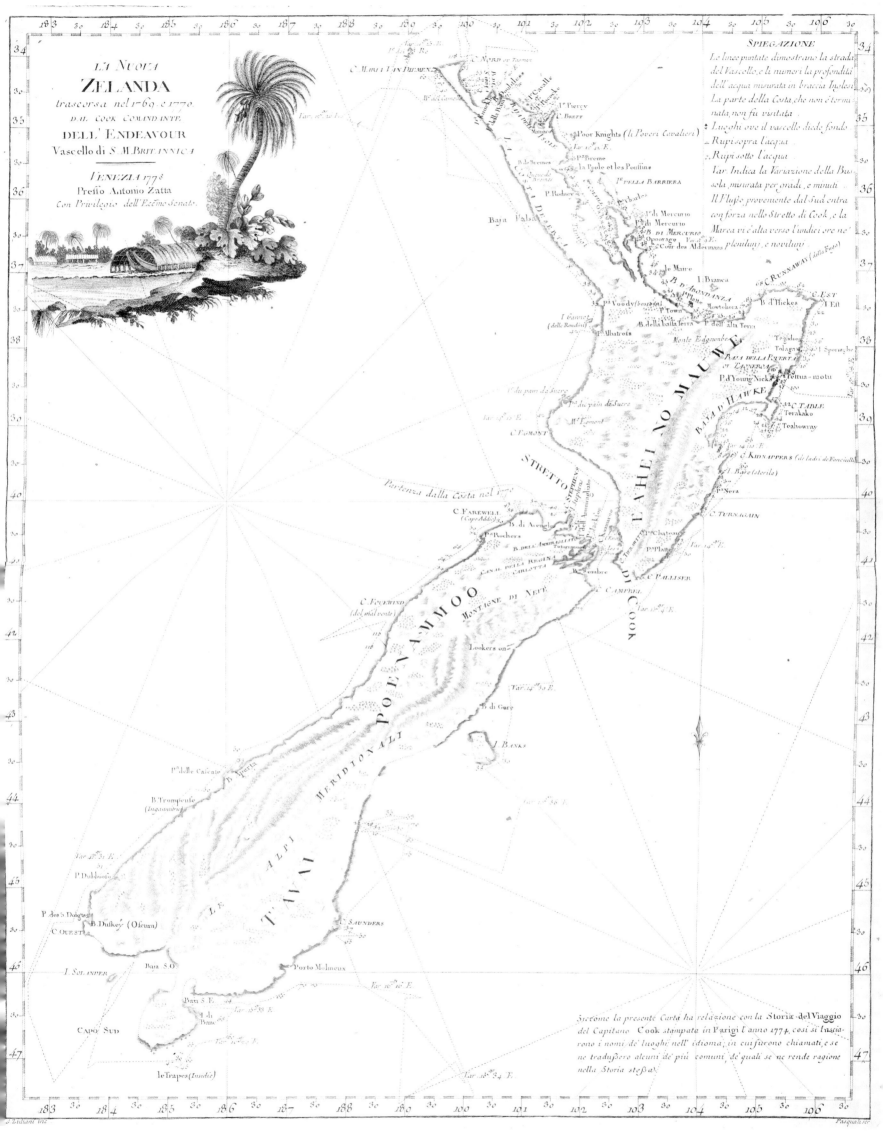

Before Raki, the Sky Father, wedded Papa-tua-nuku, the Earth Mother, each of them already had children by other unions. After the marriage, some of the Sky Children came down to greet their father's new wife and some even married Earth Daughters. Among the celestial visitors were four sons of Raki who were named Aoraki (Cloud in the Sky), Rakiroa (Long Raki), Rakirua (Raki the Second), and Rarakiroa (Long Unbroken Line). They came down in a canoe which was known as Te Waka o Aoraki.

They cruised around Papa-tua-nuku, who lay as one body in a huge continent known as Hawaiki. Then, keen to explore, the voyagers set out to sea in their enormous canoe, but no matter how far they travelled, they could not find land. They decided to return to their celestial home but the karakia (incantation) which should have lifted the waka back to the heavens failed. Their craft ran aground on a hidden reef, turning to stone and earth in the process and forming the South Island, which became known as Te Waka o Aoraki.

The waka listed to the east, and settled with the west side much higher out of the water, forming Ka Tiritiri o te Moana, the Southern Alps. Aoraki and his brothers clambered onto the high side and were turned to stone. They are still there today: Aoraki is the mountain known in English as Mount Cook, and his brothers are the next peaks, Rakiroa or Mount Dampier, Rakirua or Mount Teichelmann, and Rarakiroa or Mount Tasman.

The island was not fit for human habitation, so a benevolent god, Tu Te Rakiwhanoa, took on the job of shaping the land. He created important features such as Horomaka (Banks Peninsula) and Mawhera (the Grey River valley), but his most important work was in Fiordland where he used his great axe, Te Hamo, to gouge out the fiords.

Further shaping of the land was carried out by chief Rakaihaitu, who arrived on board the first canoe bearing the Waitaha people to the South Island. While his son sailed the waka around the coast, Rakaihautu travelled through the interior, digging out the great lakes with his magic ko, or digging stick.

For the first few years of European settlement Aoraki retained its name, possibly because it was seldom seen. The first European settlers to record a sighting of Aoraki, in May 1846, were New Zealand Company surveyors Charles Heaphy and Thomas Brunner, and the company's Nelson agent William Fox (later Premier of New Zealand). Accompanied by the Maori guide Kehu they had set out in March from the young Nelson settlement, travelled northwest to the tip of the South Island and then fought their way south along the coast, battling steep coastal cliffs and raging rivers, and finally running out of food before they reached Cape Foulwind. Here they were rewarded with the sight of snowy mountains that floated, mirage-like; 'beyond [Arahura] the long range of snowy mountain that Captain Cook denominated the Southern Alps is seen stretching away to Cascade Point, where, their peaks only showing above the sea horizon, they appear like ice islands lying off the coast.' Local Maori gave them food, and rested and fed the party continued down the coast to the Arahura River, just north of present-day Hokitika, where they could clearly see 'Te Hau rahi [Hauraki or Aoraki] which the natives assert is of the highest of any in this island.'

But during Brunner's subsequent epic exploration of the West Coast, which began later the same year and saw him and various Maori guides, including Kehu, spend 18 months travelling from Nelson as far south as Lake Paringa before turning around, he made no mention of sighting Aoraki or the high mountains again. It seems that for weeks or even months the weather was so bad that they remained hidden in cloud.

Right: Sir William Fox's painting shows the glacier that would later be named in his honour during a visit to the West Coast in 1872. Over page: Charles Heaphy painted this view of 'Mount Cook, Greenstone country, Middle island' from the West Coast in 1846, when he, Thomas Brunner and William Fox became the first Europeans to record seeing Mount Cook.

Five years later a new name was bestowed on the mountain. Captain J.L. Stokes was in charge of the British steamer HMS *Acheron* which had been carrying out a survey of the coasts and harbours for the Admiralty, beginning in 1848. In March 1851 the *Acheron*, accompanied by HMS *Otago*, was sailing up the West Coast when Stokes noted 'a stupendous mountain' that he decided to name Mount Cook, in honour of the Pacific Ocean's greatest European navigator-explorer. He estimated its height at 13,000 feet.

The mountain was formally known as Mount Cook for nearly 150 years, until as part of the 1998 settlement between the government and Ngai Tahu Maori, and in recognition of the significance of the mountain to Ngai Tahu, its name officially became Aoraki Mount Cook.

Not all Maori place names have been lost. The Waitaki River, for example, which includes the slopes of Aoraki Mount Cook within its vast catchment, retains its southern version of the common Polynesian name Waitangi. The exact reason for its naming has been lost over time, but it literally means 'the waterway of tears'. The Waitaki is often referred to in whaikorero or Maori oratory as representing the tears of Aoraki, which spill into Lake Pukaki and eventually make their way down the river to the coast.

While Aoraki Mount Cook towers over the other high peaks in the central Southern Alps, it is the striking spire of Mount Aspiring that dominates the skyline to the south. This dramatic four-sided pyramid was usually known to Ngai Tahu Maori as Tititea, meaning 'glistening peak', but it had other Maori names as well. Makahi Te Rakiwhanoa means a wedge belonging to the benevolent land-shaping god Tu Te Rakiwhanoa, while a more obscure name, Otapahu, was perhaps a reference to a type of dogskin cloak.

Naming goes hand in hand with exploration. On 7 December 1857 John Turnbull Thomson, Chief Surveyor for the Otago Province, who would later become New Zealand's first Surveyor General, embarked on 'by far the most interesting of my explorations', a trip to explore the upper Waitaki River. His daunting task was to map the Otago Province, which in those days included what is now Southland. He had begun a year earlier with a map that was little more than the coastline as charted by HMS *Acheron*, and soon after had met the Maori chief Reko on the Mataura River. Reko had guided farmer Nathaniel Chalmers, the first European to visit Central Otago and to see lakes Wakatipu, Hawea and Wanaka, in 1853. Reko drew a map in the earth showing Turnbull Thomson the lakes and rivers, as well as a pass he had crossed while following a well-established Maori trail on his way south through the Mackenzie Country to the Clutha River. Turnbull Thomson followed Reko's route, and after crossing the low pass named it the Lindis Pass, because a rocky outcrop and the rolling contours of the land reminded him of Lindisfarne Castle.

After crossing the pass he climbed a peak he called Longslip Peak, after the great scar on its flank, which gave him a 'commanding view of the surrounding countryside'. To the north were the Southern Alps, 'abounding in precipitous slopes and sharp snowy peaks'. Among the peaks to the west 'a very high mountain was conspicuous [at a] distance [of] 60 miles'. He also mentions it in his field notebook as the 'very high Snow Mt'. Two days later, on 18 December, he added in pencil in his notebook the sentence 'at the head of Hawea, distance about 40 miles, is a very lofty snowclad peak which I called Mt Aspiring'. Six months later he wrote 'Mt Aspiring forms a magnificent spectacle not only owing to its great altitude . . . but owing to its bold and symmetrical shape of a steep cone or spire.' Because its distinctive shape is reminiscent of the Matterhorn in the European alps, Aspiring is often also referred to as the Matterhorn of the South.

Mount Aspiring wasn't the only name about which Turnbull Thomson changed his mind en route. His second view of the mountain was from a peak he initially called Black Knob Hill, but even before leaving the summit 'I changed its name in my fieldbook to the more euphonius Grandview.'

Turnbull Thomson doubled back over Lindis Pass to

the north, and on Christmas Day 1857 scrambled up the slopes of the Benmore Range, becoming the first European to record seeing Mount Cook from the east. He sketched the scene in his field notebook, and later used it as the basis for a painting. Two days later, after finally managing to cross the flooded Ohau River, he travelled up the side of Lake Pukaki, then scrambled up the slopes of the Ben Ohau Range to a point 'commanding a perfect view' of a mountain which seemed to fill him with ambivalent feelings:

Mount Cook, the monarch of the southern mountains, was full in view, distant about 25 miles and towering 13,000 feet above the sea. It was clothed in snow from its tapering peak to its base, and supported as it is by rugged precipitous sides, surrounded by desert and utterly barren mountains and valleys; its appearance, however, calculated to excite the admiration of the lovers of the picturesque. For it possessed with its magnificence, so much of the appalling and forbidding in its barren dreary wildness, that most visitors would unconsciously turn aside and relieve their eyes with the more tame and rounded grassy downs to be seen stretching for many miles in the direction from whence they had approached.

Turnbull Thomson calculated the height of Mount Cook to be 12,460 feet, much closer to the then correct height of 12,349 feet (3764 metres) than Captain Stokes' guess. Then, as a tribute to the Captain's marathon efforts mapping the coasts, he named a prominent snowy mountain Mount Stokes.

In 1857 a dispute between the Otago and Canterbury provinces over the exact location of their shared boundary flared up, so during 1858 and 1859 Canterbury Surveyor Edward Jollie and his assistant William Spearman Young were sent on several expeditions to explore and survey the Mackenzie Basin and Lake Wanaka area. On one trip they climbed to a peak near Shotover Pass, where Jollie remarked 'Thomson has called that mountain Aspiring; we must call ours Perspiring.' The name was duly noted on their map, but later became the more prosaic Mount Motutapu.

Turnbull Thomson's work surveying and mapping Otago was well in hand by the time the Canterbury provincial government began to recognise the importance of mapping all of their enormous province — which at that time included Westland — and of finding what mineral resources existed, especially gold, as gold fever had hit the country. They hired a German immigrant, Julius Haast, as their Provincial Geologist, in the dual role of geologist and surveyor, and in 1861 he made his first exploring and surveying trip to the Rangitata-Ashburton area of the foothills of the Southern Alps.

In January 1862 Haast led a party of 'men used to horses and rough country', including Assistant Surveyors Arthur Dobson and William Young, to begin an exploration of the Mackenzie Basin. Haast was an indefatigable observer and place-namer, and many features in the Southern Alps owe their monikers to him. It wasn't long before he had irritated Turnbull Thomson by renaming some of his features: Thomson's Upper Waitaki River, which flowed down 'The Valley of Sand' to Lake Pukaki became the Tasman River, and Mount Stokes was renamed Mount Sefton, after William Sefton Moorhouse, the Superintendent of Canterbury.

Haast poured tributes upon Dutch navigator Abel Tasman, who ended up with the second highest peak, the largest glacier and a river named after him. He also tended to favour the names of other geologists and scientists, as well as local politicians, although during his survey further north the previous year he had used

Over page: This view of Lake Howick was painted by Sir William Fox when he was the Nelson agent for the New Zealand Company. He took part in a number of explorations around Nelson and the West Coast, most famously with Charles Heaphy and Thomas Brunner. February 1846.

LAKE HOWICK

Clyde, Havelock and Lawrence, all names of generals from the British Army's Indian Mutiny campaign. He was very fair in the geographic spread of his acknowledgements: British biologist Charles Darwin, French geologist Elie de Beaumont, British geologist Sir Henry de la Beche, French geographer Victor Malte-Brun, Australian botanist Dr Ferdinand Müller and German chemist Justus von Liebig were among the many men of science whose names he bestowed on a landscape he found 'magnificent'.

As I never expected that alpine scenery on such a gigantic scale could be found in New Zealand, the grandeur of the landscape astounded me . . .

Between 1861 and 1863, Scotsman James McKerrow completed Turnbull Thomson's pioneering survey work in Otago, to produce the first realistic map of the interior. McKerrow gave the Southern Alps in the vicinity of Mount Aspiring the flavour of Greek mythology: Mount Somnus was named after the Greco-Roman god of sleep, and Momus, Nox, Chaos and Cosmos are also figures in Greek mythology.

Westland District Surveyor Gerhard Mueller added a distinctly nautical flavour, naming a river after the coastal vessel *Waipara* and continuing the maritime theme in tributaries called the Companion Ladder Rapid, The Binnacle, The Third Mate, The Cook and The Cabin. From the summit of a Mueller-named peak ex-navy man and mountaineer Paul Powell paid tribute to 'one of the few examples of imaginative naming in the New Zealand mountains':

Below us, the growl and thunder of ice avalanches shook our summit. The wind of their passing blew to the sails of the Haast Range bringing the names a tang of the sea — Stargazer, Moonraker, Skyscraper, Main Royal — all names of sails on a full-rigged ship, they thrill a sailorman.

During the 1920s and 1930s John Pascoe and friends from the newly formed Canterbury Mountaineering and Tramping Club made a number of first ascents, naming a number of previously unclimbed peaks in the Arthur's Pass and North Canterbury areas. But it was a journey in the footsteps of Victorian runholder and satirist Samuel Butler that led to their biggest 'find'.

Navigator names

Cook and Tasman aren't the only navigators honoured in the roll call of the highest mountain peaks; they have for close company many other seafaring explorers such as early buccaneer William Dampier; Cook's navigator on his first voyage, Zachary Hicks; the famous French navigator Le Comte de la Perouse; and George Vancouver, who once served with Cook. On his 1791 voyage to New Zealand, Vancouver visited Dusky Sound but like Cook before him failed to see the mountains. Other landforms are named after the Spaniard Alessandro Malaspina, who visited New Zealand in 1793; and also Torres, Drake and Magellan.

In late 1934, after ascending the Rangitata Valley, crossing the Main Divide and making the first traverse of the Perth Glacier on the west coast side, Pascoe and three others reached a great unknown ice plateau.

Priestley Thomson suggested a biblical theme, his idea inspired by a play on the name of the nearby Adams Range. His companions agreed. So the great expanse of snow and ice became the Garden of Eden, and the rivers of ice spilling over its southern edge were named the Eve Icefall, and the Serpent, Cain and Abel Glaciers.

There was also Angel Col, and Eve's Rib. The group returned the following year and continued with the biblical theme, adding the Arethusa and Beelzebub icefalls.

Although the Geographic Board initially rejected formal approval of most of the biblical names many had already passed into general use in the mountaineering community and were subsequently recognised by the board. By 1940 the neighbouring ice field had been named by anonymous mountaineers, in gentle satirical counterpoint to the Garden of Eden, the Garden of Allah and Satan's Saddle.

Some names speak less of poetry than they do of frustration, such as a sequence of names above the Burke River near Haast Pass: Chaotic, Mistake and Blunder spurs. Creek names in the same area are a wonderfully imaginative set of variations: Jostling Water, Brisk Water, The Twirligig, Hidden Rivulet, Restless Torrent, Churn Rapids and Raving Torrent. They bring to mind explorer Charlie Douglas's comment from 1891 that:

A fellow traversing new country has to put names or Numbers on peaks and Knobs to keep the run of them, and suffers fearful mental agony in so doing . . . Let anyone sit down and try to name say twenty natural features and see how difficult it is.

Douglas had the opportunity to name many features of the Southern Alps during his 40 years of exploring, often placing classical names on his maps. He had strong opinions on the appropriateness of names, especially when:

Government Clarks and Survey apprentices supplied the illustrious names and the towering Peaks don't tower at all, but are simply knobs on a Mountain Mass bearing about the same proportion to it that the teeth do to a Saw . . . It has always been the acknowledged right of an explorer to affix names to places, and unless the said names are absurd or very inappropriate they are allowed to remain. I have no objection to my names being taken off, if those put in their place are more appropriate or sonorous, or even shorter, thereby taking up less room, but why should a name short and sonorous like Hyllus be altered to Flannigan's summit, who in blazes is Flannigan.

Flannigan was in fact the chief draughtsman in the Head Office of the Lands and Survey Department, tasked with turning Douglas' field maps into departmental maps.

The last word on names must also go to Douglas, with the following penned in his inimitable style and spelling, during his four-month exploration of the Waiatoto River in 1891:

Sketched in the Pickle Haub [Pickelhaube] glacier and the flat. . . . The name Pickel Haube is a puzzel. Who or what it is? Is Pickle &c the name of some celebrated German Proffessor or was he a Mongol General, or is it the name of a New Sauce, invented by some Philanthropest to make Rabbit Stew more palatable than it is? I must enquire and get a bottle.

A pickelhaube is in fact a distinctively shaped German helmet.

Over page: Sir Julius Haast made this field sketch of 'Mount Cook and Lake Pukaki' during his first exploration of the Mackenzie Basin in 1862.

ICE

The weather has left its signature across the Southern Alps in flourishes of bold white rivers of ice. Glaciers are gigantic earth-moving machines, capable of grinding down mountains, yet they trace their beginning to one of the most beautiful — and ephemeral — things in nature: a snowflake. On its own a snowflake is fleeting and insubstantial, but en masse snow combines with mountains to create glaciers; and in glaciers, great mountains have met their match.

The snowflake and the Tasman Glacier

The intricacy and delicacy of snowflakes bring to mind works of art, yet they are purely the result of physical laws operating on a simple chemical structure, and for all their beauty, snowflakes are just frozen rain. Whether liquid or frozen, rain is one of the most powerful destructive forces in the alps; while rock and tectonic processes build mountains, rain and snow conspire to wear them away.

The tale of rain and snow is intertwined with the story of wind. New Zealand straddles a part of the globe where the winds blow consistently from the west. This westerly drift is part of a planet-wide wind system which is driven by the difference in temperature between the equator and the poles. The direction of the wind here is a result of air currents moving heat north to south from the tropics to Antarctica, being deflected by the spin of the earth. The South Island lies squarely in the path of the so-called Roaring Forties, whose winds average a speed of about 45 kilometres per hour at an altitude of 3000 metres. Winds are at their strongest in spring, when there is the biggest difference in temperature between the tropics and Antarctica, which is just emerging from an icy winter.

The westerly wind moving over the Tasman Sea collects water vapour evaporating from the sea surface, and by the time it arrives at New Zealand's West Coast the air is saturated. Within a few kilometres of the coast the three and half kilometre high mountain barrier of the alps lies directly across the path of the wind, and forces it to rise. This begins the process of orographic precipitation, which can intensify a rain-producing weather system by a factor of ten or more. Because atmospheric pressure declines with altitude the rising air begins to expand and cool, as does the water vapour it contains. The cooling vapour condenses around minute particles of dust into tiny drops of water and, as it gets cool enough, into ice crystals. These water droplets and ice crystals mass together and become visible as clouds, inside most of which it's cold enough for them to combine to form snow.

Once the contents of the cloud become too heavy they

A heavily crevassed icefall cascades onto the head basin of the Tasman Glacier.

are released; although most of what leaves the cloud is snow, warm air temperatures mean it has usually melted to rain by the time it reaches the ground. It takes a while for the rising clouds to reach this critical mass and dump their heavy load of water, so the amount of rain falling up the slope of the mountains increases until it reaches a maximum about ten kilometres inland from the Alpine Fault. Although most of the rain falls on the West Coast some spills over the Main Divide into the headwaters of the east coast glacier and river catchments, where it is an important source of water for the country's major hydro rivers and lakes.

A typical transect from west to east across the Southern Alps shows an annual rainfall of two to three metres at the coast, five metres on the low slopes, between 12 and 15 metres or more in the 'wet zone' of the mid-slopes, four metres at Aoraki Mount Cook village on the eastern side of the Divide and just over half a metre in Timaru.

Once the air has crossed the high point of the Main Divide it begins to lose altitude as gravity pulls it down, and the process here is the reverse of what happened earlier. The air compresses as it drops, and begins to warm. As the air is dry it heats much faster than it cooled on the west coast so by the time it reaches the Canterbury Plains it is hotter than it has been at any stage on its journey. Lower

air pressure on the eastern side of the Divide, known as a 'lee trough', gives it momentum, resulting in the hot strong wind known as the nor'wester.

The wind gains extra force as it's funnelled down long valleys, such as the Rakaia River and its tributaries, out onto the plains, and it creates wind and storms with wind speeds that may gust up to 195 kilometres per hour. Vast amounts of dust can be blown around during such storms, and deep deposits of wind-blown soil, or loess, on the Canterbury Plains show intense nor'west winds have been blowing across them for millennia.

Attempts to measure rainfall in the mountains are made extremely difficult by high winds; a rain gauge at Almer Hut on the Franz Josef Glacier was eventually abandoned, as the wind was so severe that rain often flew past the gauge rather than fall into it, and the solar panels for the system were blown off the hut. Despite such setbacks scientists have managed to collect many rainfall measurements across the alps, and discovered that most rain falls during storms following a northwest front, which last on average one to five days. Two thirds of the time the rainfall begins at the same time along the length of the alps, and the rest of the time it begins in the southwest first and rain quickly progresses up the island. Regardless of how long the storm lasts a graph of the amount of rain accumulating during a storm follows an S shape, with most rain falling in the middle of the storm.

On the far bank of the island we heard sickening thuds as a muddy torrent hurled boulders down in the flood. The flood surged past the bank in yellow waves . . . Of all the macabre sounds of Alpine travel in Canterbury, the worst is the thud as boulders are rolled over in the river as if they were pebbles.

John Pascoe describing the Rakaia River in flood, 1931

The wettest places on earth

Parts of the Southern Alps undeniably receive a lot of rain, a lot of the time. A fair annual average for the West Coast's 'wet band' is 12 to 15 metres of rain. How does that compare with the rest of the world? There are two places that are commonly cited as being the wettest places in the world, and unsurprisingly they are both mountainous. Quoted averages for Mount Wai'ale'ale on the Hawaiian island of Kauai vary between 11.68 and 13 metres per year, while Mawsynram in the Himalayan foothills in India gets 11.87 metres, the difference between them being that it rains almost every day on Mount Wai'ale'ale and it only rains during the six months of the monsoon at Mawsynram. On average then, sites such as the Cropp River regularly get more rain than the places which have traditionally been regarded as wet. The Cropp River's all-time record of 18.44 metres in one year at the Waterfall rain gauge, however, is eclipsed by the rain which fell between 1 August 1860 and 31 July 1861 in Cherrapunji, not far from Mawsynram: an astonishing 26.46 metres. From a global perspective the Southern Alps don't get the heaviest rainstorms — that privilege falls to places that get seasonal monsoon rain or are more tropical, as warmer air holds more water — but for a temperate country our rainfall is up there with the best, and the alps are responsible for much of it.

Mountain waves

The nor'west wind has very distinctive cloud signatures. Commonly known as hogsbacks, the smooth, sinuous curves of lenticular, or lens-shaped, clouds appear above the mountains and out to the east, often ahead of a cold front. The hogsbacks are the crests of standing waves of air that form in the lee of the mountains in the same way 'wave trains' or standing waves form in the rapids of a river. As the wind pours over the judder bar of the divide, having been pushed upwards on the western side, it begins to oscillate as a wave that can sometimes spread hundreds of kilometres downwind from the alps. The crests and troughs of the waves remain in the same place as air moves through them at speeds of up to 150 kilometres per hour. As the air rises into the crest it expands and cools, becoming visible as the hogsback cloud; as it descends into the next trough it warms and the cloud dissipates. So even though the clouds appear stationary they indicate high winds aloft.

The nor'west arch is a line of clouds with a marked gap of light sky behind that appears along the western edge of the Canterbury Plains, and can run almost the length of the South Island. It is part of the same wind pattern that has created hogsback clouds, and it announces the arrival of strong, hot winds on the plains even as it's pouring with rain in the mountains.

These 'mountain waves' have a particular significance to glider pilots, which is why Omarama, situated in the Mackenzie Basin just east of the alps, has become such a gliding Mecca. The front of each wave has a smooth, powerful zone of lift which gliders can use to soar rapidly to great heights, although they often have to fly through very turbulent air to reach the wave.

When the wind gets too strong waves can over-develop, just as in the ocean, and begin to break like surf. On rare occasions in spring, when the polar vortex (a persistent low-pressure system) spreads north from Antarctica as far as the alps, the mountain wave can extend out of the troposphere, the zone of atmosphere closest to the earth's surface, into the stratosphere, giving glider pilots the possibility of setting new gliding altitude records.

A clearly defined mature nor'west arch has formed over the alps, in advance of a weather front which will bring heavy rain to the mountains, and hot dry winds on the Canterbury Plains. The peak of Nun's Veil is in the background.

Truly in South Westland one is never out of the sight and sound of running water. Whether it be of the great rivers hurrying to the sea, or the white cascades or stream rippling fetlock-deep across the track, that voice of many waters is always in one's ears. There are times when the fierceness of the rivers fills one with a sense of impotence. A wide river-bed strewn with tree trunks and enormous boulders when the flood comes down — and they chafe and roll in wild turmoil — is an awesome enough sort of place. And the more you have to do with New Zealand rivers, the stronger becomes the awe in which you hold them.

Maud Moreland, 1911

Rain is only the warm half of the alp's precipitation story: the snowflakes that build New Zealand's glaciers begin life when conditions are sufficiently cold that clouds become snowflake factories.

Water usually freezes at 0°C, but the water in clouds becomes supercooled, which means the temperature is below zero but the water is still liquid. However, once the temperature falls below -10°C some of the droplets begin to freeze as tiny ice particles, and more of the surrounding water vapour begins to condense on their surface, causing them to grow. At this stage the snow crystal has a hexagonal shape which is already obeying certain rules that will determine its future structure. Due to its chemical structure, water — H_2O — freezes into an ice lattice with six sides, and so the hexagonal nature of the snow crystal is predetermined by a molecule ten million times smaller than itself.

As the snow crystal grows it begins to develop six arms, their particular pattern determined by the exact temperature and degree of water saturation in the cloud at the time it forms. The developing crystals are being buffeted around inside the cloud, and as they move they are exposed to subtly different temperatures which begin to influence how they grow and what shape they take. The most ornate fern-like dendritic stars develop when temperatures are between -12°C and -18°C. Each crystal follows its own unique path within the cloud, which is why no two are exactly the same.

The snow crystals are heavier than air so they're always falling, but at the same time they are being tossed around by updrafts; as a result the inside of the cloud is a blizzard of snow crystals which begin to collide with each other to build snowflakes. Eventually the mass of snow inside the cloud becomes so heavy that it begins to fall through the updrafts.

If it's cool enough the flakes will survive their 20-minute journey to land as snow. Depending on the day, the falling snow might be made of columns, needles, plates, feathery stars or, more usually in New Zealand, blobby flakes. Most of the snowflakes fall through supercooled water droplets which condense on their surface as rime, and by the time they arrive on the ground they are covered in frozen droplets.

Precipitation which falls as rain spends only a fleeting time in the high alps before gravity moves it downhill, but precipitation which falls as snow can have a lifetime measured in hundreds of years. This, the journey of a single snowflake in the Tasman Glacier, begins in the year AD1430.

From its moment of landing at 2500 metres altitude on the high slopes between Elie de Beaumont and Hochstetter Dome on the Main Divide, the rime-covered snowflake begins to lose what remains of its delicate shape. The sharp points of its arms blunt and wear as it lands, then it is rolled around by the wind and becomes buried under the weight of more falling snow. Water vapour evaporates from the tips of its arms and condenses on larger grains, and before long the once-beautiful snowflake has become an indistinguishable granule of ice. The compacting snow has become sugar-sized crystals known as firn, or old snow.

In the winter of the snowflake's fall, about ten metres of snow collects in the accumulation basin, or névé, on Elie de Beaumont. Each year more than eight metres of precipitation falls in this part of the Southern Alps, as either rain or snow. Snow is light and fluffy, full of air, and takes up about three times the volume of its constituent water, so it translates into a much greater depth of snow. High winds also blow fresh snow around, stripping it from exposed ridges and accumulating it in sheltered places. By the end of the snowflake's first summer the thick snowpack from the previous winter has melted significantly and settled as a blanket of firn about three metres thick. The pristine white of the snow has become sullied with wind-blown dust and tree pollen from the surrounding lowlands, and some from as far afield as Australia.

With each passing year the summer melt is followed by new layers of winter snow, and the firn becomes increasingly dense as the air in and between the ice granules is gradually forced out. Each year adds another layer of winter white and summer black to the annual zebra-patterned layering of the snowpack. The snowflake is now an ice crystal buried tens of metres below the surface. Under pressure at depth the once-white firn granules are melding together into larger crystals that might be four or five centimetres across; eventually this packed firn becomes blue glacial ice. In the central Southern Alps, with its high summer rainfall, high winter snowfall, warm summer temperatures and high melting rate this change is very rapid, taking place within five or so years, whereas in extremely cold, dry areas of the world it may take a hundred or more years.

The enormous accumulation of ice doesn't remain in the head basin; pulled by gravity, ice is continually on the move, flowing downhill as a frozen river, albeit moving about 100,000 times more slowly than water. The top 20 or so metres of ice behaves as a brittle crust, but below that the ice is viscous, like putty. Molecules within ice crystals align themselves in microscopic parallel planes which can slip over each other, and this gliding within ice crystals, as well as between larger cleavage planes, allows the glacier to deform and move.

Over page: A heavily crevassed glacier flows through a steep icefall on the Olivine Ice Plateau.

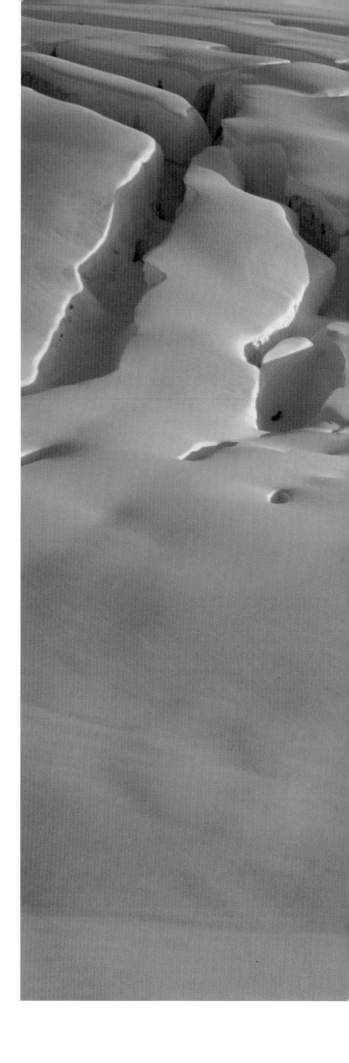

As well as movement within the ice, the glacier is sliding on the rocky bed below. The pressure of ice moving over a rough bed combines with rain and melted snow to provide a film of water that allows the glacier to slide along, in an abrasive, elephantine version of the melting action which allows a skater's blades to slide across ice.

The snowflake begins its journey 300 years after the beginning of the Little Ice Age, during one of a number of cool periods the Earth has experienced since the end of the last great ice age more than 10,000 years ago. Temperatures are, on average, more than 1°C cooler than today, and the world's glaciers are accumulating lots of ice and expanding in size.

As the deeply buried ice crystal begins to move away from Elie de Beaumont and Hochstetter Dome it moves slowly at first, then gradually gathers speed because of the increasing amount and depth of ice. The mass of ice doesn't all move at the same speed; there is more friction along its sides and bottom, so the ice in the centre moves most rapidly. The deep ice is viscous and absorbs the variations in speed, but the brittle surface crust cracks under the strain, tearing apart and forming blue-walled crevasses that are seldom more than two or three metres wide, but may be 30 metres deep. Each winter all but the largest crevasses seem to disappear, painted out by a dusting of new snow which partially fills and bridges them, but the crevasses are still there and reappear the following summer when the snow melts.

After two kilometres or so the glacier encounters a steep drop. As it gathers speed and pours over, the ice between the crevasses is under increased tension and splits, forming chaotic rows of spectacular towering pinnacles, known as seracs, some of which are several storeys high. On a still day deep cracks and groans can be heard as the ice settles and shifts, and there is an occasional crash and rumble

A lone skier is dwarfed against crevasses at the head of Fox Glacier. Winter snow has filled many smaller crevasses, which will become visible again when the snow melts in summer.

as a serac collapses. From a distance the surface of the icefall has the look of a scrunched-up sheet; up close it's a complicated maze.

Once it has raced through the icefall the ice reunites, coalesces again, and slows down; the glacier is now more than 300 metres thick and thickening rapidly. The ice crystal is now three kilometres from where it started, and has been on the move for more than 30 years. From a distance the glacier still appears pristine white, with a surface as smooth as a baby's skin, but as it travels the glacier is gathering rock, and underneath it's far from white and clean. Initially the sole and sides of the glacier are plucking rocks and boulders from the valley floor. As the glacier carries along this load of glacial till, as it is known, it becomes a giant grinding machine, wearing away the rock bed below. Trapped and rolled between the hard valley floor below and the rough debris overhead, small, soft rocks are ground to a fine dust known as glacial flour; large boulders, on the other hand, might survive intact during their journey in the clutches of the glacier. Some rocks are slowly drawn up from below into the deep ice.

Meanwhile the glacier is completing its role as a giant earth-moving conveyor belt by also collecting debris from above. Shattered greywacke on surrounding rock bluffs is loosened by continual freezing and thawing and falls along the edges of the glacier, sometimes as single rock falls, at other times as large rock avalanches. Many other smaller glaciers poised high above the Tasman Glacier are also shedding debris. By the time the Tasman Glacier rounds the corner towards the Darwin Glacier flowing in at right angles from the east, it has collected a line of medial moraine from the bluffs above Darwin's corner along one side, and further ice and debris that has tumbled down from the Constance Knox Glacier perched high on its western flank.

Aerial view from the head basin of the Tasman Glacier across to the cloud-covered west coast. Mount Green is in the middle right, with Elie de Beaumont at the far right.

A straightforward definition of a glacier is that it is a mass of ice that accumulates above the permanent snowline, and creeps downhill to be melted away at lower, warmer altitudes. However, it was anything but a straightforward job to count how many glaciers existed in New Zealand.

The New Zealand Glacier Inventory was based primarily on a set of oblique aerial photographs taken during the autumn of 1978. To be counted as a glacier, the body of ice had to be larger than one hectare (the size of a rugby field), and it had to have survived the warmest years during the previous two decades. After all possible glaciers were identified it then took a further ten years to double-check them. The tally was 3153 glaciers, which included 18 glaciers around Mount Ruapehu in the North Island, and nine active rock glaciers in the arid Inland Kaikoura Range, which are glaciers that are so covered in rock that no ice is visible.

Far and away the largest glacier in New Zealand is the Tasman Glacier; 29 kilometres long, and covering an area of nearly 10,000 hectares, it is twice the size of the second largest glacier, the Murchison. Together, the ten largest glaciers account for nearly half of all the ice held in glaciers. Most glaciers are small, steep cirque or alpine glaciers, between four and eight hectares in size, and just a few tens of metres thick. In total the glaciers were found to cover an area of 1160 square kilometres, and were estimated to contain 53.3 cubic kilometres of ice.

In Fiordland and Westland, where it is cool and wet and more snow falls, glaciers usually occur at 1600 metres above sea level. In the warmer north and drier east they occur much higher, at least 2200 metres above sea level. South-facing glaciers that are shaded from the sun tend to be 300 metres lower in altitude than north-facing glaciers exposed to the melting effect of the sun.

Although the Glacier Inventory still stands as the official verdict on the number of glaciers in New Zealand, and will remain so until UNESCO deems it necessary to repeat the World Glacier Inventory, the area covered by glaciers is shrinking. Glacial ice shrank by a quarter between the late 1800s and late 1970s, and since then many small glaciers have disappeared entirely in response to climate change. For example, between 1969 and 1975 intensive surveys were made of the Ivory Glacier, in the Waitaha catchment on the West Coast. However, glacial recession allowed a terminal lake to start growing, and by 2000 the Ivory Glacier had disappeared, 'eaten by its own glacier lake'.

The Tasman Glacier, on the other hand, is so large that it is considered to be out of equilibrium with the current climate. Its great mass of debris-covered ice is still adjusting to warmer temperatures, and although its surface has lowered it didn't lose any length until the early 1990s, when the Tasman Lake formed.

Since 1977, the Southern Alps have seen an interesting small reversal in the usual trend of shrinking glaciers. In most years there has been more snow accumulating than is being lost; as a result, the glaciers are now estimated to contain 59.25 cubic kilometres of ice, an increase of more than 12 percent. The extra snowfall and the advances of many glaciers are the result of changes in atmospheric circulation patterns, such as El Niño events, and an increase in the number of years when southwest rather than northwest winds dominate New Zealand's weather. The Tasman Glacier has responded to increased snow accumulation by becoming slightly thicker, rather than lengthening.

Crevasses are narrow blue ice canyons formed as the brittle surface of a glacier tears under tension. A crevasse that is just one metre wide may be as deep as 30 metres.

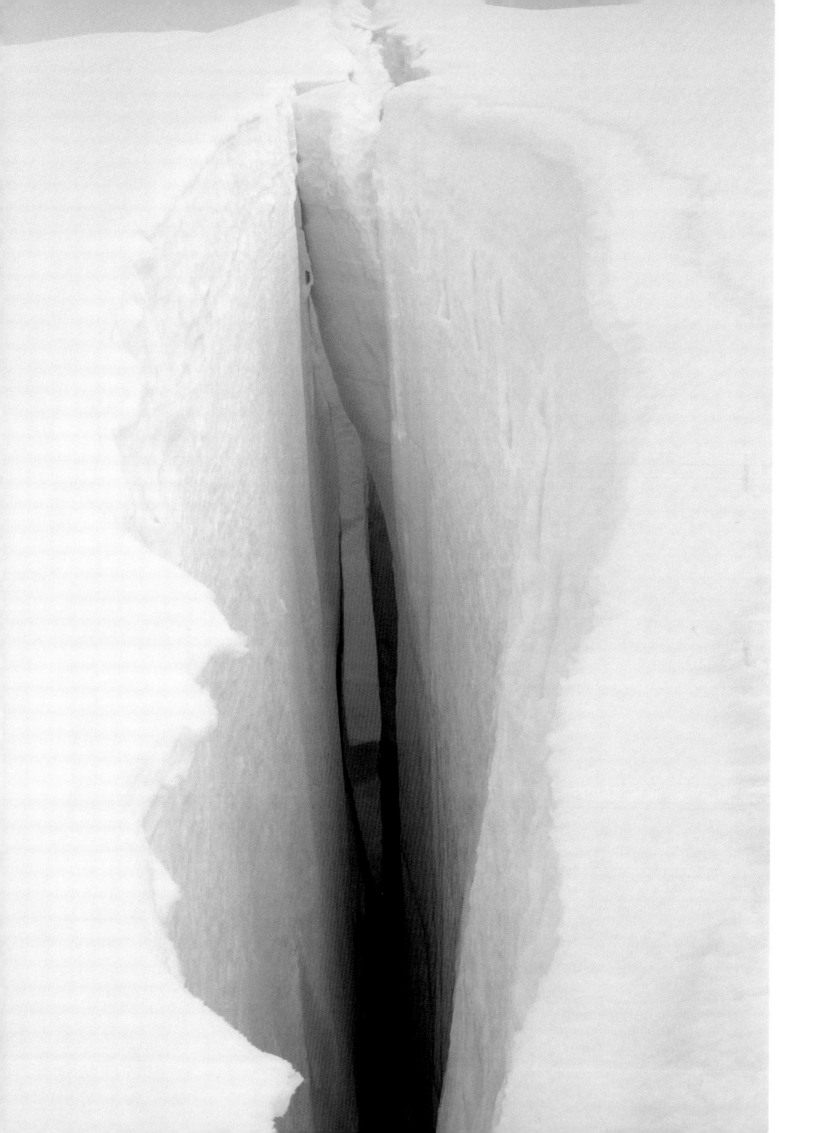

Windy westerlies

The Southern Alps are a complex obstacle and they affect the weather in many ways other than creating precipitation. Not all the westerly wind blows across the mountains; much is diverted around either end of the alps, which is why Cook Strait and Foveaux Strait suffer so many days of gale-force winds. Captain James Cook, in the *Endeavour*, noted that northwesterly storms in the Cook Strait region were:

. . . sometimes violent and troublesome, owing to the neighbouring mountains (always at these times laden with vapours) which, not only increase the force of the wind but alter its direction in such a manner that no two blasts follow each other from the same quarter.

Occasionally low-level air is very stable and resists rising upwards over the mountains. Instead it is deflected by the land and blows parallel to the alps in a strong current known as a barrier jet. This current not only causes gales at either end of the island, but it also acts as a 'virtual mountain', forcing incoming air to rise over it before reaching the actual mountains. When this happens orographic rain falls over the West Coast, rather than in its more usual mountain zone.

The general weather pattern for New Zealand is a series of alternating depressions and anticyclones, which move from west to east across the country at intervals of about seven days. The most common wind directions are northwest and southwest, and though the average situation in the alps is a fair-weather anticyclonic southwesterly, it is the northwesterly winds which more usually create memorably bad weather. In the mountains wind speeds of 160 kilometres an hour are not uncommon, with wind gusts reaching more than 240 kilometres per hour. During the first traverse of Mount Sefton in December 1910, Australian climber Freda du Faur, accompanied by mountain guides Peter Graham and David Thomson, experienced windy conditions very typical of the Southern Alps:

We climbed a snow slope leading to the saddle between two peaks, and turning to the left followed the steep arête leading to the higher one. In the process we received a severe buffeting with the wind, which threatened to blow us over the other side. There were times when I could not stand upright against the force of it, being the lightest of the party, so crouched forward and crawled. The gale had excavated a hollow on the west side of the summit, and into this we crept, trying to evade the worst of the icy blast. We just walked on to the actual summit and off again — it was too bitterly exposed for human beings. Mists were driving around us, being blown apart now and again, and disclosing great banks of white cloud racing before the gale over the low passes and hurling themselves against the defying walls of the high peaks. The cloud-level was at about 8000 feet, and out of it towered the summit of Mount Cook like a giant rising from a sea of foam.

Local topography plays a significant role in channelling winds to great speeds. The destructive power of such mountain winds was shown in 1977 when the Three Johns Hut, above the Mueller Glacier in Aoraki Mount Cook National Park, was torn from its anchors during a violent storm; tragically the four occupants were killed as the hut was hurled over a high bluff. The replacement Barron Saddle Hut is shaped like a barrel lying on its side, to offer less wind resistance.

Over page: Looking across the Caroline face of Aoraki Mount Cook towards the head basin of the Tasman Glacier. As it travels down the valley the large glacier accumulates rocky moraine on its surface as smaller glaciers join from the sides.

The Darwin Glacier is the first significant tributary glacier to merge with the Tasman Glacier. It is a small valley glacier that is itself the product of a glacial merger, and it already bears several wide grey lines of surface glacial till. The Tasman Glacier is so much larger than the Darwin that it barges on regardless, the incoming ice from the Darwin Glacier swept up as a narrow, dirty-grey band along the eastern side of the Tasman.

By the time it draws near the Darwin Glacier, the ice crystal has dropped 800 metres in altitude, and journeyed more than four kilometres in about 45 years. The Darwin Glacier is a significant milestone: it marks the equilibrium line, the location on a glacier where winter snowfall and summer melt balance each other, and the glacier changes from accumulating snow and growing, to losing mass and beginning to shrink. It is also where the glacier reaches maximum velocity, and where the ice crystal stops being buried deeper and deeper in the glacier and begins very slowly rising towards the surface. This line is the end of summer snow line, and is always at its clearest in late March, when the previous winter's snows have melted to their highest level, and when the first snows of the next winter have not yet fallen. Below the equilibrium line the surface of the glacier is now melting ice, fighting a losing battle with the sun and with rain, which sometimes sends streams coursing across it.

The glacier has been moving steadily in its upper section, covering about 25 centimetres a day, although it gained speed as it dropped through the steep icefall. This extra speed was a consequence of an increasing volume of ice and a deepening of the glacier and then, as it rounded Darwin's corner, of being funnelled into a narrowing valley. The glacier continues to move steadily, but is now slowing as compressive flow begins to push ice upwards to replace that being lost to melting at the surface.

The gentle sweep of ice that fills the valley from side to side gives the impression of icing on a cake; a thin, decorative topping perhaps. But strip away the ice and the valley would look very different indeed. Millions of years of grinding have worn an unusually deep U-shaped groove in the valley floor, which is now nearly 500 metres below the surface of the ice. The groove continues to deepen down-valley, so while the surface of the ice maintains a smooth gradient, the ice below is becoming thicker and thicker. By now the glacier surface has long, thin medial moraines that run like stretch marks in the direction of downhill flow. Added to this are concentric arcs of rocky avalanche debris deformed by flow to bulge downhill and spread across the glacier from side to side, as friction grabs the sides of the glacier and slows it down while the middle continues to move more rapidly.

The original Malte Brun Hut was a popular overnight destination for tourists taking guided walks from the Hermitage at Mount Cook. This 1905 photograph looks down the Tasman Glacier towards Mount Cook.

No. 257. Mount Cook
from Maltebrun.

The awful and solemn silence of the mountains, broken only now and again by the crash and thunder of an ice avalanche or the screech of a solitary kea, the complete desolation, the loneliness and remoteness from the haunts of men, all tend to inspire one with deep thoughts and feelings. One line in Walter C. Smith's 'Hilda' expresses more than pages of mine would do — The silence of the mountain spoke unutterable things.

George Mannering on being in the New Zealand mountains

Pink snow and ice midges

During the 1890s alpine guide Peter Graham reported after a summer trip to the Burton Glacier in the Maximilian Range that 'All the slopes on the north side of the glacier were covered with a bright pink snow. We could dig down in this for some six inches and it was like pink granulated sugar.' What he had observed was coloured snow, sometimes known as watermelon snow, caused by a bloom of snow algae. Coloured snow is usually pink or red, although it is sometimes orange or yellow, it is a feature of old waterlogged snow during warm summer months. The algae probably spend the winter in rock crevices, the soil or in permanent snowfields, accumulating on the snow's surface when it melts and blooming as more light penetrates the snowpack.

Coloured snow is a worldwide phenomenon, and the six genera of snow algae found in New Zealand are globally widespread. Coloured snow occurs throughout the Southern Alps, and on mountains in the North Island, at altitudes between 1500 and 2500 metres, and can colour large patches of snow to a depth of 15 centimetres.

Snow algae aren't the only surprising lifeform that thrives on ice and snow. Tiny chironomid midges, colloquially known as 'ice worms', live only on West Coast glaciers. They are found in ice caves, crevices and shady melt pools, between 400 and 600 metres above sea level, where they feed on wind-blown plant and insect material. The male midges have small wings and can't fly, although they have long, stout legs and comb-like claws which give them good grip as they hop across the ice. The females have large wings, and are probably able to fly across the ice to find mates, and also to find places to lay their eggs. They are the only midge which lives solely on glacial ice.

By the early 1500s the ice crystal, still well buried in the depths of the glacier, is passing more alpine glaciers poised above: the heavily crevassed Ranfurly to the west, the Turnbull, Malte Brun and Beetham in the east. Those in the west have been feeding debris to the sides of the Tasman, which now has several permanent grey streaks of dirt and rock running down its western side. Still moving at more or less the speed it did in the névé, it takes a further 65 years to travel the six kilometres from the Darwin Glacier to the next big glacial intersection, where the Rudolf Glacier sweeps in from the west from behind the De la Beche Ridge. The Rudolf stands in stark contrast to the Tasman Glacier; although the surface of the Tasman is now wrinkled like the skin of the elegant centenarian that it is, it is nonetheless still mostly white. The Rudolf Glacier, however, is a grubby urchin, covered in a thick grime of disintegrating greywacke. The larger Rudolf Glacier is more assertive than the Darwin Glacier, which the Tasman just pushed to one side, and it slides in confidently alongside the larger glacier. Seen from above the white glacial surface begins to narrow as a wedge of dark, till-covered surface widens alongside it. A slight ridge of debris marks where the lateral moraine on top of the Tasman's ice joins with debris carried on the Darwin.

Although unsightly, the metre or so thick debris layer acts as an anti-aging treatment which will prolong the glacier's life. It's a lumpy sunscreen, preventing the rays of the summer sun from reaching and melting the ice. Under the debris the rate of melting and evaporation is up to 90 percent less than on white ice. Even where the surface of the glacier remains more or less white, rates of melting vary depending on how smooth or rough the ice is; smooth ice melts less, while rough ice has a greater surface area, and melts more.

Well-protected from melting in the midst of this icy mass, the ice crystal continues to saunter downhill, although it is slowly drifting upward through the glacial ice. Around the turn of the seventeenth century, and five kilometres further down the valley, the Tasman Glacier enters a collision zone. The Hochstetter Glacier icefall is an unruly jumble of heavily crevassed ice tumbling down from the Grand Plateau, an enormous level apron of snow and ice slung across the wide hips of Aoraki Mount Cook and Mount Tasman, which gathers up ice falling from higher glaciers such as the Linda. Where the Rudolf Glacier was content to join the Tasman's slipstream, the Hochstetter icefall barges into the Tasman in a distinctive shear zone, assertively adding a sizeable wedge of white ice alongside the debris legacy of the Rudolf Glacier which, for a while, is relegated to the centre of the glacier.

After the collision comes a time of rebuilding, as ice and rocks from the Tasman and Hochstetter glaciers reunite and amalgamate into one mass. By all measures the glacier is now a behemoth; it is ice all the way down for more than 700 metres, as far as the thickening slurry of debris being dragged along the valley floor. The large amount of incoming ice from the Hochstetter gives the Tasman Glacier a hurry-along, and it accelerates from its previous 90 metres a year to 160 metres or so a year, sprinting down the next three kilometres in just 20 years.

By the time it draws alongside the next significant landmark, the Ball Glacier, the snowflake has been on the move for more than 200 years, and has travelled two thirds of the length of the Tasman Glacier. But although it's covered most of the distance, it still has a long journey ahead, as the glacier's speed is slowing back down to a stroll. The debris-covered Ball Glacier is angled against the flow of the Tasman Glacier, and the incoming ice and debris has to be dragged into line.

Since it passed the Hochstetter icefall the Tasman Glacier has been collecting a new load of debris along its western side, which amalgamates with the Ball Glacier debris and sprawls across onto the narrowing wedge of ice from the Hochstetter icefall. Not far beyond the Ball

Over page: The Rob Roy Glacier, which once extended down the Rob Roy Valley to the West Matukituki Valley, is now a much-shrunken hanging glacier. Mount Aspiring National Park.

Glacier junction a thickening blanket of debris almost completely covers the whole width of the glacier.

Even though the Little Ice Age still grips the country, and although snow still covers the glacier each winter, each year more than 15 metres of ice disappears from the surface of the glacier, whisked away by melting and evaporation in a process known as ablation. By the time Abel Tasman and his men become the first Europeans to sight the Southern Alps in 1642, the ice crystal is moving strongly upwards in an icepack which is now only 600 metres thick and is continuing to steadily thin as the glacier bed rises. Gravel and sediment carried within the glacier is melting out onto its surface, as all the while more glacial till from underneath is being drawn up into the ice. Diverging flows carry increasing amounts of debris out to the side, where it is accumulating as walls of lateral moraine.

By 1670 the ice crystal passes the last major side valley, the eastern home of the Murchison Glacier. Second only in size to the Tasman, the mighty Murchison Glacier doesn't make it all the way down its valley to meet its larger cousin, but finishes several kilometres back from the valley mouth. The Tasman Glacier bulges into the open valley, while its growing side wall of lateral moraine confines the meltwater river flowing in from the Murchison Glacier against the side of the valley.

This prevents the river from eating into the glacier itself, but in many other ways water has become a major force that is sculpting and eroding the Tasman. In summer, streams flow across the surface of the glacier, carving deep channels, collecting in pools of meltwater or disappearing down sinkholes known as moulins or mill holes. They join streams fed by meltwater and rainwater that find ways to flow through cracks and channels in the ice. The subterranean waters make their way beneath the glacier until they pour out at its snout, or terminus, in a grey river that is silty with rock flour. The flowing water sculpts the glacier, creating beautiful ice tunnels and ice caves as big as ballrooms.

Around 1717 a violent earthquake shakes the Southern Alps. It is a massive magnitude 8 quake, emanating from the Alpine Fault itself. On the West Coast, as the Alpine Fault ruptures it moves the Australian and Pacific plates apart by eight metres horizontally and three metres vertically. To the east of the Main Divide the shock dislodges ice and rock, sending innumerable avalanches cascading off most of the peaks and ridges. Hundreds of millions of cubic metres of debris come crashing onto the Tasman Glacier.

By the time Captain James Cook and his men sight the Southern Alps from the Tasman Sea in 1770 all New Zealand's glaciers are as large and long as they've been for more than 10,000 years, although Cook's glimpse of mountains offers him neither summits nor glaciers. The Little Ice Age is at its peak worldwide, and on the other side of the world, during London's cruel winters, people are lighting fires and skating on the frozen River Thames.

More than 50 years after the great earthquake there is little damage showing; winter snow has covered scars on the mountainsides. As the Tasman Glacier continues to grind its way slowly down the valley the earthquake debris has been carried away from where it fell, and has become part of the general chaos of the glacier surface. The lower glacier is now a shrinking block of ice, less than 400 metres thick, firmly wrapped on all sides in an expanding envelope of gravel, dust and rocks. The debris layer beneath the glacier is now 400 metres thick. The ice crystal is little more than two kilometres from the snout of the glacier, but its speed has reduced to a crawl.

By the mid 1800s, when Europeans begin exploring the Southern Alps, the Little Ice Age has ended, and the climate is becoming warmer and milder. But the Tasman Glacier is like a lumbering old-time sailing ship, unresponsive and slow to react, and still growing slowly. In 1862,

During fierce storms in the alps wind speeds may average more than 160 kilometres per hour, with gusts reaching 240 kilometres per hour. Wind-blown snow, Temple Basin, Arthur's Pass.

when Julius Haast and Arthur Dobson spend two months studying and surveying the mountains and valleys at the head of lakes Pukaki, Tekapo and Ohau they call it 'the Great Tasman Glacier'. Upon seeing it for the first time on a fine late summer morning Haast wrote:

. . . the terminal face of a gigantic glacier filled it [the valley] from side to side. For more than fifteen miles the eye could follow the course of this enormous ice stream up to the vast snowfields in which the noble mountains at the head of the valley were almost entirely enveloped.

The terminus of the glacier is moving so slowly that grasses and alpine plants are flowering amongst the thick surface debris. Keen to look beyond the glacier terminus, but turned back by dense thickets of prickly matagouri and speargrass along the side of the glacier, Haast and his party climb onto the glacier and begin to pick their way across it. It's a tiring journey, scrambling over the rough, uneven surface and picking their way around meltwater pools, but they make their way as far as the Murchison Valley, where they get the first glimpse of the terminus of the Murchison Glacier.

By the time the next person ventures onto the glacier seven years later, the ice crystal has barely moved 70 metres, as much upwards as forwards. Despite the difficulty of travelling on the glacier Edward Sealy carries his bulky and heavy wet-plate camera up the glacier as far as De la Beche corner, taking the first-ever photographs of Hochstetter Dome and Mount Darwin, 'this being the first time that this striking peak has been seen from this side of the island', as well as views of Mount Cook and the glacier itself.

By 1882, when Irish climber William Spotswood Green, Ulrich Kaufmann and Emil Boss camp on the flat at the junction of the Ball and Tasman glaciers during an attempt to climb Mount Cook, the Tasman Glacier has reached its full height, and towers over its lateral moraines. Green describes how 'above our spring the boulders were piled into a rampart about sixty feet high, over which the ice of the glacier rose in a vertical wall of from twenty to thirty feet.'

By 1890, when surveyor T. Noel Brodrick is three years into his pioneering measurements of height of the glacier and its speed of travel, the ice has had a final growth spurt, and even breaches the moraine wall in one place.

The climate is beginning to warm, and across the Southern Alps glacial ice begins to melt rapidly. The ice crystal continues to inch down the glacier, and get closer to the surface that melts down towards it. There is less snow falling, and smaller cirque and alpine glaciers, along with the highly responsive Fox and Franz Josef glaciers, begin to retreat. The snout of the Tasman Glacier stubbornly refuses to move, but overall the glacier is losing height, about a metre a year, slowly subsiding below the top of its moraine walls. What was once a climb up onto the top of the glacier becomes a steep slide down an increasingly unstable moraine wall. The sides of the glacier are covered with more and more rocks and debris tumbling from the moraine wall; during heavy rainstorms, avalanches of debris pour down the walls. During the summer of 1955 all the glaciers of the Southern Alps experience their greatest recorded summer melt; a series of photographs taken that year by the Royal New Zealand Air Force shows a record low amount of residual snow remaining on the mountains by the end of summer.

New measurements made 70 years after Brodrick's first measurements show that the glacier is now 82 metres lower next to the Ball Hut site. The ice crystal hasn't yet melted out at the snout of the glacier, but whereas it once had 600 metres of ice above it, it is now in a narrowing wedge only 200 metres thick.

In the late 1960s the terminus begins a very rapid disintegration; the first signs are increasing meltwater

Right: As the Tasman Glacier calves into the Tasman Lake, the resulting icebergs carry with them a thick coating of grey rocky moraine. Over page: On 16 April 1862 Sir Julius Haast sketched a view of the 'Great Tasman Glacier, source of the Tasman River' and described the glacier as an enormous river of ice.

207 208

Mt.
Delabeche

209

210

From Centre of
Tasman Glacier
31st March 1862. —

ponds in the centre of the glacier, and a small lakelet which begins to develop on the eastern edge of the glacier, where water from the channelled Murchison River has begun to leak through the moraine wall as a series of springs. The dirty grey colour of the ponds, most of which are between 20 and 45 metres deep with ice on the bottom, shows they are part of the decaying glacier's system of streams and flowing channels that connect with the river flowing from the glacier's base; the pretty 'blue lakes' on the western side of the glacier, upon which Haast once remarked and which have become a popular tourist attraction, are true meltwater moraine ponds, collecting cleaner water from the glacier surface, and are not associated with the decaying glacier ice.

In 1977 the fortunes of all the Southern Alps glaciers change, as a little more precipitation begins to fall in their head basins. Within five years the Franz Josef Glacier, followed as usual by the Fox six months later, begins to advance. The Franz Josef and Fox glaciers are the fast movers of the New Zealand glacier community. They travel at speed, and their snouts dash back and forth in quick response to climatic changes; compared to these two the Tasman Glacier is a sedate lady.

The western slopes of the Main Divide are much steeper than those in the east, and the annual rain and snowfall is extremely high, especially between 1800 and 2300 metres above sea level. As a result both the Fox and the Franz collect large amounts of snow in their expansive head basins, and a correspondingly large amount of ice is then channelled down steep narrow valleys, coming to an abrupt halt just 300 metres above sea level.

Right: Tasman Lake first appeared at the terminus of the Tasman Glacier in the early 1990s, and recently it has increased significantly in size as it eats back into the glacial ice.
Over page: The Waiho River, which pours out from under the Franz Josef Glacier, is silty from the fine 'rock flour' which the glacier has produced as it grinds against buried rocks and bedrock below.

Franz Josef Glacier/Ka Roimata o Hine Hukatere

Franz Josef Glacier/Ka Roimata o Hine Hukatere is New Zealand's third largest glacier. The first recorded European sighting of Westland's great glaciers was made from sea in 1859, when the ship's log of the boat *Mary Louisa* noted:

We saw what appeared to be a streak of mist running from between the two peaks . . . At noon abreast of Mount Cook, close inshore, we could see distinctly that it was an immense field of ice, entirely filling up the valley.

The Maori name Ka Roimata o Hine Hukatere means 'the tears of the avalanche girl'. In Maori legend a woman named Hine Hukatere often ventured into the mysterious world of mountains and snow. One day she persuaded her lover Tawe to join her, but he slipped and fell to his death, and Hine's endless tears of grief were frozen into a stream of ice.

In 1865 Julius Haast gave it the name Franz Josef, after the Austro-Hungarian emperor. The Franz Josef is fed by a number of other glaciers; its largest tributary is the Agassiz Glacier, which is in turn fed by the Chamberlin and Davis snowfields. In 1837 the Swiss scientist Louis Agassiz was the first to suggest that ice ages had dominated the world's climate at various times.

The Franz Josef Glacier reaches below 300 metres above sea level, after a rapid descent from an expansive head basin down a steep narrow valley. View of glacier from Sentinel Rock.

Fox Glacier/Te Moeka o Tuawe

Fox Glacier/Te Moeka o Tuawe, meaning the resting place of Tu Awe, falls dramatically from the western slopes of Mount Tasman from 1500 metres above sea level to just 300 metres, in only seven kilometres. In 1872 former explorer and four-time Premier Sir William Fox became the first tourist to visit the West Coast glaciers, having been inspired by Julius Haast's lyric descriptions. Haast had already given the name of Prince Alfred to the slightly smaller and more southerly of the two glaciers, but it was renamed in Fox's honour. Fox visited and painted both the Fox and Franz Josef glaciers.

Explorers Charlie Douglas and Arthur Harper made the first observations of the Franz Josef Glacier, and there have been many scientific surveys since then to measure its speed, which have been confirmed by the occasional more whimsical event. In 1950 a Tiger Moth plane crashed onto the icefall of the Franz Josef Glacier, 5.6 kilometres from the glacier's snout. The pilot and passenger walked to safety, and 14 years later the plane arrived at the bottom and fell off the steep terminal face, having travelled at top speeds of between 1.5 and 1.8 metres per day. This is pretty much par for the course for the Franz Josef, which can trot along at up to 2.5 metres a day through its steep icefall, although it's been known to gallop along at an astonishing seven metres a day after heavy rain.

One wouldn't describe the Fox Glacier as sluggish either. In 1967, Jonathon Pascoe, nephew of mountaineer and prolific writer John Pascoe, was in a climbing party at the head of the Fox Glacier névé when he lost his cigarette lighter, an elegant Ronson lighter engraved with his name, which had been given to him by his future wife. In 1996 it was discovered 12 kilometres away, below the glacier's lower icefall, by glacier guide Rob Kirkwood, who traced it back to Jonathon. Now a confirmed non-smoker, he was nonetheless delighted to have his wife's gift returned. In 28 years the lighter had travelled almost the entire length of the glacier, moving at an average speed of 1.17 metres per day, and covering 426 metres each year. This corresponds pretty well with speeds of 1.3 metres per day which were measured near the glacier terminus in the early 1960s.

The snouts of the Franz Josef and Fox glaciers are very sensitive climate instruments which reflect how fluctuations in temperature and snowfall are affecting the glaciers as a whole. They respond to changes in their head basins within just five to seven years. This extreme sensitivity comes from the high amounts of snow and ice collecting in their névés, and the steep topography which causes them to move at high speeds.

Between the 1920s and 1960s the two glaciers were in rapid retreat during warmer than average years, making small advances during the late 1940s and the mid 1960s, when their snouts advanced as much as 1.9 metres per day. Then during the 1980s and 1990s both glaciers began to make rapid advances, which coincided with a period of frequent El Niño weather events which began in the late 1970s and resulted in cooler temperatures and higher precipitation. From 2000 onwards they began to retreat slightly again.

Research shows that the Franz Josef Glacier has the highest rate of ablation, or ice loss, reported for any glacier anywhere in the world, losing the equivalent of 20 metres in a year.

However, despite the increase in precipitation, the

The terminal face of the Fox Glacier clearly shows the alternating layers of winter ice and summer dirt that the glacier has accumulated over many years.

Tasman Glacier barely responds; its acknowledgement of the extra snow is a subtle thickening of ice along the edges as a slight wave passes down her length. But none of this has any effect at the terminus, where the melting is becoming increasingly catastrophic. The meltwater lakes are growing rapidly in size and depth; in just four years between 1982 and 1986 they double in size. By now there is a new kind of movement happening — rather than moving down-valley, the glacier has begun to slump into the meltwater ponds. By the late 1980s the ponds and the lakelet have merged into a single lake that is nearly two square kilometres in area. It has sheer ice cliffs on the glacier side, but there is no longer any ice below, as the lake has melted down to the thick gravel layer beneath. It is so big that it's already earned an official name: the Tasman Lake.

The ice crystal has nearly melted out from the ice cliffs at the northern end of the lake when, in 1991, the leading edge of the glacier splits dramatically, calving off a huge chunk of ice. The ice crystal suddenly finds itself launched in a 100 metre-long iceberg, floating in a lake whose temperature is barely above freezing. Soon there are six icebergs in the lake, being blown back and forth by the wind, and beginning to melt rapidly. Winter freezes the lake and gives the melting icebergs a temporary reprieve, but the following summer the ice crystal melts, to finally become water again. Tasman Lake flows out into the Tasman River, which will take the water drop out to sea in a journey much faster than its glacial travels.

Of all the glaciers it could have fallen on, the Tasman Glacier locked the snowflake up as ice for the longest period of time. It took more than 560 years in the glacier's embrace to travel nearly 29 kilometres from the slopes of Elie de Beaumont to the snout of the glacier, dropping nearly two kilometres in altitude as it did so. Perhaps one day, as water vapour, it will get picked up again by the passing wind, frozen and dropped once more on a high mountain range, to start life over as part of a glacier. And who knows — perhaps it had already been here before, during the great ice ages when glaciers truly ruled the land, unlike now, when they are fighting for their survival in the changing climate of the modern world.

Left: Meltwater ponds, which dramatically sculpt and erode the surface of a glacier during warm summers, freeze during winter months. Storm clouds above Fox Glacier.

Over page: In 1862 Sir Julius Haast described the terminal face of a gigantic glacier filling the Tasman valley from side to side. Today the view of the terminus of the Tasman Glacier is one of a lake bordered by high moraine walls.

CLIMBING
THE ALPS

Mountains mean different things to different people: while many people are content to admire them from a distance, or to walk on and around them, others are driven to climb to the top. On Christmas Day 1894, a team of young New Zealanders — Tom Fyfe, Jack Clarke and George Graham — became the first climbers to reach the summit of Mount Cook, and in 1910 Australian Freda du Faur became the first woman to climb New Zealand's highest peak.

Climbing the alps

Freda du Faur initially visited the Mount Cook area in 1906 as a curious tourist, not as a mountaineer; her visit had been sparked by seeing photos of the alps, yet her first glimpse of the mountains inspired in her a desire to climb:

From the moment my eyes rested on the snow-clad alps I worshipped their beauty and was filled with a passionate longing to touch those shining snows, to climb to their heights of silence and solitude, and feel myself one with the mighty forces around. The great peaks towering into the sky before me touched a chord that all the wonders of my own land had never set vibrating, and filled a blank of whose very existence I had been unconscious . . . To a restless, imaginative nature the fascination of the unknown is very great; from my childhood I never saw a distant range without longing to know what lay on the other side. So in the mountains the mere fact of a few

thousand feet of rock and snow impeding my view was a direct challenge to climb and see what lay behind it.

New Zealander George Mannering had a similar epiphany 20 years earlier. George and his cousin Charles Fox had arrived at the Hermitage at Mount Cook village after a two-day journey inland from Timaru, first by train and then horse and buggy:

A low mist had hidden the higher peaks throughout the day, and led to a surprise on the following morning which I little dreamt of . . . No words of mine can describe the ecstasy which seemed to pervade my whole being as on the early, cloudless morning the wonderful picture of Mount Sefton reared itself in indescribable sunlit splendour above the old bush-clad moraine close by the Hermitage. Here, indeed, was a new and a fairy-like world to live in.

Right: Brothers Alex and Peter Graham were among the leading alpine guides of their day. They are seen here with client Freda du Faur, following their successful ascent of Mount Cook. Freda du Faur was the first woman to climb Mount Cook. 1910.

The first mountaineering in New Zealand, however, was carried out not by climbers such as du Faur and Mannering, but by explorers, gold prospectors and scientists. In February 1863 the Otago Provincial Geologist James Hector, accompanied by J.W. Sullivan and I. Rayer, made the first recorded alpine crossing of the alps, from the Matukituki Valley over Hector Col to the Waipara River on the West Coast. They were equipped with a new type of ice axe and climbing rope, the first time such equipment had been used in New Zealand, but even so their journey across the heavily crevassed Bonar Glacier below Mount Aspiring was very challenging.

During the harsh winter of 1863 the miner Patrick Quirk Caples explored alone in the Routeburn area, using his miner's shovel to cut steps in the snow. The following winter was equally cold and harsh, but another prospector, Alphonse Barrington, and his two companions James Farrell and Antoine Simonin spent an arduous four months without proper equipment or clothing, and often without food, exploring from Queenstown to the Cascade, returning via the remote and difficult Olivine Ice Plateau. During 1866 rumours of gold discoveries on the Cook River on the West Coast led to more prospectors making unrecorded alpine crossings to the Copland Valley.

Between 1867 and 1870 surveyor Edward Sealy made three trips to the Mount Cook region, exploring the glaciers and taking some outstanding photographs; each photographic plate had to be developed straight away in the mobile laboratory which he had lugged two thirds of the way up the Tasman Glacier, along with his cumbersome camera and tripod. Inspired by such photos, by the 1870s the first tourists had begun to make their way to the Mount

Previous page: A group of mountaineers setting out to climb Mount Sefton in 1895. They carried food, spare clothes and sleeping blankets in swags made from sacks, and ice axes and a coil of rope were their only alpine equipment.
Right: During the 1880s and 1890s, climbers wore hob-nailed boots for grip on the ice and snow, and used long ice axes to cut steps to stand in, as these men are doing on an ice face on the Tasman Glacier.

CLIMBING ICE FACE - TASMAN GLACIER

Cook area, keen to experience the mountains and glaciers of the Southern Alps for themselves. The first visitors were mainly parties of locals; visitors from further afield had to be very dedicated:

In 1881 the foot of Mount Cook could be reached only by a bone-jarring journey over bullock tracks from the settlement at Lake Tekapo, followed by a dangerous crossing of the wide shingle bed of the Tasman River. Lake Tekapo was connected by bridged road to Albury, and from Albury there was a rail route to Christchurch . . . between it and the 'Old Country' there lay 12,000 miles of sea, to be traversed by small steamship.

In 1873, Christchurch lawyer and explorer, Leonard Harper and his wife Joanna went on to the Mueller and Tasman glaciers, possibly the first time a woman had set foot on the glaciers. Exploration ran in the family; their son Arthur Harper went on to become a mountaineer who climbed with Mannering and others, worked with explorer Charlie Douglas on the West Coast, and later became one of the founders of the New Zealand Alpine Club. Several months after the Harpers' visit the Governor Sir George Bowen visited the area and climbed the viewpoint of Mount Sebastopol. He was impressed by the tourist potential of the region and, keen to draw attention to it, issued an invitation offering assistance to any member of the English Alpine Club who wanted to attempt to climb Mount Cook. His offer was never taken up, but within eight years an English exhibition of photos of the mountains and a copy of Julius Haast's *Geology of Canterbury and Westland*, illustrated by some of Sealy's photographs, inspired the Irish clergyman Reverend William Spotswood Green to make an attempt.

In 1882 Green, and his Swiss climbing companions, hotelier Emil Boss and mountain guide Ulrich Kaufmann, had to travel halfway round the world just to reach New Zealand. Climbing here was quite a different proposition to climbing in Europe, where well-appointed alpine huts and porters provided comfort and support; here they had to work very hard to carry heavy loads and establish camps in the remote Mount Cook area before they could launch their climbing attempt. Equipped only with nailed boots, a rope and ice axes for cutting steps they came within several hundred feet of the summit before being faced, in the late afternoon, with a large, gaping crevasse that was impossible to cross. On their way down they were caught out by nightfall, and had to spend a night in the rain standing on a narrow ledge, attempting to stay awake so as to not fall off. It was an epic adventure, and although they failed by the narrowest of margins to reach the summit of Mount Cook they were fêted by the press, and their efforts inspired the next generation of climbers. With a week to spare before their boat sailed they also made an attempt to climb Mount Earnslaw at the head of Lake Wakatipu, but were again defeated by bad weather.

The following year, in March 1883, Austrian explorer and biologist Robert von Lendenfeld and his wife Anna visited the Mount Cook area intent on exploring the Tasman Glacier. Accompanied by New Zealander Harry Dew they established a camp up the Tasman Glacier under Malte Brun, and from there made the first ascent of Hochstetter Dome; this achievement took them 24 hours, and was the first alpine ascent of a major New Zealand peak.

In 1885 Charlie Douglas and Westland chief surveyor Gerhard Mueller explored together up the mighty Arawata River as far as Williamson's Flat. John Pascoe wrote in *Mr Explorer Douglas* that:

. . . the highlight was the first ascent of Mount Ionia, a fine peak from any angle. Although only 7390 feet, its shapely cone rises 6000 feet above the Arawata with a graceful

Explorer Charlie Douglas and Arthur Harper, who later became one of the founders of the New Zealand Alpine Club, undertook many alpine climbs during their West Coast explorations. With dog Betsey Jane in the Cook River Valley, 1894.

A perfect deluge

Reverend William Spotswood Green, Emil Boss and Ulrich Kaufmann had made it halfway round the world, and as far up the Tasman Glacier as the Ball Glacier, when they had their first taste of the changeable and ferocious weather which proves so often to be the biggest barrier to climbing in the Southern Alps:

. . . About midnight the wind increased to a furious westerly gale, accompanied by a perfect deluge. The tent could not blow away, the floor and sides being all in one, unless it carried us with it, but we felt certain it must soon split. It fluttered and banged every now and then with reports like pistol shots, and the rain kept up such a constant roar that it almost drowned the thunder which now began to crash about the mountain peaks. Sleep was out of the question, so we lay as patiently as was possible reading the barometer at intervals by the light of a match and hoping that every squall might prove the last. Dawn came but the weather was as bad as ever. At 9 a.m. we were ready for breakfast, but preferred to remain in shelter rather than make any attempt to light a fire. Hitherto the tent had kept out the rain, but now Kaufmann discovered that his bag was soaking the wet through the tent wall, then a pool formed in our opossum rug, and it was no longer possible to keep dry. We sat shivering in the tent listening to the rain and the howling of the storm, and watched the surface of the little lake every now and then lashed into a sheet of white foam by the fury of the squalls. At twelve the rain ceased, so we lit a fire and warming up the parrot soup enjoyed a hot meal. Then as the rain began afresh we retired to our shelter . . . Meeting with a repulse in this early stage of our undertaking was not a little disheartening, but we buoyed ourselves up with the hope that the morrow would be fine enough for a fresh start. Vain hope!

It proceeded to rain for a further 36 hours, eventually turning to snow, until finally rewarding the damp mountaineers with a sunny day on which to dry out their wet clothes and sleeping bags. Yet they were lucky; bad weather in the alps often lasts for more than a week, and even two weeks at a time.

William Spotswood Green's painting shows himself and Swiss mountaineers Emil Boss and Ulrich Kaufmann attempting the Summit Rocks, 'the worst bit on Mount Cook'. 1882.

symmetry. Mueller wrote *"I have never seen anything to approach in awe-inspiring effect the view from Mount Ionia . . . It took me two days and half hard climbing to get to the top of Ionia. The rope had to be used again and again, both in ascending and descending, and for well nigh half a mile steps had to be cut in the frozen snow to get footing."* It has been said that as ice axes were then unknown in Westland, Douglas cut the steps with a bill-hook or slasher . . . This ascent was enterprising by any standards.

In the early years of New Zealand climbing the motivation to make first ascents was very strong, and while there were almost limitless possibilities, the lure of climbing the highest peak remained a focus. The next climbers in the Mount Cook region were New Zealanders. Inspired by Green, Boss and Kaufmann's unsuccessful attempt on Mount Cook, and keen that the peak should be climbed first by New Zealanders, Mannering decided it was something he would like to attempt, despite having no experience in alpine climbing. Accompanied at various times by his cousin Charles Fox, Marmaduke Dixon, Charles Inglis, Percy Johnson, Malcolm Ross and Arthur Harper, he put in a concerted effort to climb Mount Cook, making four attempts between 1886 and 1890. Although these attempts brought him within 50 metres of the summit, he never succeeded.

Despite his goal eluding him, he remained in every sense a true adventuring mountaineer:

There are pleasures in the pursuit of adventure amongst the great snow-fields and glaciers which only those who are initiated can thoroughly enjoy. Ask the man who goes climbing what those pleasures are, and he cannot tell you, he cannot define them — yet he feels them, and they are ever luring him on. They are indefinite, inexpressible; but there is a sort of "mountain fever" which comes when one has "lost one's heart to the great mountains." In the

work all a man's best physical, and many of his mental, powers are brought out and strengthened. There is the energy, perseverance and patience to last through a day's swagging, the pluck to face all sorts of dangers amongst the snow, ice and rocks, combined with the prudence to know when, for the safety of oneself and party, to give in and restrain enthusiasm. There are the qualities of organisation and system, for which plenty of exercise is found; indeed, one cannot overstate the benefits which accrue.

In 1891, mountain climbing in New Zealand came of age when Mannering, Harper and Ross formed the New Zealand Alpine Club, although after ten years it went into a decline, to be resurrected in the early 1920s. In 1893 Dixon and Mannering made another attempt on Mount Cook, and were joined by Timaru plumber Tom Fyfe, who was proving to be a great rock climber. On this attempt they had homemade skis, manufactured from reaper blades with upturned ends, to make the crossing of the Grand Plateau easier. During their ascent:

We found the trail of a rabbit on the ice plateau. What on earth this enterprising rodent was about wandering on this elevated snow field at 7000 feet, I cannot imagine; but the fact remains, and if that rabbit gets to the top of Mount Cook, it is greatly to his credit, though I am afraid he will not get the honour due to him.

As it turned out, neither the rabbit nor the men made it to the summit; it was the fifth unsuccessful attempt for the indefatigable Mannering.

For the rest of that summer Fyfe carried on climbing, building his alpine skills and experience by making a solo ascent of Malte Brun, successfully climbing De la Beche and the Footstool with young Waimate man George Graham and, with 18-year-old Jack Clarke, guiding a German climber on the first ascent of Mount Darwin.

May Kinsey was one of a number of women who visited the Mount Cook area to climb with guides who were based at the Hermitage. One of the guides' main jobs was to cut steps for their clients. 1895.

By the following spring there was news that an English climber, A.E. Fitzgerald, was bringing the famous Italian guide Mattias Zurbriggen from Europe with the intention of climbing Cook and Tasman, and the New Zealanders redoubled their efforts to get there first. Finally, after several unsuccessful attempts, the young team of Fyfe, Clarke and Graham succeeded in reaching the summit of Mount Cook's high peak on Christmas Day 1894.

Pipped at the post by the Kiwis, Fitzgerald and Zurbriggen made a number of significant first alpine crossings and ascents in the Mount Cook region, including mounts Sefton and Tasman, the latter in the company of Clarke, who would go on to become a well-known climbing guide. Fitzgerald and Zurbriggen brought a new style of climbing to New Zealand: they used crampons for better grip on ice, pitons to be hammered in to provide vital anchors on rock, and they travelled light and fast. One of Zurbriggen's outstanding achievements was the second ascent of Mount Cook, a climb which he began with John Adamson, the manager of the Hermitage, but which he completed solo, following a different route to that used by Fyfe, Clarke and Graham less than three months earlier. It was a busy climbing season in the central alps, and the beginning of several busy years, although it would be another ten years before anyone climbed Mount Cook again.

In 1897, after injuring his leg while climbing on the West Coast, Tom Fyfe limped into the Hokitika surgery of the newly appointed Westland Hospital Medical Superintendent Dr Ebenezer Teichelmann. This meeting inspired the little Australian doctor to discover more about the mountains which dominated the inland skyline.

In 1901 the English Reverend Henry Newton arrived on the West Coast to be the vicar of Ross and South Westland. He was also a keen climber, and before long he had teamed up with Teichelmann, and with the brothers Alex and Peter Graham. These four were to pioneer and shape mountaineering on the West Coast. Over five years they climbed extensively in the alps, making many first ascents, including seven significant peaks in one season; in 1905 they were part of only the third party to climb Mount Cook. Newton passed on his snow- and ice-craft to the Graham brothers, marking the beginning of a strong guiding tradition on the West Coast which complemented that developing on the Hermitage side of the mountains.

In 1908 Teichelmann, Peter Graham and Dennis Nolan made an ambitious attempt to climb Mount Aspiring, approaching from the west up the rugged Waiatoto River, but they ran out of time and decided to retreat before bad weather trapped them in the remote, difficult valley. The following summer guides Peter Graham and Jack Clarke returned with English climber Captain Bernard Head as their client, and succeeded in climbing the mountain after approaching it from the West Matukituki valley.

For more than 20 years guides were an integral part of climbing in the alps, and New Zealand and overseas climbers alike hired their services. Responsible not just for route-finding and safety, one of a guide's most important tasks was to cut hundreds of steps. But from the mid-1920s keen amateur climbers began to attempt increasingly difficult climbs, without guides but with the use of crampons, and by the end of the Second World War guiding had almost faded as a tradition. In the latter part of the twentieth century, however, there was a resurgence in alpine guiding, and today guided parties take their place in the mountains alongside a robust and enthusiastic community of independent climbers.

Until the 1950s it was possible to find unclimbed peaks and to claim a piece of history by being the first person to climb them. With the first ascents all taken, people turned their attention to other milestones: to

Jack Clarke was one of three Kiwis who successfully made the first ascent of Aoraki Mount Cook from the Hooker Glacier on Christmas Day 1894.

Oh, the misery of it!

Between early 1886 and late 1890, the indomitable George Mannering made five unsuccessful attempts to be the first to climb Mount Cook. This scene from the second unsuccessful attempt by Mannering, Marmaduke Dixon and Charles Inglis in 1887 shows not only how bad the worst mountain weather can be, but the qualities of stoic endurance and humour that the three climbing companions shared:

The wind now began to rise from the nor'west, and clouds of dust were sweeping down the valley, so we lost no time in pressing on to a patch of Irishman scrub a mile or so below the terminal face of the [Tasman] glacier. We hurriedly cut some bedding and pitched the tent before the rain came on, in rather close proximity to an old creek-bed, which had apparently been dry for some time. That creek made up for lost time during the night, and soon the rain came down in bucketsful as we lay our wearied limbs to rest in our oiled calico blanket-bags. The thunder crashed and the lightning flashed, and the Tasman River began to roar, and by one o'clock such a quantity of rain had fallen as to convert the dry creek-bed into a roaring torrent, whose waters threw up a bank of shingle, and turning its course (horror of all horrors!), came right into our tent. In less than a minute from the time that we felt the first trickle there was a foot of water in the tent, and all our impedimenta of every description were sopping or floating about in the dark, and in imminent danger of being washed away.

Hurriedly we collected all we could into our blanket-bags, got into our boots somehow, and made for higher ground. We could not see a rise in the ground, but after wading about found a small portion out of water, and with much strong language and trouble, succeeded in repitching the tent — after a fashion!

Ah! well do we remember the miseries and discomforts of the scene. Wind blowing in fitful gusts, rain coming down in sheets, while thunder and lightning and the incessant roar of the Tasman all tended to make the scene one of terror and discomfort. Matches nearly all destroyed; bread reduced to a state of pulp; blankets and clothes wet; instruments, boots, ropes, ice-axes all muddled up anywhere, some in the tent, some being silted or washed away from the spot where the tent was first pitched; the floor of the tent now hard, wet stones, in lieu of comfortable dry tussock. Oh, the misery of it!

We lay in our wet clothes the rest of that night, all the following day, and the next night. Inglis and I scarcely stirred but to eat some disgusting, soppy mixture or to light our pipes; but Dixon

pluckily rigged up a windbreak with an old tent left by the Birch Hill shepherds, and after three hours' persistent labour kindled a fire, improvising a chimney out of a pair of white flannel trousers and sundry other garments!

We were quite hemmed in by water, and were in a constant state of anxiety lest the river should make depradations in our direction, as it was quite close to us, whilst in the creek on the other side we could hear the rocks being rolled down by the force of the water.

Nine inches of rain had fallen during the forty-eight hours, but on the Sunday it cleared, and once again the warm sun shone out, the birds began to sing, and the waters subsided as quickly as they had risen, and our spirits rose again as we spread out our wet belongings on the scrub and donned a hat, shirt, and a pair of boots apiece, and set out for a visit to the scene of devastation at the face of the glacier, whence the river issues. The costume was airy but convenient, as we had to cross several streams before reaching our destination.

The famous Italian mountain guide Mattias Zurbriggen arrived in New Zealand in 1894, and made the second ascent of Mount Cook on his own, as well as completing significant first ascents and routes on other peaks. Seen here with his 'pet mountain', Mount Sefton 1896.

climbing solo, finding new routes, harnessing new technology and skills to climb routes that were once considered impossible, and to the first descents by ski, snowboard, parapente or hang-glider.

But although mountains bring out in many people the desire to be first, to go where no one else has gone, that is far from being the only motivation. Each climber has their own reasons for wanting to climb, and ultimately the experience is as much about the person themselves as it is about the mountain they are climbing.

Paul Powell's particular mountaineering passion was Mount Aspiring during the 1940s and 1950s. He wrote:

. . . I will always climb there for the fascination of untrodden places, for the beauty of form and line where rock and snow curve to the sky, or for the friendships that are made on mountains. Part of the reason has been vanity, sometimes a drive to get-there-first. When I have been brash the mountains have chastened me. I've been afraid there many times, but my friends have helped me overcome my fear.

And John Pascoe wrote:

As did an Italian mountaineer in the Himalayas, I find in mountains "the bread and the passion of life" . . . We conquer ourselves, not the mountains. In acclimatising to fatigue, overcoming fear, strengthening links of comradeship, one can seem linked closer to mother country, even if that mother is a barren tuft of scrub above a horrible rock slab. And to be close to one's friends or to one's country is a good destiny.

The English Reverend Henry Newton (seated, centre) and the 'little doctor' Dr Ebenezer Teichelmann (crouching, right) joined forces to climb in the alps, passing on their skills to West Coast brothers Peter Graham (second from left) and Alex Graham (second from right) who went on to become guides. R.S. Low at left. 1906–08.

Beyond the trees, and below the permanent snow, the Southern Alps are girdled by a broad mosaic of alpine gardens. Hidden under snow in winter, during summer these gardens are revealed as a lush patchwork of beautiful flowers, low bushes and graceful snow tussocks, set among rocks and streams.

The heart of an alpine garden

The wealth of New Zealand's alpine gardens comes not just from a great diversity of species, but from an ecological complexity we are only just beginning to discover. Plants and invertebrates rely on one another in a tangled web of interdependence that is at once universal across the alps, yet also unique to each particular place.

Snow tussocks, or snow grasses, are the mainstay of New Zealand's alpine grasslands and herbfields. Although they have the stature and appearance of a garden, they are as long-lived and structurally complex as a forest.

There are currently 23 recognised species of *Chionochloa* tussocks, whose Greek genus name means snow grass; the group has recently been taxonomically revised and there are also a number of subspecies. Twenty-two of the species in this group are found only in New Zealand, with just one species occurring in Australia. Up to 14 of the snow tussocks occur in the alpine zone.

There are two lines part-way up the slopes of the Southern Alps which illustrate how much temperature falls with increasing altitude. New Zealand's sharply delineated treeline marks the point above which it's too cold for trees to either establish or survive. This ranges from roughly 1500 metres above sea level in the central North Island down to 900 metres in Fiordland. The other clearly defined line is the permanent snowline, above which it remains cold enough year-round that snow and ice don't melt, and plants, as a rule, don't grow. In between these two lies the alpine zone, and the plants that live here have to be able to cope with what seem to humans to be extreme conditions.

Ecologically it is a 1000 metre wide band of vegetation that for ease of description botanists often divide into the low-alpine and high-alpine zones. The alpine zone begins where trees end, which is generally

Plentiful water plays an important role in the alpine zone, and numerous streams, tarns and wetlands are significant features in the grasslands and herbfields.

where average summer temperatures are less than 10°C. For the first 200 metres immediately above the treeline, especially above podocarp-dominated forests such as those on the West Coast, snow tussocks and large-leaved alpine flowers often grow among shrubs in a dense tangle that can reach head height. This is sometimes referred to by trampers as the subalpine zone. Between 200 and 400 metres above this mixed shrubland, tall snow tussocks alone dominate.

The high-alpine zone begins where the average temperature in the warmest month is around 5°C; here the vegetation is sparse and low, and plants hug the ground. A thousand metres above the treeline, where the average temperature of the warmest month is close to zero, and there are frequent days and nights when temperatures sink below freezing, conditions are too harsh for plants; only a few hardy lichens survive above here in the nival zone of permanent ice and snow.

Like other alpine plants, snow tussocks are tallest near the treeline, where they can reach 1.5 metres in height; as they ascend the mountain slopes they become shorter. In the low-alpine zone some species thrive in rich, well-drained soils on recently disturbed sites, while others prefer wetter sites with poorer soils in more stable areas. At higher altitudes snow patch tussocks cope with late-lying snow, and are often short and flattened against the ground. Short snow grass is notorious among trampers for being very slippery when wet or snow covered.

New Zealand snow tussocks are usually referred to as tussocks, a word which is derived from an Old English word describing a tuft of hair, but another more northern name for the group, bunch grass, refers to the way the plant's stems bunch together.

This life story focuses on a single snow tussock plant, and unravels some of the intimate complexity of the alpine community to which it belongs. The exact mix of species is unique to this community, and has developed in response to subtle local variations in climate, topography and soil, but the principles and processes apply equally to any other mountain community in the alps.

It's a late summer afternoon, several hundred years ago, on a warm, still mountainside, 1400 metres above sea level, on the western side of the Main Divide, towards the southern end of the Southern Alps. It's a rare perfect day in the mountains; a high pressure weather system sits across the country, ranks of snow-capped mountains brush against a pure blue sky and, rarely for these temperate latitudes, there is no wind. A light curtain of heat haze shimmers above the ground. It's remarkably quiet, the only sounds a lone cicada rasping rhythmically, the indistinct murmur of an out-of-sight stream, and a single distant call from a kea flying over the forest edge 200 metres below.

A gentle breeze springs up, its arrival announced by a rustling which grows louder as the whole hillside begins to ripple. Thousands of snow tussock stalks, heavy with seedheads, sway in tawny waves until the slight zephyr moves on and everything settles back into stillness.

This stunning sight is the result of a mast seeding year; after several years of little seeding, the snow tussocks have synchronised in a heavy mass flowering and seeding.

The gentle breeze which shakes the ripe seedheads in passing portends a change in the weather, as do the first barely noticeable white threads of cirrus cloud high above. By the following morning the sky is full of clear signals of the arrival of the nor'west wind, and each peak wears a hogsback cloud as a jaunty hat. A hot wind is buffeting the tall flower stalks of the snow tussocks, whipping them back and forth and shaking loose the seeds from within the florets where they have developed and matured during the previous six weeks. The flowering adult snow tussocks produce thousands of tiny seeds, each weighing just one milligram.

The seeds don't travel far, less than two metres. Many

In spring and summer the alpine zone becomes a rich flower garden. Mountain daisies (*Celmisia verbascifolia*) blooming in the Valley of the Trolls, at the head of the left branch of the Routeburn River, Mount Aspiring National Park.

Coping with the cold

Globally, nearly three percent of the world's land area is classified as alpine, and four percent of the world's higher or vascular plants, some 10,000 species, make their home there. They have become adept at coping with drought and freezing, the former often being a consequence of the latter. Many alpine plants have evolved from lowland species, able to make the transition as the same adaptations that allowed them to tolerate drought and dehydration enabled them to survive the cold.

In New Zealand, however, drought is not a feature of the alpine zone; even in the dry rainshadow areas there is usually a year-round surplus of water. But although they have it easy when it comes to water supply, the plants that live in the Southern Alps must be able to tolerate temperatures that average between 0°C and 11°C, and range from 25°C to nearly 15°C below freezing. Even in the middle of summer frosts are frequent, and it's rare for much longer than a week to pass without the temperature dropping below zero. Air temperatures are highest close to the ground, especially in the lee of rocks or plants, which is why most alpine plants are low-growing and hug the ground. Shape is important, allowing many plants to generate their own shelter: it can be many degrees warmer inside the base of a snow tussock than outside, and even warmer just inside the windproof tangle of short stems and tight-growing leaves that typify cushion plants.

Many plants wear the natural equivalent of a warm coat, their leaves covered in a dense hairy fuzz, which traps warm air against the leaf surface and cuts down wind chill. This also has the advantage of minimising water loss. Even though soil water is never lacking, New Zealand's strong winds quickly wick water away from the surface of the plant as it transpires. Snow tussock leaves are folded or rolled in on themselves to shelter their stomata from the wind.

Cold is not the only enemy; on a summer's day in the mountains it can get surprisingly hot, a situation made worse by high levels of ultraviolet radiation. UV levels are naturally higher at altitude, and New Zealand's clean atmosphere lacks many dust particles to filter the UV rays. As well, in January the Earth is several million miles closer to the sun than it is in July, so UV levels during a southern summer are about seven percent more intense than during a northern hemisphere summer. All up that's a sure-fire recipe for lots of damaging UV radiation.

Luckily, many of the tricks plants have evolved for coping with cold and drought are as effective at blocking out UV rays. Hairs, such as those on the leaves of many mountain daisies, and thick shiny cuticles, such as those on Mount Cook buttercup leaves, work as a natural sunblock.

With more than 60 species, mountain daisies are a striking and common sight in the alpine zone. *Celmisia semicordata* can grow to more than a metre across, with large flowers atop stems which may be half a metre high.

of the seeds fall on unfavourable ground — the alpine zone is a crowded place, and there are not many 'safe' sites for a seed to germinate and put down roots. But fortunately, and unusually, there is a good opportunity nearby, where a speargrass has succumbed to old age and died, leaving an open area covered in a rich, rotting mass of dead leaves. A few seeds land here, and although some are blown away by the gusting nor'wester, some lodge within dark, moist gaps between the decaying leaves.

In the middle of the night the front arrives, and rain begins to fall. This is no gentle shower; the first few drops are fat and splash as they land, and the rain quickly becomes a heavy downpour. Within minutes, rivulets of water begin to streak across rocks and down leaves, and soon sheets of water pour across the already wet soil. Heavy rain like this is the norm here, where more than six metres of precipitation falls in most years.

By morning, when the rain finally stops and the wind has swung to the southwest, 50 centimetres of rain has fallen, and the mountain streams are full and boisterous as they drain away water steadily soaking through the sodden soils. In the valley 1000 metres below, the river rose more than a metre overnight and is a sullen, surging torrent, ripping at its banks and moving and grinding boulders along its bed; it can be heard from above as a distant roar. The seedheads of the snow tussocks hang wet and heavy, drops of water along their drooping stems glistening in the early sun. The air is cool, but the late summer sun is warm, and soon a miasma of steam hangs over the mountainside as the sun wicks moisture away. Many of the seeds that fell the previous day were washed away completely, or pushed against rocks and among the larger plants, but half a dozen remain nestled firmly in the rotting speargrass.

The warmth and damp are triggers, urging the seeds to germinate, and within seven weeks three of the six remaining seeds have sent down their first long root into the rich humus, and the first pale shoots sprout like fine hair. But although the days are still warm, they are rapidly getting shorter, and the nights are longer and cooler. In early April, the next rainstorm falls higher up the mountain as snow, although it quickly melts. One night the first hard frost whitens the mountainside.

Over the next two months the frosts become more intense. Each night the surface layer of rich humus from the rotting speargrass freezes slightly, and during the day it thaws. As it freezes, the moisture within it expands and pushes the humus and plant roots upwards; each time it thaws they soften and slump. Two of the tiny seedlings are dislodged by this constant frost heave, and they quickly desiccate when their spindly rootlets are exposed to the air. By June, when the first winter snowfall settles on the ground without melting, only one snow tussock seedling remains.

Temperatures continue to drop, but the snow now acts as a blanket, staying at a constant temperature and buffering the seedling against the extremes of the outside air. August is the coldest month, and a series of fierce storms roll in from the Tasman Sea, but the seedling is oblivious to the gale-force winds and hail which accompany more snow; all growth has stopped, and the seedling waits, cocooned in dim dampness.

In September, spring arrives slowly. The soil is still cool, but on warm days the snow softens quickly, and begins to melt where it is thinnest, or where it sits against dark rocks which warm in the sun. At the edge of the snow bank covering the snow tussock seedling, bright yellow petals begin to unfurl beneath the thinning snow. The flower buds of the New Zealand marsh marigold *Psychrophila* (or *Caltha* as it was previously known) were fully developed in the autumn, but needed exposure to freezing temperatures before they would open. This way they gain a head start on other alpine flowers, and the first pollinating hoverflies and moths to emerge give these unexpected sweet-smelling splashes of colour on the drab slopes their undivided attention. As the snow retreats up the mountain slopes, the honeysuckle-scented *Psychrophila* flowers follow, opening later and later the higher up the mountain.

In winter snow acts as a blanket, insulating alpine plants from extreme air temperatures and protecting them from wind damage. Compared to more continental areas, winters in New Zealand are quite mild.

The spring days slowly lengthen over the next two months, and most of the snow melts, except for a few deep drifts lying in shady gullies. For a few weeks as the snow melts the entire mountainside becomes as squelchy as a bog; on still days there is the sound of water dripping and percolating through soggy soil, of thousands of tiny temporary watercourses finding a way around plants, dribbling across rocks and eventually merging as larger streams that gush and burble down rocky streambeds. Dark mosses and lichens revel in the wetness, coating damp rocks. For the first days after they are freed of snow, most of the plants look battered and lie flat against the ground, but after they've been exposed to the sun for a while they begin to grow, reorienting themselves upright and unfurling new green shoots and leaves.

Most of the plants in the alpine zone are evergreen like the snow tussocks, keeping their leaves through winter. But a few are 'summer greens', which die back during the winter and sprout new leaves each summer. Among them are the great mountain buttercup, often misleadingly called the Mount Cook lily, the largest buttercup in the world and one of the largest and most striking flowers in the Southern Alps.

Near the snow tussock seedling a great mountain buttercup bursts spectacularly into life. Smooth, glossy, dark green leaves unfurl, each the size of a large dinner plate, then a branching flower stalk thrusts upwards to nearly a metre in height. Opening on the tips of the branches, the dozen large, striking flowers have a bright yellow centre, surrounded by up to 20 dazzling satin-white petals.

They don't have the marsh marigold's seasonal head start, but nevertheless the great mountain buttercups still manage to be one of the earliest flowers in the mountains, and are a magnet for pollinating insects. On each flower at least one and often more small black hoverflies or beetles congregate, feasting on nectar and becoming dusted in pollen which they move to other plants as they search the hillside for more flowers.

The snow tussock seedling is growing steadily, sending short rootlets out sideways, and also deeper into the soil below the rotten speargrass, anchoring it firmly in place. It is developing its first leaves, and as the plant grows they will become organised into the tillers which are such a distinctive feature of the snow tussock family. In an adult snow tussock each tiller is a short stem supporting a group of four leaves, held together at their base by a tough enfolding sheath. At first just one leaf emerges, then another, enclosed within the protective embrace of the older leaf. By the end of its first full summer the snow tussock seedling is barely two centimetres high, a scrawny bundle of a few leaves which are cinched together at the base by the roots.

Another of the surviving seeds germinated during the spring and begins to grow, but doesn't manage to send down long-enough roots to survive a brief dry period in midsummer. Larger snow tussocks fare better as their leaves effectively intercept water droplets from damp ground-level cloud and mist, channelling the drops along grooved leaves to their roots.

Following the previous year's mast seeding, none of the adult snow tussocks are flowering this year. The tillers which contained the flower stalks have died back, and the plants focus their efforts on sprouting new tillers that have developed, each with its own set of juvenile leaves, below the now-dead flowering tillers.

The summer has been generally dry but cool; by the time winter approaches and the first snow settles the marsh marigold has shed its dry seeds and is in full bud, ready for next spring. The great mountain buttercup begins to die back in the cold, until just its short thick rhizome and associated roots are left underground. The seedling and the fields of snow tussock ride out the winter storms tucked under an insulating snow blanket.

The following summer is warmer, and there is a succession of hotter than usual late January and early February days, when average temperatures reach nearly

Every few years *Chionochloa* tussocks synchronise in spectacular mass flowering and seeding events which give the alpine grasslands the appearance of a rich wheatfield.

A black and white world

There are two recurring colour themes among the animal and plant life of New Zealand's mountains: white flowers and black invertebrates. Many of the white flowers are large and conspicuous, yet they have a simple structure, and their nectar and pollen are easy for insects to reach. The common explanation for the high proportion of white, and to a lesser extent cream and yellow, flowers is that there are few specialised pollinators such as long-tongued bees and butterflies in New Zealand. Our insect pollinators are more primitive generalists, such as flies, beetles, moths and some bees, all of which have short tongues and lack sensitive colour vision. So unlike elsewhere, where flowers have evolved alongside specialised pollinators, and have developed bright colours and complex structures to attract particular insects, New Zealand flowers have evolved simply to attract the greatest number of native insects.

Interestingly, many white alpine flowers have bright relatives overseas, and in the New Zealand subantarctic bright, showy flowers are also the norm. Yet there are many hints and traces of colour among alpine flowers here; the underside of petals may be coloured, so a bud shows colour until it opens to reveal the white interior, while other flowers have coloured veins.

Amongst the invertebrates, black is the best colour when it comes to soaking up heat in a cold environment. Alpine cicadas are black and hairy, and bat-winged flies have a dark body and wings that act like solar panels, as do black mountain ringlet butterflies. Dark-coloured rocks that hold warmth are favoured sunbathing spots. Black mountain ringlet butterflies give their eggs a solar head-start by laying them not on the more usual plants but on rocks which act as natural incubators; the drawback to this strategy is that the caterpillar hatchlings must find their way from the rock to nearby plants to begin feeding.

Right: *Ourisia caespitosa* plants creep along the ground and form loose mats, usually in damp or shady areas in the low alpine zone. Harman Pass, Arthur's Pass National Park.
Over page: *Chionochloa* tussocks are the long-lived mainstays of New Zealand's alpine grasslands. Above Haast Pass on the slopes of Mount Armstrong.

12°C. These warm days, combined with the long summer daylight hours, synchronise the adult snow tussocks, which begin a period of physiological change in most of their mature tillers known as floral induction. By April they have all begun producing tiny buds, just a few millimetres long, nestled deep inside many of their older tillers. New tillers grown since the previous flowering season are too immature and don't respond; neither does the young snow tussock, which is barely larger than it was last summer.

By the end of summer, the rotten speargrass is barely visible: neighbouring plants have spread onto its margins, and another snow tussock seed from the masting year two years previously has germinated, although the other surviving seed finally succumbed to rot. A different seedling has also appeared, the offspring of one of the expanding neighbours. The seedling belongs to a *Raoulia*, a genus of plants which grow on these wet mountain slopes as distinctive loose, shaggy mats, and on drier slopes as tightly packed cushions. Above ground the seedling is just a pair of cotyledons, its first young leaves, but below ground it is already sending down what will eventually become a large, woody taproot.

The young *Raoulia* is tucked between the snow tussock seedling and a dark grey boulder the size of a rugby ball, rounded from a long lifetime exposed to the elements. The rock has rested in this site for hundreds of years, and wind and water, heat and cold, have thickened its exterior into a rough, weathered rind. A patchwork of grey-green and yellow lichens have marked the passage of years in slow-growing rings that spread across its upper side, fitting around each other where they meet. The rock is a benevolent hot-water bottle for the young plants, gathering heat from the sun during the day and slowly radiating welcome warmth during cool nights.

A number of species in the *Raoulia* genus grow as tightly-packed cushion plants, some of which may spread more than two metres in diameter. While some species have soft hairs on their leaves which give the cushion the feel of velvet, others have harsh rough surfaces.

The following summer is another mast seeding year for the snow tussocks, and the mountain slopes again appear to undulate with tall flower stalks waving in the wind. By the time the seeds fall, there is barely any open ground on what remains of the rotten speargrass, and only a couple of fresh seeds find a toehold and germinate by the time the winter storms arrive and snow settles thick on the ground. The tiny seedlings, however, fail to last until the following spring, and the older seedling is left to monopolise the site.

As a rule tussock seedlings grow exceptionally slowly, but this one is in a very good position; well nourished, and sheltered from the worst of the weather by the rock, it's making rapid progress. By the time it's ten years old it is almost 15 centimetres high, although it still has only about ten tillers. By the time it reaches the age of 20 it is 20 centimetres high, and is slowly beginning to bulk out. It has begun to be absorbed into the complex alpine community around it, and has become a target for hungry herbivores.

The great grazing herds of the alpine meadows are the flightless short-horned grasshoppers. They are just one to three centimetres long, and the higher up the mountain they live the larger they become; the biggest grasshoppers are found on high, open stonefields, where they can easily bask in the warmth of the sun. By mid-summer they are present in multi-hued hordes of green, grey, brown and tussock tan at astonishing densities of more than 18,000 animals per hectare; even the young snow tussock has half a dozen grasshoppers living in and around it, belonging to three different species. When disturbed they leap crazily in all directions, making a sound like falling rain as they land, leaping again and again away from danger. Otherwise, they mostly bask in the sun. They spend just ten percent of each day eating, but in that short time they are extremely efficient — each year, the grasshoppers may eat up to

five percent of the growth produced by all the plants in the alpine grassland. Eating in short bursts is their alpine survival strategy: it allows them to hide from bad weather for long periods of time if necessary.

For the snow tussock, the grasshoppers' appetite means the loss of a few leaves — hardly a calamity considering each leaf lasts only three years. Every year, each tiller unfurls a new inner leaf, as the outermost one, which has died back from the tip a little more each winter, finally dies; with this constant replenishment the number of exposed leaves in each tiller remains a constant four.

Even during February, the warmest month, nights are cool, and at dawn the mountainside is quiet. But as the sun rises, activity slowly increases, and it's not long before the young snow tussock is the centre of a bustling insect metropolis. A small black alpine cicada emerges from his night-time shelter at the base of a nearby Armstrong's mountain daisy, *Celmisia armstrongii*, and climbs one of several stout 25 centimetre-tall flower stalks until he almost reaches the large white flowerhead which is held enticingly aloft. It sways in the light breeze, both flowers and cicada warming in the morning sun. Clumps of Armstrong's mountain daisy dot the mountainside, flaunting their bold white flowerheads; their bronze, sword-like leaves with fuzzy white undersides provide a striking contrast to the rest of the green and grey-green plants.

A small butterfly crawls out from the underside of the lichen-covered boulder; as if unfurling a small array of solar panels, the Butler's ringlet spreads its chestnut-brown wings to their full four centimetre span, and basks.

After half an hour the male cicada begins to make his distinctive, rhythmic, rustling call, a rapid *er-chit-er-chit-er-chit*. A few metres away in a rock jumble another high-alpine cicada adds his call, competing for any females in

Top right: This little short-horned grasshopper is still awaiting formal identification, and in the meantime is known as *Sigaus* 'blue'. Its cryptic patterning blends in well with the *Raoulia* in the background.
Bottom right: Both the plants and animals that live on greywacke scree slopes are coloured to match the rocks. Alpine grasshopper *Brachaspis nivalis* next to a flowering *Stellaria*, Torlesse Range.

the area. It is late in the season for the cicadas, and the last few individuals are in a rush to mate. The Butler's ringlet takes off, and begins to fly a low weaving search, tacking back and forth into the gentle breeze to catch a whiff of nectar, perhaps, or pheromones advertising the presence of a female.

The rock is a popular resting spot, and the butterfly's place is soon taken by a strange fly. Its ordinary fly body is just over a centimetre long, but its dark wings, from which it gets the name bat-winged fly, are each well over a centimetre across; they are extravagant creations, the fly equivalent of a satin ball gown with enormous puffy sleeves. It may be dressed like a debutante, but the bat-winged fly is a ruthless predator that thrives in these damp western alpine gardens and, like the butterfly, uses its wings as solar heat collectors.

A gangly mountain crane fly that appears all flimsy wings and long delicate legs, hence its other name of daddy-long-legs, flies slowly toward the mountain daisy. It lands, probing the flowerhead's yellow centre for sweet nectar. Alerted by the movement, the bat-winged fly takes off, and begins a low, zigzagging hunt towards the crane fly, which finishes feeding and takes off just in time, foiling the attack. The bat-winged fly continues its darting search for prey, heading closer to the tiny stream which even after a few rainless days is still fed by meltwater from a late snow patch high above, and contains enough water to maintain small waterfalls and energetic riffles, as well as calm pools. The bat-winged fly puts on a burst of speed and grabs an unwary caddis fly in mid-air, before landing on a nearby rock to devour it. With its four pale wings the adult caddis fly looks much like a moth as it flies in search of flowers and nectar, although unlike moths, caddis flies lead lives tied to water.

The cold water in the alpine stream is sparkling clear and rich in oxygen, providing perfect conditions for the development of the immature stages of a number of kinds of flying insect. Several caddis fly larvae cling to the underside of a large rock in mid-stream, feeding by scraping algae off the rocks. The caterpillar-like larvae are protected in cocoons they have spun from silk, incorporating a few tiny pebbles and bits of plant matter to make their disguise more effective. A keen-eyed giant lacewing larvae that targets fly larvae for food is living behind a little waterfall, kept constantly wet by splashes of water.

The soil along the sides of the stream is wet and moss-covered, prime real estate for invertebrates that need water in their life, without needing to be immersed. Hidden in a long U-shaped tunnel it has dug into the wet bank, the ugly boggle-eyed larvae of a mountain giant dragonfly waits out the day; under the cover of night it will move to the tunnel entrance and use its extendable mask-like lower jaw to grab passing insects, such as moth larvae specialised to feed only on wet moss. The dragonfly larvae has been growing slowly in its lair for five years, moulting its hard outer skin each time it has increased in size, and it will undergo its final moult, into a winged adult, next summer.

This stretch of stream is part of the large territory of an adult mountain giant dragonfly, which rests on a prominent warm rock. Its face is completely dominated by its huge bulging eyes, which give it exceptional vision — the tens of thousands of facets which make up each eye enable it to see well above and below, and by turning its head it can effectively see 360°. Some distance away it sees another dragonfly, and immediately lifts straight up like a helicopter and flies quickly and directly to see the intruder off. The giant dragonfly is an awe-inspiring sight — the second largest dragonfly in New Zealand, it has a wingspan of nearly 12 centimetres, and like others of its kind is one of the fastest fliers in the insect world. As soon as the other dragonfly moves away, the territory holder comes to a complete mid-air halt, turns and begins to

---

Top right: The extraordinary bat-winged fly (*Exsul singularis*), seen here with a flowering *Celmisia*, has a wingspan of more than two centimetres, and lives in very high rainfall areas.

Bottom right: With a wingspan of up to 12 centimetres the mountain giant dragonfly (*Uropetala chiltonii*) is the second largest dragonfly in New Zealand, and it is a fierce aerial predator that lives in wet alpine areas.

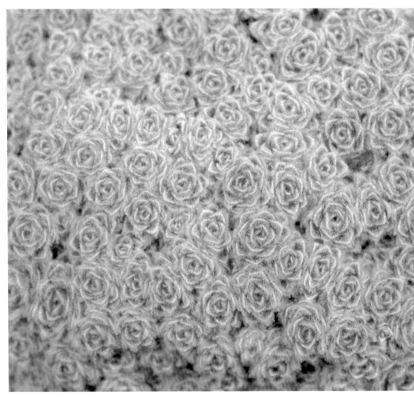

make short rushes close to the ground, changing direction frequently. The mosses alongside the stream are busy with flies touching down for a drink, and it isn't long before the dragonfly has successfully caught a fly, which it devours back on its usual lookout rock.

There are many kinds of flies, including blue blowflies, with their familiar buzzing, and fast-flying hoverflies gorging on pollen and nectar from the late flowers. There are also brown and orange tussock butterflies, and many day-flying moths, the latest in a series that have hatched sequentially since spring, none living more than a few weeks. All of the flying insects are in a rush to breed before the shorter, cooler nights of autumn arrive. Many of the female moths are flightless and unable to move far from their host plant, so they waft pheromones to advertise their presence. Once a male has successfully tracked one down and copulated with her, she lays her eggs on the sheltered underside of leaves. The young snow tussock is now large enough to have become an enticing nursery, and a flightless female *Proditerix* moth, fat with eggs, makes a rare sortie from a neighbouring snow tussock to lay her clutch near the base of its leaves. Her task completed, she dies, her body joining a growing layer of rotting leaves and debris that is becoming trapped within the base of the snow tussock. These are not the only eggs for which the snow tussock provides a nursery; attracted by the very specific scent of snow tussock, a female Butler's ringlet has also laid her eggs on the leaf bases, while a blowfly soon seeks out the decomposing moth body in which to deposit her own eggs. Soon it'll be the turn of the lanky crane fly to add her eggs to the accumulating debris. The mountain grasshoppers, meanwhile, are laying their eggs in the soil around the base of the plant. A flat giant stoner nymph is wedged in the base of the tussock, feeding on

Clockwise from top left: Alpine cicada (*Maoricicada mangu mangu*) on orange lichen; Butler's ringlet (*Erebiola butleri*) basking on tussock; tightly packed woolly leaves of the vegetable sheep *Raoulia mammillaris*; the Cascades gecko (*Hoplodactylus* 'Cascades') joins a growing list of high altitude New Zealand lizards which are remarkably cold-adapted.

the fine threads of fungi that are growing on the damp, decaying litter.

Other alpine plants are being targeted by their own suite of egg-layers: a *Raoulia* mat plant has resident *Notoreas* moths, which live out their entire lifespan on a single plant. They lay their eggs in the deep, damp compost that accumulates among its low, dense branches; the tightly packed leaves feed hungry caterpillars while its small midsummer flowerheads provide sweet nectar for the adult moths. A *Gelophaula* moth has laid her eggs among the leaves of the mountain daisy; when these hatch next spring the caterpillars will bore into the flower stems and eat them from the inside, safely hidden from predators.

An alpine cicada lays her eggs in the low stems of a speargrass growing next to the boulder, carefully posting each egg in a slit in the stem; when the larval cicadas hatch they will burrow down into the soil beneath the rock, feeding there on roots. Well above ground a giant flightless speargrass weevil slowly chews the edge of a leaf, well clear of its fearsome spiked tip, while deep in the rosette of leaves its larvae also feast on the plant. The larvae are well hidden but still not safe from the plant's resident predator, a mountain jumping spider with distinctive headlamp-like eyes, which for the moment hunts among seed clusters on the metre-high flower stalks.

By the time darkness arrives, the day shift has long gone into hiding, prompted by falling temperatures. But the alpine garden is as busy by night as it was by day; night-flying moths emerge, as do alpine cockroaches and beetles, rummaging through decaying plant matter, and feasting on fresh leaves and flowers. From a burrow at the base of a large snow tussock an enormous alpine giant weta, *Deinacrida pluvialis*, emerges. Elephantine in size — this female weighs 11 grams — and fearsome in appearance, she is however a benign vegetarian, who busies herself browsing flowers and grazing on whatever leaves she can reach. There are many smaller ground weta, too, out

foraging for insects, small seeds and fruits, flowers and leaves. The unexpectedly large, white, juicy fruits tucked inside a low, sprawling snowberry are a treat for which the ground weta pay an easy price: the seeds inside the fruit pass through their digestive system intact, and are deposited in their droppings as they travel around the alpine garden.

An adult giant stoner emerges from its hiding place in a permanently damp hollow filled with scree and rocky rubble, to begin searching for a mate. The shady hollow is covered with snow until late each summer, which provides a steady larder of wind-blown frozen insects for the stoner. This giant stoner is nearly two and half centimetres long and, like nearly a quarter of the more than 100 stonefly species found in New Zealand, is flightless. Lowland stoners are associated with streams and rivers, but both the adults and nymphs of the alpine species have adapted to a terrestrial lifestyle. Just half its size, the alpine green stoner is also out and about on this still night; it possesses wings but when it flies it flutters clumsily.

There are hunters about, too — a fast-running, long-legged hunting spider, a many-legged centipede with fearsome jaws, and a gaudy red flatworm in search of worms to eat. An intricately patterned giant leaf-veined slug, nearly four centimetres long, rasps at threads of fungi.

Many of the invertebrates in the damp alpine garden survive as adults for just a few summer weeks, some as briefly as a few days. By March, as temperatures begin to slowly fall and the last alpine flowers start to fade, the mountainside becomes quieter and quieter. The moths, butterflies and flies have laid their eggs, which will survive the winter tucked in soil or litter at the base of plants; most of the adults have already died. In some species, caterpillars have turned into pupae, which will exist in a state of suspended development until they metamorphose in spring. Under the boulder a female mountain jumping spider guards a dense silken web filled with eggs, which will soon hatch. The thick silk will shelter her and her brood through the winter. Long-lived nymphs such as the giant mountain dragonfly and cicadas continue slowly growing,

The fierce appearance and large size of the alpine giant weta (*Deinacrida pluvialis*) belie its gentle vegetarian lifestyle.

well insulated from the vagaries of the outside world in their long underground tunnels.

The grasshoppers have the most flexible life cycle, with surprising variations in the speed of development during their various life stages, depending on nuances of temperature. Depending on how early or late eggs were laid during the summer, and the occurrence of cool or warm weather, some grasshoppers live for three years and others for four. They can survive the winter as either eggs, nymphs or even adults, and may spend more than a year at each stage. This way their numbers are spread more evenly from year to year, and broods from different years get an opportunity to interbreed.

During winter the alpine garden is buried in a thick snow blanket; just the tops of the tallest snow tussocks poke through in places to face the harshness of snow and ice blown by fierce winds. Some of the larger alpine invertebrates survive the winter as adults by entering a state of torpor or diapause: they stop growing, and their bodily functions are slowed to a minimum. New Zealand's alpine weta and cockroaches are famous for their ability to freeze solid and then fully recover; their blood contains particular sugars and amino acids which prevent ice crystals damaging delicate cells. But for most of the winter, regardless of how cold the air is, soil temperatures hardly ever drop below freezing; by burying themselves in the ground, or in the litter accumulated at the base of the snow tussocks, most invertebrates are well protected from ice and frost.

Come spring, the invertebrates that survived the winter as adults pick up where they left off the previous autumn, each occupying a particular lifestyle and space on

Top left: The white-bearded mountain jumping spider — seen here devouring its prey — belongs to the Salticidae family, and is a roving hunter rather than a web-builder.
Bottom left: In nutrient-poor alpine bogs, carnivorous sundews catch insects on sticky droplets, and then slowly consume them. Here a sundew has trapped a blue damselfly (*Austrolestes colensonis*).

the mountain. Eggs begin hatching into larvae and nymphs, and as summer advances synchronised waves of different species emerge, flourish and then disappear, but not before they have established the following generation. The base of the young snow tussock is alive with crane fly maggots, known as leatherjackets, and blowfly maggots. Slightly higher up the plant, feeding on its leaves, are several kinds of moth caterpillars, as well as Butler's ringlet caterpillars. The pulsing of invertebrate life echoes that of the flowers, which provide an ongoing smorgasbord for the many nectar feeders.

Every few years the mountainside takes on the appearance of a bountiful wheatfield, as the adult tussocks experience another spectacular flowering and seeding year, but more than 50 years pass before a warmer than usual January finds the young snow tussock finally mature enough to join them. By April it is developing tiny flower buds, just a millimetre or so long at first, deep inside a few of its older tillers. Its annual growth spurt, which began as soon as the spring thaw started, and saw its new leaves gain nearly 36 centimetres in length, has stopped by March as it focuses all its resources into next season's flowering. Protected like the over-wintering invertebrates deep inside the plant, the tiny buds wait out winter. As soon as the spring snow thaw starts they begin to grow quickly, remaining short as the buds develop; finally in December the flower stalks elongate, rapidly pushing the flower heads to over a metre in height. On each stalk up to a dozen long, slender stems separate and droop gracefully from the top portion of the main stalk. Each stem in turn dangles half a dozen fine threads, along each of which lie as many florets, still folded in upon themselves, and sprouting fine hairs from their tips.

This intricate dance of development and growth is synchronised across the Southern Alps, until the perfect choreography reaches its pinnacle in late January. For just a couple of hours each day, in the late morning, millions of snow tussock flowers mature, their stamens splitting to release billions of tiny, lightweight pollen grains. Snow tussocks don't rely on insects for pollination: they depend on the wind to blow pollen to neighbouring plants. If it's too calm for pollen to travel, a snow tussock is able to 'make do' and use its own pollen for fertilisation. After the long build-up to this moment the pollen urgently needs to reach female stigmas, as it remains viable for less than an hour.

The snow tussocks don't need the help of insects, but there are some insects which are totally dependent on the tussock flowering. In early December, as the closed florets emerge from the stem, but before the flowers even begin to emerge, a tiny fly called *Diplotaxa similis* has begun to lay eggs within the protective bracts, or modified leaves, which enclose them. The fly is black with yellow markings and less than three millimetres long, while her white eggs are comparatively enormous, three quarters of a millimetre long. Within a couple of days the numerous eggs hatch into large transparent larvae, which soon appear green from the unripe flower parts that quickly fill their stomachs. The larvae, which have a distinctive pair of breathing tubes, or spiracles, quickly develop through different stages, or instars, and as flower parts ripen to gold and rose colours, so the colour of the larvae changes to match. Within a couple of weeks the first larvae have turned into pupae that are as large as the adults. By mid January, as the snow tussock flowering declines, the larvae have finished their flower-feeding frenzy and are all pupating.

Several weeks after the *Diplotaxa* invasion begins, more eggs start to appear in the opening florets. These ones are small and orange, and they rapidly hatch into small, mobile larvae that are transparent except for a distinctive orange centre. They belong to a different kind of fly, a cecidomyiid newly classified as *Eucalpytodiplosis chionochloae*. As they grow they become more orange, feeding on fertilised flower ovaries that are developing into seeds.

Speargrass plants belong to the genus *Aciphylla*, and are often called spaniards. Although they are members of the carrot family they are armed with memorably sharp leaf tips; male and female flowers are borne on separate plants. Arthur's Pass National Park.

Temperature and altitude

When it comes to temperature in the mountains, there is a simple truism: the higher you go, the colder it gets. Known as the lapse rate, a standard drop in annual average temperature of around 0.6°C for each 100 metre increase in altitude applies in New Zealand and around the world.

During a vegetation survey on Mount Armstrong, near Haast Pass, ecologists recorded hourly temperatures over two years, at three different sites: near the treeline at 1200 metres altitude, in the low-alpine zone at 1600 metres, and at the upper limit of the high-alpine zone at 2000 metres. During February, the warmest month, the mean air temperatures at these three sites were 11.45°C, 8.9°C and 6.44°C respectively. During the coldest month, August, mean air temperatures at the same sites were 0.48°C, -1.44°C and -4.83°C.

But average temperatures tell only part of the story: the warmest air temperature recorded at the treeline site was 21°C, but in the same December that site also recorded a low of -1°C, which means the plants and animals that live there must be able to cope with constantly fluctuating conditions that vary day by day, and indeed hour by hour. At the highest site, 200 metres below the mountain's summit, air temperatures reached as low as -13°C. Compared to mountainous areas in other parts of the world, however, these temperatures are not extreme, and indeed these moderate temperatures are among the defining characteristics of New Zealand mountains, and allow snow tussocks to dominate the alpine zone.

Air temperature only affects those parts of plants that grow above ground; their roots have to cope with a different set of temperatures. Like air temperature, soil temperature declines with increasing altitude, but it tends to be more stable and less extreme than air temperature. At 20 centimetres deep, the soil never gets as hot or as cold as the air above, although it can still reach nearly 20°C and sink to -3°C. The most difficult time for plants physiologically is when the soil freezes, which can happen any time during the coldest four months at treeline level, and over eight months of the year near the summit.

And as if these two flies weren't enough, the larvae of a moth, *Megacraspedus calanogonus*, join the feeding frenzy early on in the season. Pale with long red stripes, the moth larvae are comparative giants, six millimetres long, but the flies make up for their much smaller size by sheer abundance.

Together the larvae of these three insects make up a guild of *Chionochloa* specialists that are such voracious feeders they are often called predators; the early appearing *Diplotaxa* flies and *Megacraspedus* moths are flower predators, while the later cecidomyiid flies are seed predators. They are the reason why the snow tussocks don't flower every year — their irregular mass seeding is an attempt to outmanoeuvre the enemy, to prevent their numbers building up and causing even more damage.

After six weeks the surviving seeds have ripened, ready for another warm wind to shake them across the crowded alpine garden. Although the fly and moth larvae

have destroyed large numbers of flowers and seeds they haven't made an appreciable impact, and millions of seeds remain. Across many kilometres of alpine grassland several thousand seeds rain down on each square metre, to be gorged upon in turn by many other opportunistic invertebrates such as cockroaches and grasshoppers, and by pipits, which temporarily forsake hunting invertebrates to join the seed feast.

The lifestyles of the flower and seed predators part company here; the *Diplotaxa* pupae hatch into adults in late summer, and it is these which survive the winter. The following summer there are hardly any snow tussock flowers, and even though they take advantage of almost all the flowers available most of the numerous *Diplotaxa* adults die without successfully reproducing. Within a single year their numbers have dropped dramatically.

The *Megacraspedus* moths follow the same life cycle, and their population crashes as well. But the cecidomyiid

The delicate but hardy black mountain ringlet (*Percnodaimon pluto*) has dark wings which act as solar panels, allowing it to absorb warmth from the sun.

fly plays the snow tussocks at their own game, and has developed a cunning longer-term strategy. The larvae drop from the snow tussock seed heads to the ground, and spend the winter in the soil in a state of diapause. Many will pupate the following summer and hatch in midsummer and, like the *Diplotaxa* adults, fail to find any snow tussock flowers. But some larvae continue in a state of diapause, waiting out a further one, or perhaps even two winters, when their chances of coinciding with the next mast flowering year are that much greater.

The relationships between the predators and their hosts are only just being unravelled by scientists. There are many complicating factors, with the flies competing with each other as well as trying to outwit the snow tussocks. The two flies don't like to share, but the *Diplotaxa* flies get a head start, so by the time the cecidomyiid flies come along many of the snow tussock flower heads are spoken for. But *Diplotaxa* females lay only a few, large eggs, while the cecidomyiid females can lay up to a hundred, making them better able to take advantage of a superabundance of seeds. Overall it seems that the snow tussocks are still winning the fight, but that the cecidomyiid flies are making better headway against their survival strategy than *Diplotaxa*.

This biological game of wits has been evolving for millions of years, and as a result New Zealand's snow tussocks have the most variable flowering of any plant in the world. In about half the years there is no flowering at all, while there are other years in which every mature plant flowers heavily. This strategy comes at a cost to the plants: they lose opportunities to reproduce during non-flowering years, and their seeds face much greater competition for space and resources such as food and water. And a mass flowering effort depletes the number of mature tillers, which must be renewed before they can flower again. This extreme mast seeding only works because snow tussocks

Alpine gentians (*Gentianella patula*) are among the last alpine plants to flower in late summer. They are one of New Zealand's white alpine flowers which show strong hints of colour on the outer faces of the petals.

are long lived, and their seeds long lasting, able to germinate after several years lying dormant in the ground.

Incredibly, this whole strategy pivots around something that is seemingly random: it all hinges on a particular average temperature being reached, when day length is at least 14 hours. Botanists trying to understand the subtleties of this phenomenon believe it is the only known example in the plant world of chaotic behaviour, and possibly that is why it works, somehow unpredictably maintaining a balance between plants and their predators.

It's the end of the young snow tussock's first flowering summer, and thousands of empty seed heads still wave gently across the mountain slope, giving no hint of the epic evolutionary battle of wits they have been hosting. Splashes of white on the mountainside come from clusters of delicate white gentian flowers, which are among the last of the summer flowers. Unlike the snow tussocks, the gentians are short-lived — this will be the only time

they flower. The young snow tussock, however, will get many more opportunities. This year's flowering tillers will die back, adding to the growing collection of leaf litter in the base of the plant. Each flowering tiller buds off one or two new tillers, which won't be old enough to flower themselves for at least ten to 15 years.

As the annual cycle of seasons come and go the snow grass slowly reaches full maturity. By the time it is 100 years old, its more than 1000 tightly packed tillers form a base 30 centimetres across, spraying out in a canopy nearly a metre tall and covering an area of nearly a square metre. Nearly 100 generations of annual insects such as flies and moths have come and gone among its leaves, while more than 30 generations of grasshoppers and cicadas have hatched, lived and died in the soil around its roots. This soil is now an extraordinarily complex and abundant self-contained ecosystem containing a myriad of microscopic organisms: in the top two centimetres of soil alone there are hundreds

Haast's buttercup (*Ranunculus haastii*) lives only on mobile scree slopes. Its underground rhizome lies in the moist soil layer under the surface scree, and its delicately attached summer leaves easily break off if the scree moves.

of mites; thousands of beetles; tardigrades (also known as water bears) and rotifers; tens of thousands of nematodes; and an uncountable number of bacteria. In this world inside a world there are vegetarians, omnivores, carnivores and decomposers; there are creatures specialising in eating fungi and others that live on bacteria.

From a distance the alpine garden is the same, many textured patchwork of plants and rocks, but during the hundred years there have been many subtle changes. Unstable boulder patches have shifted and moved downhill slightly, while others have stabilised and been colonised by plants. The snow tussocks have endured, but as other plants have died, new ones have taken their place, so while the deck of plants remains the same, they have shuffled and re-dealt themselves across the slope.

In the following hundred years, the alpine ecosystem has to face another challenge: strange new mammals, such as brown hares, chamois, thar and red deer, which have enthusiastically taken up residence in the naturally mammal-free mountains. Himalayan thar are mountain specialists related to wild goats and sheep, which have adapted very well to the Southern Alps. They were officially introduced to New Zealand in the early twentieth century by the government, which wanted to create a hunting resource for local residents and foreign visitors. The first 13 animals were gifted by the Duke of Bedford from his captive herd at Woburn Abbey, and were released near the Hermitage at Mount Cook in two lots, in 1904 and 1909. They established rapidly, and by the early 1920s the population was over 100.

Males began to wander early on, and by the early 1930s breeding populations of females had also begun to spread. By the mid 1970s they had expanded into all the suitable country containing the snow tussock basins, low-alpine scrub and steep rock bluffs they require. Following ten years of intensive aerial hunting their

Chamois were introduced from Austria, and this 1907 photo shows the cage release system for ten animals liberated in the Tasman Valley near Mount Cook.

range contracted, and they now inhabit the central alps from the Rakaia and Whitcombe rivers in the north to the Haast and Hunter rivers in the south. The latest population estimate suggests that there are between 6000 and 9000 thar, and to minimise habitat destruction their numbers and distribution are controlled by recreational and guided hunting, and by official aerial hunting when required.

Thar are striking animals; the larger males have distinctive long winter manes, and both sexes have large horns. They are social animals, and outside the breeding season form into large bands of females and young animals, and all-male groups. During the winter rut male and female groups blend, and adult males follow and guard receptive females to ensure they get exclusive mating access.

Groups of thar rest high on rock bluffs, and descend up to 500 metres each day to feed in lower vegetation. They feed mainly on snow tussocks, flowering alpine plants and bushes such as matagouri; their diet varies through the season depending on what is available. In winter animals are less active, to conserve energy, and spend only half the time they do in summer feeding. This behaviour is a specific adaptation to varying food availability in the New Zealand mountains, and is accompanied by an extraordinary physiological change: the useable digestive surface of the animals' stomachs shrinks to half its usual size during winter, also to save energy. In summer, when there is plenty of food, it returns to normal.

Also feeding on the tussock are alpine chamois, a type of goat-antelope that hails from Europe. Chamois were

Above: Chamois (*Rupicapra rupicapra*) are a type of European goat-antelope. They established so successfully in the South Island mountains that within 30 years of their release government cullers were employed to control their numbers.
Right: Himalayan thar (*Hemitragus jemlahicus*) were introduced by the New Zealand government to establish a hunting resource. They have thrived here, although the original Himalayan population seems to be declining. During the breeding season male thar develop a striking ruff around their neck and chest.

introduced from Austria as a gift to the New Zealand government from Emperor Franz Josef II, at a time when they were scarce and hard to catch in the European alps. Ten animals were released near the Tasman Valley at Mount Cook in 1907, and another pair was released in 1914, although the male was shot after it attacked tourists.

Chamois have established extremely successfully, and have spread at a rate of more than nine kilometres a year. In fact, they were so successful that within 30 years of their release government hunters had to begin culling them.

They occupy steep areas in the high- and low-alpine zones and extend down into the Westland forests, and from northern Fiordland throughout the alps as far as the Seaward Kaikoura Range. A very rough guess puts their population at 18,500. Like thar they eat grasses, woody shrubs and flowering alpine plants. They are more solitary than thar, however, and as result are more widely dispersed. They are also very elusive and wary of humans, which makes them hard to find.

Thar and chamois do not co-exist well, and the much smaller chamois are pushed out of areas with strong herds of thar. There are currently no systematic programmes in place to control chamois numbers, although government shooters kill some each year in the course of their work with thar and goats.

The once tiny snow tussock is now a venerable giant, fit and vigorous. In a flowering year more than 400 flower stalks may wave above this single plant, and it produces nearly 9000 seeds. Like the adage of grandfather's axe with its many new heads and handles, nothing remains of the original tussock although the plant itself endures, constantly renewing itself. So how long will it live? While many suggest 100 or even 200 years, botanist Professor Alan Mark goes one step further. On field trips into the mountains he answers this question with a challenge: 'Find me a dead snow tussock.' Invariably, everyone returns with the report that they have found no such thing; and with a twinkle in his eye Professor Mark declares his belief that snow tussocks are 'potentially immortal'.

So these young mountains are populated by a suite of possibly immortal ancients, individual plants that may well have been here since before the first humans stepped ashore. New Zealand's alpine flora and fauna are the extraordinary products of this country's geology, topography, weather, isolation, history and the serendipity of which species reached here. Universal patterns and processes may repeat across mountain ecosystems, and alpine plants and animals from different parts of the globe may share survival and life strategies, but our evergreen snow tussocks dominate uniquely New Zealand alpine gardens.

Left: The penwiper plant (*Notothlaspi rosulatum*) lives on fine stable screes. After growing for several years each plant flowers and seeds just once before dying; the sweet-smelling flower spikes may be up to 25 centimetres tall.
Over page: 'Potentially immortal' is how botany professor Alan Mark describes the *Chionochloa* snow tussocks which are such a defining feature of New Zealand's alpine zone.

CROSSING THE ALPS

People who venture into the mountains today do so knowing they are going where others have gone before. However, their journey will still be an elemental one of an individual pitting their psychological strength and physical stamina against the unpredictable might of mountain and weather.

Crossing the alps

Modern mountaineers and trampers come to the alps well prepared with light equipment, warm clothing and briefed by long-range weather forecasts. They can rely on mountain huts for shelter, radios and satellite phones for instant communication, and helicopters for easy transport — and rescue.

Having all this at our disposal today makes the achievements of those who went first even more remarkable. The pioneering explorers who first ventured up mountain valleys in search of gold and alpine crossings; the first geologists and surveyors trying to measure and piece together the topography and put it down on maps; and the early mountaineers, both amateur and professional, who dared strive for the summits. For these men and women, journeys took weeks or even months, and getting to the foot of the mountains was a long and arduous undertaking in itself.

Early European exploration around and across the Southern Alps was motivated by two things: grazing and gold. During the 1850s all of the eastern plains, across the tussock-covered foothills as far as the base of the alps, the wide expanses of the Mackenzie Basin and the area around the Southern Lakes, were quickly taken in a land-grab which saw runholders claim all the land considered capable of supporting sheep and, less commonly, cattle. Gold rushes in California during the 1840s, and in Australia during the 1850s, kindled the idea of gold in this new country, and the discovery of gold at Gabriel's Gully in Otago in May 1861, and shortly after on the West Coast, sparked gold fever. Gold the mineral, and later the 'gold' of trade and tourism, created another need: for routes across the alps, which could be developed as horse trails and later roads.

In their earliest incarnations there were three provinces in the South Island: Otago took up the bottom third, the enormous province of Canterbury spanned the centre of the South Island from east to west, while Nelson occupied the top. One of the early challenges for the provincial governments was to find good routes across the Southern

This watercolour of Arthur's Pass was made by Theodore Hurt in his field sketchbook sometime in the late 1860s.

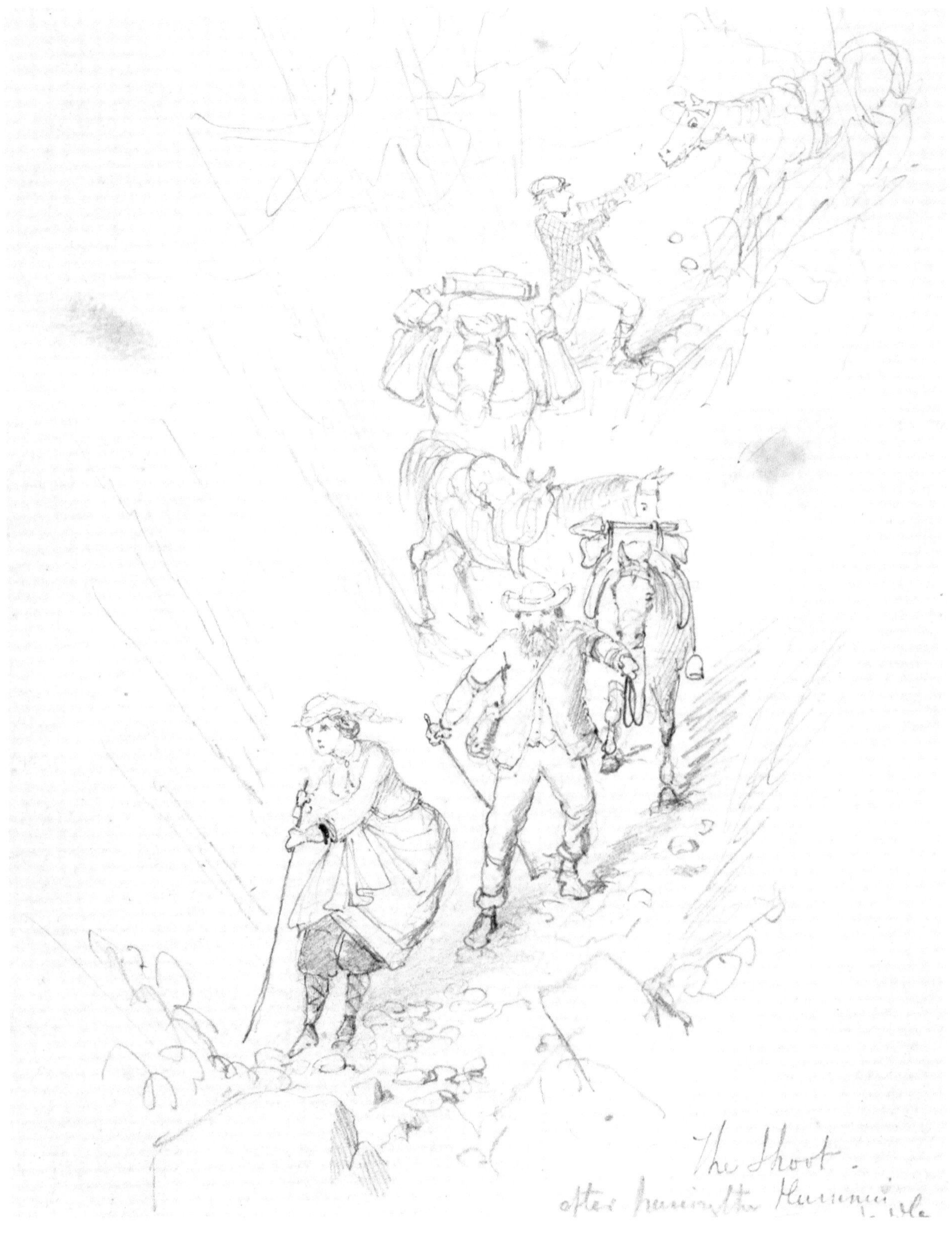
The Shoot -

Alps between the growing settlements and farms on the east coast and the isolated west coast, which at that time was accessible only by boat. Much of the early exploring of the foothills and lower slopes of the Southern Alps was carried out by runholders and gold seekers, but a lot of it was ad hoc and these men left few records of their experiences. That job generally fell to provincial surveyors and geologists, who were given the task of mapping the sheep runs and the countryside, and searching for minerals such as coal and gold.

There was a small community of people involved in these busy endeavours, and their professional and private lives frequently overlapped; in Canterbury this was often through the auspices of the Christchurch Club. Canterbury Provincial Engineer Edward Dobson and his wife Mary, for example, were good friends of Provincial Geologist Julius Haast. The Dobsons' two sons, George and Arthur, were both surveyors, and Arthur Dobson worked with Haast in the Mount Cook region before becoming involved in the development of the pass that would come to bear his name. The Dobsons' eldest daughter Mary later married Haast.

Early exploration was incredibly difficult work. There were no maps, no marked routes, hardly any settlements apart from Christchurch, Nelson and Dunedin, and just a scant knowledge of Maori routes. The bush was dense to the point of impenetrable, and most of the travel was on foot. Even the simplest journey was usually deserving of the description 'epic'.

In late 1857, following a route that was well-known to Kaiapoi Maori, Edward Dobson and Hurunui runholders Henry Taylor and George Mason became the first Europeans to cross a significant inland pass between the east and west sides of the Main Divide. Their route led up the Hurunui River from Lake Sumner on the eastern side

When artist Nicholas Chevalier and his wife made a trip from Christchurch to the West Coast in 1866 they crossed what was then called Hurunui Saddle (now Harper Pass) and discovered the steep muddy 'shoot' on the western side of the pass.

and crossed a pass into the headwaters of the Taramakau River, where they were turned back by bad weather and rough terrain.

Early settlers called it the Hurunui Pass, until it was named Harper Pass in honour of the next European to cross it, making it all the way out to the west coast. Twenty-year-old Leonard Harper had heard stories from chief Tainui of Kaiapoi of how some Maori had fled across the pass to the West Coast to escape a war party. He enthusiastically persuaded the chief to allow his son Ihaia Tainui and two other Maori to guide him and a Mr Locke on a private trip across the pass, promising not to divulge details of the route. They began in October 1857 and, after abandoning their horses in the upper Hurunui Valley when they could go no further, they carried their own swags as they faced dense West Coast bush, a dangerous river, and bad weather. They ran out of food, until the Maori guides caught some eels and birds to eat. West Coast Maori usually travelled up and down the Taramakau River to the pass using canoes, but as none were available, Harper's party finally resorted to building a raft from bundles of flax sticks, and spent two risky days floating downriver to the sea, during which time Harper lost nearly all his clothes overboard.

Once they had reached the west coast the party explored as far south as Okarito or thereabouts, accompanied by local Maori chief Tarapuhi; they didn't have a tent, and Harper had only half a blanket and no spare clothing. This was no mean feat, as even the beaches were almost impassable, as this description of the West Coast by Arthur Dobson on another expedition shows:

The whole of the country up to the snow-line and down to the water's edge was covered with thick forest. Every flood brought down to the sea quantities of timber, which was thrown up on the beaches, and excepting where the coast was cliff-bound the timber piled up in such vast masses that it was quite a climb to get over it into the

bush beyond. In many places the timber was stacked up from ten to fifteen feet in height, and from two to three chains in width . . . The scrub on all the low ground was almost impenetrable, small trees up to three and four inches growing thickly together, tied up with a mass of supplejack and lawyer vines.

After nearly three months away, Harper planned to return to the east coast via a pass at the head of the Otira River which local Maori had told him about, and which would eventually become known as Arthur's Pass. However, bad weather and a lack of boots convinced him to return the way he had come, still accompanied by chief Tarapuhi. By this time his only piece of clothing was half a ripped shirt, which he draped around himself as a modest apron, and which didn't provide much warmth during the snowstorm they experienced at the pass. When the party arrived back at Henry Taylor's sheep run at Waitohi, Harper hid behind a tree while Locke went to borrow some trousers for him.

Although Harper kept his promise not to publicise his trip, others already knew of the pass. By the early 1860s it still offered the only sure possibility for a route between Canterbury and the west coast. As a result, Herbert Charlton Howitt was engaged to cut a track suitable for horses up the Hurunui and across to the west coast.

The 1860s saw a lot of activity in trying to find passes across the alps. Three years earlier Englishman Samuel Butler had managed to discover and procure one of the last available sheep runs, in the high reaches of the Rangitata River. Classically trained and self-described as 'Samuel Butler, gentleman, of Canterbury', he had come to New Zealand to make his fortune, and after four years here would return to England where he became famous as a satirical writer, basing his best-known work *Erewhon* on his experiences in inland Canterbury. At the end of 1860, 25-year-old

---

This view of Samuel Butler's cob cottage homestead on the high country sheep station of Mesopotamia, in Canterbury's upper Rangitata River, was painted by William Packe circa 1868, four years after Butler returned to England.

SUMMIT OF ARTHURS PASS. No 508 J.R.

Butler and 20-year-old surveyor's assistant John Holland Baker began to explore the enormous headwaters of the Rangitata River in the hope of finding more grazing land, perhaps on the other side of the mountains. They tried up the Havelock Branch, but couldn't find a route. They tried again early in 1861, this time up the Clyde Branch, but again found their way blocked by impassable mountains. On their third attempt, up the Lawrence Branch, they could see a pass at the top, and were sure this would be what they were looking for. Butler wrote:

I was within ten minutes of the top in a state of excitement greater, I think, than I had ever known before. Ten minutes more and the cold air from the other side came rushing upon me. A glance. I was not on the main range. Another glance. There was an awful river, muddy and horribly angry, roaring over an immense river bed, thousands of feet below me. Another glance, and then I remained motionless.

There, across the Rakaia, they could see what they had been seeking: a saddle crossing the alps, and on the other side, the west coast.

Ever persistent, they returned to their horses and made their way back to Mesopotamia to restock. Then they set out to ride the long way around to Lake Heron and the pass they had seen. The pass proved an easy climb, and they ventured 'some distance down the other side until we were within 20 miles from the west coast, but found the valley so densely timbered that the chance of finding open country seemed hopeless.' Butler and Baker were curious, but pragmatic; they were only interested in land that could graze sheep, so having discovered the second route across the Southern Alps, they returned to Mesopotamia, and each carried on with their business.

Butler's name remains associated not with this Main Divide pass, however, but with the frustrating saddle between the Rangitata and the Rakaia rivers. Instead, this pass was named after an attempt in April 1863 by Henry Whitcombe and Jakob Lauper to cross the pass and follow the route all the way to the coast. They were woefully ill-prepared for their journey, carrying very little in the way of food, and Whitcombe was tragically drowned. In his memory the pass became known as Whitcombe's Pass.

Following his explorations with Butler, Baker turned his attention south, looking for more sheep country in the southernmost reaches of the Canterbury province around the heads of lakes Wanaka and Hawea. In March 1861 Baker and E. Owen were exploring around the Makarora River at head of Lake Wanaka and became the first Europeans to reach what would become Haast Pass, although they didn't cross it. As with the Whitcombe Pass, Baker was interested in finding grazing land, and not in forcing a route through dense forest.

Rival claims to have been the first across Haast Pass are usually associated with prospector Charles Cameron and a party led by Julius Haast in 1863, but although Cameron was almost certainly first across the pass he

---

The first route across Arthur's Pass was built during 1865–66, and by 1866 the first overland telegraph had been erected. The initial narrow road was soon made wide enough to accommodate horse-drawn coaches.

didn't make it all the way out to the west coast, as Haast did. By this time Haast had completed his survey work in North Canterbury, in his friend Butler's part of the world and around Mount Cook. He was now looking for gold-bearing deposits, with the usual secondary goal of looking for a route to the West Coast. Haast and others knew there were two well-known Maori routes crossing from South Westland to lakes Hawea and Wanaka: Tiori Patea, meaning 'the way ahead is clear', which would become known as Haast Pass, and the so-called Maori Saddle which crossed between the Blue and Okuru rivers.

In mid-January 1863 Haast and his party, which included young surveyor William Young, made an uneventful crossing of the Main Divide from the Makarora River, using the low, forested pass Tiori Patea. Haast wrote of the 562 metre pass that '. . . a most remarkable pass was discovered, which in a chain of such magnitude as the Southern Alps of New Zealand, has no equal.' But it then took them nearly a month to make their way to the coast down what was then called the Awarua River. They faced with stoicism the usual hardships and difficulties: Haast slipped on loose boulders in the river and cut his leg badly, rats ate their cache of food, and heavy rain and flooded rivers made the route impassable for days, confining them to camp. They survived on weka and kakapo caught by their dog Prince.

Fortunately they had much better luck with the weather on their return across the pass, making it back to Makarora in just ten days, 'all in rags, nearly shoeless and without any provisions'. Well pleased with their efforts, Haast rewarded himself with the name of the pass and the river, and Young with the naming of a river and a mountain range.

In 1880 a packhorse bridle track was cut across the pass. However, despite the easy gradient on the Makarora side of the pass and its official status as a favoured route, it was nearly 100 years before Haast Pass was fully developed as a road and connected with a road down the west coast.

Arthur Dobson headed to the west coast in mid-1863 to carry out a survey of the northern part of the coast; among the first news he received was that of the drowning of Whitcombe, with whom he had previously worked, and also the drowning of Hewitt and his men in Lake Brunner. They had successfully cut a trail across Harper Saddle 'so that it was possible to get horses down to the Teramakau [sic] river, by taking all the gear off and letting them slide through the bush, from the top of the saddle to the riverbed.'

After months of hard surveying he returned briefly to Christchurch the following February, but was soon heading back over to the west coast with his brother Edward. This time he took a route up the Waimakariri, 'discovering' the pass which chief Tarapuhi had pointed out to him, as he had to Leonard Harper a few years earlier. It proved to have easy access from the east side, but like Harper Pass was steep on the western side, and dropped into a steep gorge in the Otira River. Edward returned east, while Arthur continued across the new pass with the help of the local runholder and one of his men. It was so steep they had to build a ladder from light poles lashed together with flax, and they lowered the runholder's dog down using a rope they made from flax. Arthur reported how on:

. . . *returning to Christchurch I made a sketch of the country I had been over, and handed it with a report to the Chief Surveyor. I did not name this pass, but when the gold-diggings commenced on the West Coast a committee of business men offered a prize of £200 for anyone who could find a better or more suitable pass, and at the same time my brother George was sent out [by Edward Dobson senior] to examine every available pass between the watershed of the Teramakau [sic], Waimakariri and Hurunui. He carefully examined the pass at the head of every valley, and reported that Arthur's Pass was by far the most suitable for a direct road to the coast.*

Sir Julius Haast was the provincial geologist and explorer for Canterbury when he painted this field sketch of the 'view towards the sources of the Rakaia River from the junction of Whitcombe's Pass Stream' circa 1866.

So it was that Arthur's Pass got its name, and in mid-1865 Edward Dobson senior set a contractor the task of opening up a good horse track 'as fast as thirty good axemen can cut their way through the dense scrub.'

In the meantime, gold had been discovered on the West Coast and people had been pouring across Harper Pass, which was now in a bad state of repair from all the use, especially as herds of sheep and cattle were also being driven over the track. In mid-1865 Haast wrote that the bridle track resembled a 'morass canal: sharp stones, roots and dead trees made progress very difficult; the horses sank up to their knees and could only work themselves out with difficulty.' The creation of the more direct Arthur's Pass route removed much of the traffic from Harper Pass, although it was still used as stock route until the 1870s; since then Harper Pass has been used only as a tramping route.

The search for an alpine pass and the decision as to which one to develop was a controversial and public discussion, played out in the press of the day. For several years Browning Pass, which crossed the alps just south of Arthur's Pass, was considered a strong contender as a route, and in 1865 and 1866 a stock route was cut across it. However, as Austrian geologist Ferdinand Hochstetter had pointed out in his 1863 book on the geology of New Zealand:

. . . the so-called North Rakaia Pass has no claim to the title [of being a real pass]; its eastern face being simply a wall rising abruptly from the valley to a height of 1500 feet, and being at so great an elevation as to be buried deep in snow during eight months of the year.

Once Arthur's Pass became a viable alternative, Browning Pass was quickly abandoned as a route.

As soon as the provincial government approved

The route across Arthur's Pass traverses some difficult and unstable terrain, as seen in this drawing of Wallace's Point in the Otira Gorge, on the western side of the pass. From the *Illustrated New Zealand Herald* 1876.

the formation of a metalled road across Arthur's Pass instead of a mere horse track, about 1000 men were set to work with axes, picks, shovels, wheelbarrows, rock drills and explosives. The winter of 1865 was exceptionally cold, but the men worked through and by 1866 a road had been completed from Christchurch to Hokitika. The section through the Otira Gorge was an incredible engineering feat; the road zigzagged precariously across the edge of a massive unstable scree slope, the result of several enormous historic rock avalanches, and passed below a mountain face of highly fractured rock which constantly dropped debris onto the road below. In places the road was partially dug into the cliff, in others cantilevered on wooden trestles. The road was suitable at first for drays, but was soon widened just enough to accommodate horse-drawn coaches. A twice-weekly passenger and mail service began operating, although passengers had to get out and walk on the steepest sections, and slips and flooded rivers were constant problems. By 1866 the overland telegraph was established over the pass, and thousands of sheep and cattle were driven over to feed hungry goldminers on the West Coast.

By 1880 railway lines had been built as far as Brunner in the west and Springfield in the east, although coaches were still needed to link them through the mountainous section in the middle. The railways continued to creep towards the pass, and the final obstacle to overcome was the building of the Otira tunnel. The first explosive charge was fired in 1908, and the epic engineering feat was concluded in 1923 with the first train to travel all the way between Greymouth and Christchurch. At the time of its completion, the 8.45 kilometre Otira rail tunnel was the seventh longest in the world, its construction all the more remarkable for the difficult geology, terrain and weather that had been encountered.

Another pass across the alps existed to the north

During the early 1860s Browning Pass, seen here from the Wilberforce valley in a 1866 painting by Sir Julius Haast, was considered a strong possibility as a route between the west and east coasts.

of Arthur's Pass, at the southern end of the Spenser Mountains, but its development wasn't regarded as a priority as it didn't link directly with the West Coast gold diggings. This 863 metre saddle was another Maori route, which was given the name Lewis Pass after Henry Lewis, who crossed it in the early 1860s. Its development mirrored that of Haast Pass; during the 1890s a bridle track was cut, and during the 1930s Depression, relief labour was used to develop a road. This opened in 1937, providing an important road link between Canterbury, Westport and Nelson.

In 1929, work had begun further south to turn the Haast Pass bridle track into a road. Initially the project began as a job-creation scheme during the Depression. Construction was interrupted by the Second World War, and it wasn't until the 1950s that work resumed, finally resulting in 1960 in a road linking Wanaka and the small settlement of Haast. In 1965 the final piece of road was built, linking Haast with the glacier towns of Fox and Franz Josef. It was now finally possible to circumnavigate the Southern Alps by road and, providing winter snows hadn't closed the road, to cross the Main Divide by one of three passes.

Since then, improvements such as road sealing and the replacement of the Otira zigzag with a viaduct have made the journey faster, allowing increasing numbers of visitors access to the edges of the alps. But much of the alps remain as wild and remote as when the Dobsons, Haast and Harper set out on their explorations into unknown country; you can still choose to leave the road or the well-marked tramping tracks and pioneer your own route, to fight your way through unmarked bush, choose the best place to cross a raging river, and sit out bad weather in the shelter of a small tent. The great days of New Zealand exploration may be over, but great journeys are still possible.

The Terminus Hotel in Otira, photographed here in April 1911, was a busy staging post during the heyday of horse-drawn coaches. In 1923 the first complete train services across Arthur's Pass began through the newly completed Otira rail tunnel.

BEECH

A southern beech forest seems, at first glance, peaceful but in reality it is a battlefield where every living thing is engaged in a life-and-death struggle. The trees that provide the foundations are also in a battle with the elements; by virtue of their size they create a world for the other forest inhabitants that is largely tempered from extremes, but their reward for this role is to be under constant attack.

Catastrophe and opportunity

On a sunny summer day the interior of the forest seems gentle and idyllic. It smells healthily of sweet dampness, warm leaves and musky rotting leaf litter. A family of tiny riflemen scamper up and down tree trunks, uttering barely audible high-pitched calls as they fossick in the rough bark. A black fantail squeaks excitedly as it takes off from a small twig, snaps at a sandfly in mid-air then lands again, flipping its tail open and shut with the panache of a flamenco dancer folding her fan. Small patches of dappled light slowly rotate across the forest floor, flickering on and off as the sun slips behind branches then peeps through again.

Thick, spongy mosses drape the forest floor in a rough dark- and golden-green velvet carpet, creating a landscape of rolling hills and gentle valleys as they swaddle fallen trees, roots, soil and rocks in a wet embrace. The undulations may remain long after the logs beneath have rotted, giving the forest floor a look of substance that is purely illusory; any weight on the moss precipitates a sudden slide through the soggy fibres of a long-rotten tree trunk to soil hidden up to a metre below. The texture of the various mosses creates another illusion: a moth flying above gets an aerial view of the forest floor which mirrors that seen by a kea winging high above the forest canopy.

Rising from the sea of moss and the ghosts of fallen trees are the metre-wide trunks of living trees. Moss creeps up their straight lower trunks, joined by a lacy filigree of filmy ferns, and tough, leathery hound's tongue ferns. The living wallpaper which clings to the rough bark begins to thin as, high above the ground, the first horizontal branches reach out. Well spaced at their bases, the branches of neighbouring trees grow closer together as they widen out above 15 metres, so the canopy of the forest 20 metres above the ground appears from above as an unbroken swathe.

This is southern beech forest, a temperate rainforest distinctive in its uniformity and these horizontal spreading

Moss-covered fallen branches and tree trunks cover the ground in silver beech forest growing near the treeline. The rotting wood slowly returns nutrients to the living trees.

branches. Their small, serrated leaves identify these trees as silver beech, and they are the only trees forming the canopy in this patch of forest. This silver beech forest is growing at about 500 metres above sea level on a moderately steep west-facing mountainside, towards the southern end of the alps. A large river on the valley floor below carries water that is grey with glacial silt from the ice-covered peaks that tower above.

New Zealand was once a land of evergreen rainforests, and trees covered the country, extending from the coast up mountainsides to the edge of the alpine zone. In the last few hundred years much of the lowland forests have been cleared, first by Maori and later by European settlers. Today only about a quarter of the original forest cover remains, but that includes much of the forests that skirt the Southern Alps, which have remained more or less intact and significantly add to the mountains' feeling of primeval wilderness and timelessness.

Southern beech, or *Nothofagus*, is the classic mountain tree, but there is an intriguing anomaly: for 150 kilometres through central Westland there are no *Nothofagus* forests. In this 'beech gap' the forests are dominated by podocarps such as rimu and hardwoods such as rata, and the reason for the lack of southern beech in this area has been a question vigorously debated by botanists.

Nothofagus is a reminder of New Zealand's Gondwana connections. There are four species of southern beech in New Zealand, although one species has two distinct subspecies, so there are really five types. Red beech, hard beech and the two closely related species mountain and black beech belong together in a group known as fusca. The fusca group has its closest relatives in South America. Silver beech, on the other hand, traces its menziesii family history in the other direction, to Tasmania. Tens of millions of years ago, when New Zealand had a much warmer climate — warm enough in fact for coconuts to grow in

Southland — representatives from the third type, brassii, also occurred in New Zealand, but disappeared when the climate cooled. As a group, the *Nothofagus* beeches were once considered to be related to *Fagus* beech trees from the northern hemisphere, but have recently been classified in their own family.

Altitude, rainfall and soil fertility all determine which species grow where. Rainfall varies significantly from west to east across the alps, and while silver beech has firmly staked its claim on the wetter western slopes close to the Main Divide, mountain beech has equally decisively claimed the dry eastern slopes. While mountain beech is the most geographically widespread of all the beech species, silver beech has the most elastic ecological requirements, and occurs in the greatest variety of environments, from the heart of arid Central Otago to wet Fiordland. Red beech prefers deep rich soils and warmer, lower slopes, while hard and black beech occur away from the Southern Alps, in warmer, more northerly locations.

It is late spring, November, and the forest canopy is beginning to flush red, rather than the usual green. While the beech's leaf buds are preparing to unfurl fresh green leaves, male flowers in the buds are already unfolding and opening. Each short stalk carries one to three reddish male flowers, and as nearly every spring bud on every tree has flowered, it is this exuberance that is colouring the canopy. Almost immediately female flowers appear as well, single flowers discretely tucked between the base of a leaf and its stem. Primed by warm temperatures and dry weather the previous summer the beech trees have synchronised their flowering, and when the male flowers begin to shed their pollen there is so much that it drifts above the forest like an enormous cloud.

Although each beech tree produces both male and female flowers, those on the same tree can't fertilise each other, so the trees rely on wind to spread pollen from their male flowers to the female flowers on other trees. Unlike

Silver beech (*Nothofagus menziesii*) is one of five kinds of southern *Nothofagus* beech trees found in New Zealand. Small serrated leaves are arranged alternately along the branchlets.

the self-fertile snow tussocks which are also flowering profusely on the slopes high above, and which mass-flower to overwhelm their seed predators, the mast flowering of southern beeches seems simply to improve the chances of pollen spreading and enhance the successful production of a high proportion of viable seeds.

Once all the pollen has been blown to the wind, the fertilised ovaries of the female flowers begin to develop, and the forest canopy turns green again. A gentle rain of spent male flowers falls to the ground, where an army of caterpillars start to feast on them. The leaf litter is a rich habitat for the caterpillars of small moths; more than 50 species of moth with this lifestyle have been recorded, and their abundance and diversity are features of New Zealand's southern beech forests. In their turn the caterpillars feed predatory spiders, which hunt among the fallen leaves, and both caterpillars and spiders feed small insectivorous birds such as bush robins, which scuffle among the leaf litter to stir it up, and tomtits which search around on the litter surface. The adult moths in their turn are hunted on the wing by fantails and grey warblers.

As well as the thick carpet of moss, the forest floor is home to an open understorey of other plants. The distinctive rosettes of dark olive, rough-leaved prickly shield ferns and the softer, brighter greens of ladder ferns cluster in hollows between trees. The spindly stems of juvenile lancewoods, with their long, thin, serrated leaves held stiffly by their sides, and the airy lightness of divaricating *Coprosma*, with tiny leaves floating in a tangle of wiry stems, contrast with the solidity of horopito with its thick, peppery-tasting, red-flecked leaves.

By early January the beech seeds, which are protected in a tough woody case, have developed to full size, but it will be a few months yet before they ripen and fall. On some days an occasional harsh squawk or a quiet burbling trill, and the patter of seeds falling like rain, give away the presence of kaka feeding high in the canopy, delicately picking away at the tiny nuts with their large scimitar-curved bills and fat but dextrous tongues.

Southern beeches are evergreen, but each individual leaf only lasts for three to five years, so each year the trees shed some of their old leaves. Silver beeches begin to drop their leaves in early autumn, and soon afterwards ripe seeds begin to fall as well. The seeds are about five millimetres long and heavy for their size, although it still takes more than 300 seeds to weigh a gram. Although the seeds have small wings, they are poor fliers and the wind doesn't usually blow them very far, a few hundred metres at most; most fall within a 20 metre radius of their parent tree. The seed rain is heavy; more than 5000 seeds land on each square metre of ground, with up to 400 kilograms falling on each hectare of forest. It's late in the season, and apart from a few making an eager head start, most of the seeds will lie dormant during the winter, which is not far away.

The beech seeds will have very different fates depending on where they land, and as they won't survive beyond spring they will only get one chance to make a go of it. Some seeds have the misfortune of landing in a stream; most of these quickly become soaked and sink, although a few are swept along by the current and drift far downstream. Vivacious kakariki, bright green *Cyanoramphus* parakeets, descend to the forest floor in chattering flocks, picking up seeds along with any unfortunate caterpillars or spiders they find.

In spring, hundreds of thousands of silver beech seeds germinate almost simultaneously in the moss and pop their first two smooth, round leaves out into the light, jettisoning the outer capsule of the seed as their thin stem rockets up. Germinating from such small seeds they have limited energy reserves, so they push their first fine roots down through the moss in an urgent search for nutrients and water. It's a perilous time. After several warm days without rain the air is dry, the surface of the moss dries quickly, and many newly sprouted seeds wither and die. A dense flush of seedlings has germinated on the edge

The branches of southern beech trees have a distinctive layered appearance. Although silver beech trees can reach 30 metres in height, they become much shorter near the treeline. Rob Roy Glacier visible above high altitude beech forest, Mount Aspiring National Park.

of the forest in newly bare silt deposited along the side of a stream by a winter flood. They're both blessed with mineral richness from the silt and cursed by lack of shade to shelter them from the sun. The tiny seedlings that won the lottery to settle on the shady side of the stream fare better than those exposed on the sunny side.

Other winners in the landing lucky dip fell on a rotting log, and a swarm of seedlings hovers along its length like tiny green butterflies sporting pairs of leaves for wings. A rotting log is a prime location: it lifts the seedlings above the competitive crush and shade on the forest floor, and it is packed with nutrients. The soil in the forest is poor; most of the forest's nutrients are in the trees, both above and below ground, and living and dead. None of the adult trees are flowering this year; they're renewing their energy stores which were depleted by the previous summer's extravagant seeding.

Within a month the seedlings have added their first two true leaves to their initial baby leaves. After a further month they boast six leaves and their roots are beginning to branch. At this age the seedlings must forge a relationship that will be pivotal to their survival: with a mycorrhizal fungus. Although many fungi make their living from breaking down dead wood, these root fungi rely on an association with a living plant. They are ubiquitous in the soil and leaf litter, and soon coat the seedlings' rootlets with a closely woven weft, like a glove, effectively acting as extra roots which help draw up water and nutrients such as phosphorus.

A few seedlings succumb to less friendly fungi, others are eaten by caterpillars and a few are uprooted by bush robins digging through the moss in search of invertebrates, but most survive, especially those on the log. By the end of summer, when their tissues begin to harden in preparation for winter and they have developed resting buds, they are more than five centimetres tall.

Winter on the low and mid-slopes of the mountains is much less severe than that facing the plants in the alpine zone above, which will be covered in snow for months on end. But the adult trees must still be prepared for ice and frost, and for the weight of the occasional snowfall. They stop growing for just two or three months during the period of winter's shortest days, and the first pulse of spring growth arrives early. With it comes a shedding of small dead twigs and a few leaves, although most leaves will fall later, in autumn.

In the lingering cool of the forest interior, last year's seedlings have a slower start. Silver beech seedlings are more tolerant of shade than their relatives, but although shade and shelter were important for survival during the first summer, they become a curse by the second summer. Beech seedlings need light to grow, and while the filtered light under the dense canopy is enough to allow them to survive, their growth stalls. The forest floor is covered with a generation of potential heirs, all biding their time and waiting for the chance of light. It might be a long wait, and their growth might stall, but even if it takes 20 or more years the cohort of patient, stunted seedlings will be ready.

Many of the current monarchs of the forest won their race for a place in the sunlit canopy more than 400 years earlier. In their turn they had waited for an opportunity, which came in the guise of a fierce storm. Several days of heavy rain saturated the ground, and normally placid streams turned into raging torrents that spilled far beyond their usual confines, stripping away the beech seedlings and ferns that covered their sides, and undermining their own banks until the canopy trees along the edge became unseated and began to lean. With the rain came wind, which slammed into the forest in great gusts. The trees tottering on the subsiding river banks were shaken violently back and forth. Their wide, shallow roots, interlocked with those of all their neighbours, began to rock up and down. Huge branches began to snap and

Up to 5000 southern beech seeds may fall on each square metre of forest floor. The winners in the seed lottery are those which fall on rotten beech trees, as they provide a rich source of nutrients to the tiny seedlings.

crash to the ground, breaking other branches on their way down. The end came suddenly; the loosened roots of one tree lost their hold in the sodden soil, and its fall down the slope set in motion a giant game of dominoes. Hundreds of trees toppled, one after the other. When the storm blew itself out a few hours later, there was a ten hectare jumble of fallen and broken trees where just two days earlier had been a healthy forest.

This was no fluke event. Catastrophes like this shape New Zealand's beech forests. As a result, the forests are a mosaic of many clusters of similar-aged trees, with each cluster defined by its own catastrophe, be it rain, wind, drought, snow or landslide. In more sheltered sites the cause of death can also be old age, with single geriatric trees of 500 or even 600 years old finally succumbing to boring insects and rot; in such places the forest can be a mix of trees of many different ages.

This regime of constant disturbance has strongly influenced the evolution of the beech tree's life cycle. Far from being a disaster the wind fall is just that: a windfall. Although many of the seedlings waiting on the forest floor were crushed by falling trees, some survived intact in the gaps, and they wasted no time in seizing the opportunity. After years of barely growing they began to bolt for the light. Within just a year they had sprouted a metre, and their tufts of leaves waved at the top of lanky stems. It wasn't just light that was theirs for the taking; the fallen trees provided a shelter from wind and that priceless commodity — abundant nutrients.

The seedlings weren't the only things in the forest enjoying a bonanza amid all the damage. Litter-dwelling caterpillars suddenly had more dead leaves than they could manage to eat, and when those ran out there were many twigs and branches to go on with. Pinhole borer beetles, also known as ambrosia beetles, were attracted by the smell of fresh wood, and flew in from the surrounding forest to begin to tunnel into the logs. The males started building nesting tunnels in the soft, damp sapwood, and

the females continued them until they reached harder heartwood in the centre of the trees. Here they turned 90 degrees, staying close to the sapwood, and this was where they laid their eggs. When the larvae hatched they carried on the task of widening and extending the tunnel network, a task they attended to diligently for two years, until they pupated. A single nest could contain hundreds of larvae in what became a large network of tunnels. When they hatched from their pupal stage, hundreds of beetles flew out to begin their own tunnels. And the beetles weren't travelling alone; they took *Sporothrix* fungal spores with them which infiltrated timber along the sides of the tunnels, dyeing it dark blue and beginning to rot the tree from the inside.

Before they fell, the living trees had already been hosting beech buprestid beetle larvae in their bark. Incapable of penetrating living wood, the larvae usually only made it through their first stage, or instar, but this was the golden opportunity they had been hoping for. Soon the dead trees were under siege from a huge range of beetles and larvae. Meanwhile it was also open season for fungi and wood rot, with at least twenty different kinds targeting the wood in different ways.

The rotting trees acted as a slow-release fertiliser, which took many decades to surrender its nutrients. This was perfect for the sustained growth of the seedlings, which were now in a race with each other to form the new canopy. Their first goal was to gain height quickly, and as saplings they stayed thin and whip-like, adding about 30 centimetres to their height each year and a centimetre or so to their girth. Growing out in the full sunlight, with no competition from surrounding canopy trees, and needing to stake their territorial claim to a patch of light, the saplings began to grow branches and bush out their canopy when they were still less than ten metres high.

Across the whole ten hectare windfall 50,000 seedlings began the race, but after 50 years fewer than 5000 survived, and the numbers continued to dwindle as the trees aged

Wet heavy winter snow has the potential to break branches, but beech trees are usually able to shed most of their snow load and avoid significant damage. Forest edge at 1300 metres altitude, Craigieburn Forest Park.

and the strongest survivors shaded out the laggards. By the time the stand of trees is 200 years old, only 2500 or so trees remain. Now more than 20 metres tall and more than a metre in diameter, they are fully mature but still growing a little each year, as they will for the rest of their lives.

From early on the fresh leaves of the expanding canopy were a magnet for insects from surrounding older forest. More than 15 species of moth larvae and adult beetles now jostle for food, minimising competition with each other by targeting different parts of the canopy. Many, such as the looper caterpillars which will mature into geometrid moths, have become specialised to feed only on beech leaves. Each year a tree may lose up to a third of its leaves to these insect herbivores. Some eat leaves from the outside, while leaf-miner moth larvae hide inside the leaf and tunnel around eating the interior, leaving silvery traces of their travels. While some insects prefer new buds and leaves, others prefer old, leathery leaves. One species makes delicate lace patterns: it begins each summer chewing tiny windows between veins on the underside of the leaf, then later on munches its way from the top down through the upper layer of the leaf, until finally, late in the season, it becomes less fussy and devours the remaining leaf. Parasitic wasps and flies seek out the moth larvae and lay their eggs inside them, to become living larders for their own young.

While adult beetles feed on leaves high above the ground, their larvae attack other parts of the tree. Chafer beetle larvae lurk in the soil, feeding on beech roots, while the beech buprestid beetle larvae burrow into the bark. Other species, such as mites, climb right inside the twig or leaf, which reacts to the presence of the intruder by forming an unsightly blister or gall, enveloping it in a thick-walled pocket. One species of mite, which occurs only on silver beech, causes the tips of twigs to branch profusely and become covered with malformed, discoloured leaves. These sprays of light brown witches' brooms stand out clearly against the uniform green leaves of young trees, especially those growing on the sunny edges of the disturbed area.

In the wet silver beech forest, scale insects focus their attention on twigs, as well as leaves, and they do it by staying in one place rather than moving around. Attaching themselves firmly to the outside of the leaf or twig they insert their mouthparts into the tree to serve as a straw through which to steadily suck its sap.

In the drier mountain beech forests on the eastern, rainshadow side of the Southern Alps, scale insects play a different and far more important role. Along with red beech and black beech growing from Arthur's Pass north through Lewis Pass to Nelson Lakes, mountain beech forms a dry eastern forest, in which a substance secreted by scale insects, called honeydew, is the key component.

Inside the mountain beech forest, at 900 metres altitude, there is a strong smell of honey. It hasn't rained for a few days, and the open forest floor is dry and crisp underfoot. The airy canopy floats above in a series of horizontal layered branches. About half of the beech tree trunks are thickly covered in a matt-black wrapping of sooty mould, which spreads across the ground around them. These black trunks are covered in an exquisitely delicate tracery of white waxy threads, each half a centimetre long, with a small drop of clear fluid shimmering at almost every tip.

An olive-green bellbird alights on a trunk, clasping tightly to the rough bark with its feet as its long tongue flicks out to lick a drop of honeydew. Without having to move far it quickly gathers a dozen drops, then cocking its head in brief attention it pushes its beak into a crevice of bark and grabs a small caterpillar. Edging up the trunk a little it returns to licking honeydew drops.

Each drop of honeydew has been produced by a single scale insect buried out of sight within the bark. The white threads are the insects' anal tubes, and the drops of sugary fluid their waste products. This substance drives an ecosystem very different from that of the wet beech forests to the west and south of the alps. Whereas silver beech

Disturbance and catastrophe are hallmarks of southern beech forest regeneration. Storms, earthquakes and landslips are all capable of felling large areas of forest, creating opportunity for light-demanding seedlings. Arthur's Pass National Park.

forest is home mainly to insect-eating birds, honeyeaters such as bellbirds and tui and other sweet-toothed birds such as kaka throng to these plain but unexpectedly rich forests and fill them with beautiful song. Unfortunately, since their introduction during the Second World War, European wasps have added their distinctive buzz to the forest, and as a result of their honeydew pillaging the birdsong is now much quieter than it once was.

The honeydew-producing scale insect belongs to a genus known as *Ultracoelostoma*; other similar New Zealand scale insects belong to both this and other closely related genera. Aside from their famous honeydew secretions, these insects lead discrete, hidden lives, which pass through several distinct stages that vary according to their sex.

A female begins life as a bright pink crawler, just a millimetre long, but with well developed legs and antennae. While many crawlers walk around and settle on the same tree on which they hatched, this tiny female is swept up in a gentle wind gust and along with a few others is blown to another tree. She finds a suitable crevice in the rough bark of a mountain beech tree, which is already well populated with others of her kind, at densities of more than a thousand insects on each square metre of trunk. She inserts her fine mouthpart, or stylet, into the tissue of the tree until she has tapped into the vascular phloem and can begin to draw in the sweet sap of the tree. The female will stay anchored by her mouthparts for the rest of her life, and almost immediately produces the distinctive waxy anal tube. In readiness for her sojourn and to protect herself from danger she excretes and surrounds herself with a fluffy white waxy coat, known as a test, which gradually hardens into a solid protective shell.

Inside the hard test she moults her first skin to become a second instar scale insect. She is slightly larger, and has begun to lose her legs and antennae as she now has no use for them. Her body is now a pink sphere, tightly squeezed inside her protective chamber along with the shed skin.

By the time she sheds her skin again and becomes a third instar she is much larger, between two and a half and four and a half millimetres long, and her legs and antennae have shrunk even smaller. While she is in her second and third instar all she does is feed, and excrete honeydew continuously. She doesn't have to suck to draw in sap from the tree as fluid in the tree's phloem is under pressure and effectively pumps into her stylet; her only role is to control the rate at which she draws it in and then lets it out. The amount of honeydew she secretes has less to do with her than it has to do with her host tree, the rate at which it is photosynthesising and how much sap it is moving around between its leaves and roots.

What happens with the drop of honeydew at the end of her anal tube is also out of her control, and depends a great deal on the weather. A few days after she settles a rainstorm washes her drop away, and on another day strong wind blows the new drop away. On hot, still days the drop evaporates and shrinks to become a small, highly concentrated sugar bubble. Bellbirds, tui, kaka, the occasional kea, silvereyes, geckos and various invertebrates, including the ubiquitous and abundant wasps, also lick the drop off, getting a rich dose of sucrose and other natural sugars. The fallen sugar from millions of scale insects feeds other invertebrates and micro-organisms both in and on the soil, especially the seven species of sooty mould fungi which grow anywhere honeydew is available.

The scale insects produce honeydew year round, although they produce more in spring and autumn than they do in summer and winter. It seems that each year up to eight percent of a tree's production of carbon can be siphoned off as honeydew. Added up across all the trees this means that in some parts of the forest scale insects produce much as 4600 kilograms of sugar per hectare; that figure is all the more remarkable because that's the dry weight of sugar, and doesn't include the weight of the water it was dissolved in.

The female scale insect never leaves her post; by the

In drier eastern beech forests, honeyeaters such as bellbirds (*Anthornis melanura*) seek out sugar from honeydew droplets, as well as nectar from spring-flowering kowhai trees.

time she moults into her fourth and final instar and stops producing honeydew, her legs barely exist, and even her mouthparts lose their function as she ceases feeding.

A male scale insect shares the same life stages as the female until the end of his second instar, during which time he is also an active producer of honeydew. After he sheds his second instar skin he somehow squeezes out the tiny hole in the hard test through which the anal thread used to poke. He has become an active crawler again, a prepupa with well-developed legs and antennae; he is nearly four millimetres long and three millimetres across, bright red in colour, and no longer capable of eating. He doesn't waste much time before he heads down among the thick mat of sooty mould at the base of the tree, where he burrows in and pupates within a thin, fluffy, white cocoon.

When he emerges into his fifth and final instar he has metamorphosed into a strikingly different-looking insect. He has legs, compound eyes, a deep reddish-pink body that is four millimetres long, and he sports a pair of clear purplish-pink wings that span eight millimetres; he can now fly in search of mature females to mate with. Once he has found a receptive mature female he has to athletically mate through the small hole in her test out of which her anal thread used to hang.

After she has been fertilised the female lays 200 or more eggs within the hard test, and then slowly shrivels and dies to make way for them. The test has become a safe nursery for the pink eggs, which are covered with a dusting of white powdery wax. Once they hatch, the larvae make their way outside through the anal filament hole, and a horde of strange pink crawlers begin their quest to find an empty piece of bark that will give them access to the lifeblood of a mountain beech, unaware that they are the linchpin of an extraordinary cycle of nutrients.

Back in the silver beech forest, in early spring the air is filled with the loud, musical trills of male mohua, or yellowheads, advertising their breeding territories. Because of their size and bold yellow heads, as well as their musical song, early European settlers in New Zealand knew them as bush canaries. The female mohua are building cup-shaped nests of moss, twigs and spiderwebs within the protected confines of holes high on the oldest beech trees. In this patch of forest there are several dead trees still standing which have well-used nesting holes. Each female lays three eggs in the soft grass lining her nest, and settles in to incubate them for three weeks until they hatch, leaving only for quick feeding trips.

After the chicks hatch her mate, along with one of their chicks from the previous year, help her feed the hungry brood. These forests are rich hunting grounds for insectivorous birds, and mohua feed energetically and easily up the vertical trunks and along leafy branches. They use the long, stiffened barbs of their tail feathers as a prop to brace themselves as they hold onto the bark with one foot. A strongly muscled, broad pelvis allows them to scratch out to the side as well as back and forward, and their legs and long claws are so strong they can hang upside down from one leg as they scratch around in the mosses and leaf litter which accumulate along branches and in the crotches of trunks. As they search, a constant rain of debris falls to the ground below.

Tree holes are a highly sought-after commodity; yellow-crowned parakeets also nest in small holes, while the largest holes may be home to a pair of kaka. The parakeets forage in the canopy for scale insects and leaf miners, but if it is a masting year they will also eat their fill of flowers and, later on, beech seeds. Parakeets make the most of bonanza mast seeding years; they might breed right through summer and into the following winter, producing up to five broods of chicks.

Kaka also vary their diet between invertebrates, flowers, fruits and seeds, but they are so much larger and stronger they don't have to content themselves just with what they find on the surface. They dig into the trees themselves, gouging out bark and timber in search of large burrowing beetle larvae. A kaka might spend more

Noisy, gregarious mohua or yellowheads (*Mohoua ochrocephala*) are insectivorous birds which nest in cavities high on the trunks of mature beech trees.

than an hour extricating a single juicy grub from a living tree, although excavations on dead standing trees tend to proceed faster and be more profitable. The breeding success of the kaka also depends on the beech; they don't breed every season, only during mast seeding.

In late spring, clusters of what appear to be large yellow strawberries begin to grow out of distorted bumps on the trunks of some of the silver beech trees. These are the fruiting bodies of one of three species of fungi called *Cyttaria*, or the strawberry fungus. Alone among the New Zealand beech trees, but in common with its relatives in South America and Tasmania, silver beech has a close association with the strawberry fungus. The fungal spores appear in the dimples of the 'strawberry', and are spread throughout the forest when the fruiting body falls onto the ground. Inside an infected tree the fungal filaments infiltrate the wood, causing the tree to react as it does to invasive mites, growing a gall around the intruder. These galls can grow to be sizeable lumps, more than a metre in diameter, which bulge from the side of the tree. The contorted grain, or burr, is highly sought-after by wood turners, who appreciate its twisted beauty, but for the tree itself it's just another attempt at self-defence. If necessary a tree will carry out self-amputation of small branches to rid itself of the fungi, forming a protective seal between the branch and main stem, causing the branch to drop off. Not all silver beech trees are susceptible to the strawberry fungus, and while one tree might have a heavy infestation its close neighbours may be uninfected.

Some trees also seem to be growing sets of small, velvety, horizontal shelves from their trunks. Bracket fungi are another parasitic fungi which have invaded the tree and are stealing precious nutrients. Each year they produce spores in pores on their underside, which fall easily from there to the ground, and the lower layer wraps itself up around the curved edge of the bracket, adding to a growing collection of concentric rings that pattern the upper surface in an assortment of tan, dark brown and cream colours.

The night forest

When darkness falls in the beech forest, the night birds come out. With soft feathers as shaggy as hair, a kiwi walks slowly across the forest floor, pushing its long, probing bill into the soft soil in search of worms and insect larvae. A morepork sits on a branch, head cocked as it listens for the rustle of moth wings; alerted by a likely noise it flaps off, swoops and grabs, and returns to another branch to eat the moth's fat body, discarding the scaly wings. A mouse-brown short-tailed bat climbs out of its roost in a hollow trunk, and quickly flies off through the dark shadows. A different bat, this one long tailed, hawks outside the forest along the river edge, snapping at small flying insects. Come dawn, the bats and the kiwi retreat to roosts offered by rotten hollow trees, and the morepork settles in the crook of a branch to sleep, as once more the forest gives way to the day shift.

Top right: More than 6000 species of fungi have been catalogued in New Zealand to date, and thousands more have yet to be discovered and described. The violet pouch fungi (*Thaxterogaster porphyreum*) is one of the most easily recognisable forest fungi.
Bottom right: Beech strawberries (*Cyttaria gunii*) are the fruiting bodies of a fungus found only on silver beech trees.

In midsummer the uniform greenness of the mossy forest floor is broken by a shower of large red flowers falling from high in the canopy, and the usual insectivorous bird calls are augmented by the chimes, whistles and bells of honeyeaters such as tui and bellbird. There is not usually much in this silver beech forest to feed a sweet-toothed bird, but flowering mistletoe is worth a journey. As an added enticement, along the steep sides of the river a few southern rata trees are flowering, their red brush-like flowers carrying an enticement of nectar.

Mistletoes are another on the long list of beech bludgers, although they are not complete parasites; they have green leaves and photosynthesise their own energy, but their roots draw water and nutrients from their host rather than from the soil. Fruit-eating birds deposit the mistletoe's sticky seeds in their droppings as they perch in the canopy, and with that fertiliser head-start, the seeds waste no time in germinating and sending special roots known as haustoria into the tissues of the tree. A mistletoe can become a significant fixture in the canopy of a beech tree, sometimes reaching a diameter of up to three metres.

Two kinds of beech mistletoe make their home in the sunny canopy of the silver beech trees: red mistletoe, and the larger scarlet mistletoe. Seven of New Zealand's eight native mistletoes are found only in New Zealand, and the large red species have evolved a special interdependence with the honeyeaters. Their long flowers, up to five and eight centimetres long for the red and scarlet mistletoes respectively, are tubular, designed as a perfect match for the long, nectar-lapping tongues of a bellbird or tui. The flowers begin life sealed shut, to ensure that the right pollinating bird gets the nectar reward inside, with the added benefit of rain protection. A tui or bellbird recognises when a flower is ready by its colour, and know to twist the cap at the tip. The flower then opens explosively, showering the bird's head with pollen. As the bird dips in for a drink of nectar, more pollen brushes onto its head for good measure. At the next ripe flower the same process happens — the twist and turn, and the pollen shower — and this time when the bird seeks the sweet reward it brushes off pollen from the previous flower as it picks up new pollen.

Since late spring there has been another new bird call in the forest, a call that is a harsh drawn-out screech. Long-tailed cuckoos usually stay high in the canopy out of sight, but sometimes a few males gather and compete noisily with each other. These cuckoos are summer residents only, having spent the winter on various islands in the Pacific. They are avian parasites, which return to the beech forests each summer to lay their eggs in the nests of mohua and brown creepers. Fortunately for the unwitting foster parents, they have usually managed to successfully rear one brood of chicks before an over-sized interloper arrives in their nest to destroy their second brood and demand all the food.

Blue ducks (*Hymenolaimus malacorhynchos*) are one of only four ducks world-wide which inhabit fast-flowing rivers year-round. They are able to swim and feed in turbulent rapids from when they are just small chicks.

Blue duck

Blue ducks, or whio, are exceptionally well adapted to living in boisterous mountain streams and rivers, and they range from the alpine zone right down to low forest. From a very young age they are strong swimmers and divers. Blue ducks feed in shallow white water, scraping and sucking the larvae of aquatic insects such as caddis flies and mayflies off submerged rocks. They are well camouflaged against the grey rocks of their river home, unless the male gives himself away with his distinctive *whio* whistle. They occur in both the North and South islands.

Intricate relationships are the name of the game in the beech forest. While beautiful flowers and gorgeous song in the sunlit canopy are the hallmark of the mistletoes and honeyeaters, the subterranean realm of a beech tree's roots hold darker complexities. In spring and summer, slim dark stems push through the leaf litter around the base of some trees. When a stem reaches about 60 centimetres high, small, dark, drooping flowers shyly open along its upper length. It has none of the extravagant beauty or colour of its tropical relatives, but nonetheless this mysterious plant is an orchid. *Gastrodia*, which is also known as the potato orchid, is unable to photosynthesise, and relies instead on an intimate relationship with a fungus, *Armillaria*. The fungus has completely infiltrated the orchid's underground tubers, which are several centimetres long and were sometimes eaten by Maori as a special food. In its turn, the fungus has spread its threads into the roots of the beech tree, so *Gastrodia* is effectively an indirect parasite that is fed by both a fungus and a beech tree.

Other orchids grace the forest floor, and although their flowers are more typically orchid-like, they are still very modest members of their family. Small low-growing spider orchids have a single round, green leaf, and a single dark-purple flower. They are associated with a fungus that helped them grow when they first germinated; as adult orchids they photosynthesise and now feed the fungus in return.

Greenhood orchids are altogether more audacious than the little spider orchids. They stand boldly 20 or 30 centimetres above the forest floor, and kidnap insects. Their hooded flowers are pale green, decorated with white stripes, and have a pouting lower lip which is lowered like a drawbridge. When a flying insect lands on the lip it snaps up and in, sending the insect tumbling to the bottom of the flower. The drawbridge petal resets after half an hour or so, allowing the insect plenty of time to climb up the flower's central column, rubbing off any sticky pollen it

has collected from previous orchid visits, and collecting a new load as it leaves.

Many of these intricate beech forest relationships have been challenged and strained over the last 800 or so years. The previous generation of silver beech trees had to accommodate the arrival of the first humans in New Zealand, and their camp followers, kiore, also known as Polynesian rats. Following these arrivals, the disappearances began. First to go were the giants of the forest, the moa. Small family groups of slender, long-legged little bush moa moved easily through the thick forest understorey, using their sharp-edged beaks like secateurs to snip woody branches and wiry stems, and relying on gizzards full of stones to grind the tough, fibrous material to get nourishment from it. Sometimes enormous giant moa ventured into the forest from the scrubby river flats below. The females could stretch their heads three metres above the ground to reach leafy branches well beyond the reach of their much smaller mates and the little bush moa. The thick forest was a safe place for the giant moa, as their main natural enemy, the enormous Haast's eagle, which hunted them down and killed them with cruel talons as large as tiger claws, couldn't fly in the forest and preferred to hunt in open areas. The little bush moa, however, had to stay constantly alert for Forbes' harrier, which was a fast, agile flier, capable of manoeuvring between trees.

Less than 200 years after Maori arrived in the country and began hunting moa for food, the giant birds disappeared. With them went their great avian predators, the world's largest eagle and the biggest harrier. By now the new arrival, the kiore, was making its presence felt. The abundance of seeds and invertebrates made the forest floor a rat paradise, and with only the bush falcons to hunt them, their numbers surged and waned with the beech masting years. In a good beech seeding year Maori harvested large numbers of kiore.

With the arrival of Europeans, a flood of new species changed the beech forest forever. Beginning with Norway

Honeyeaters such as tui (*Prosthemadera novaeseelandiae*) tweak open the tightly sealed flowers of red mistletoe (*Peraxilla tetrapetala*), which open explosively to allow the bird access to sweet nectar in its base.

rats, followed by mice, possums, ship rats, stoats, deer and finally European wasps, these new invaders redrew the complex links of the forest food web. Mice and deer began to reshape the forest floor, rats and stoats climbed in search of nesting birds, possums targeted the canopy, while the wasps spread through every level of the forest.

Now in a beech flowering year, the fallen male flowers, seeds and the caterpillar army of the forest floor feed mice and rats, which begin to breed quickly. Exploding rodent numbers provide extra energy for the stoats to breed, but the surge in their numbers lags behind, reaching a peak the following summer as rodent numbers begin to subside. The hungry stoats begin to look elsewhere for food, and trapped in their nesting holes female mohua, kakariki and kaka, and their eggs or chicks, fall easy prey to these ruthless predators.

Deer and possums are having their own impact on the forest structure, although the silver beech trees themselves are left alone by the newcomers, which favour other particularly palatable 'ice cream' species. The forest understorey begins to subtly change as palatable plants become increasingly rare, leaving more room for less tasty plants such as the peppery horopito.

The rise of the introduced mammals is matched by a gradual fall in the numbers of many native species. Birds that were once a common part of the forest, such as the piopio, bush wren and South Island kokako, have disappeared completely. Others, such as South Island saddleback and kakapo, have disappeared from mainland forests, and survive only on predator-free islands. Mohua and kaka maintain a tenuous hold but their future is far from assured; in some places poisoning and trapping of predators during beech seeding years is all that assures their survival.

Red deer

The New Zealand red deer population is a combination of various strains of two forms, European red deer and the larger North American wapiti. More than 250 red deer of British stock were imported between 1851 and 1919, and by 1923 more than 1000 had been released in many places throughout New Zealand. They are now the most widespread large wild mammal.

Red deer are selective feeders, and by targeting a few preferred species they have caused major changes to the forest understorey. From the 1930s onwards they were present throughout the forests and low-alpine zone of the alps in huge numbers, and until the 1960s there were reports of herds up to 500 strong creating significant vegetation damage. In the 1950s a trade in venison began, and the advent of helicopters for shooting deer and later for live recovery for farming saw significant reductions in their numbers, especially above the treeline, where they were easiest to find.

A magnificently antlered red deer stag (*Cervus elaphus scoticus*). Despite recreational and professional hunting, red deer remain abundant in forests throughout New Zealand.

Despite all the changes that have happened around and on them, the mature silver beech trees that blanket the valley sides from the river terraces up to the treeline continue to thrive, weathering the usual heavy rains, occasional periods of drought, the summers and the winters, providing a stable home to generations of birds and invertebrates. Around their dark, mossy feet the dense sward of stunted seedlings continues its patient vigil, waiting for the opportunity of light. Twenty years old, and still only 20 centimetres high, they can grow no further for now. Their numbers are slowly dwindling; a few have run out of nutrients, and some have been destroyed by large branches snapped off during high winds and hurled to the ground.

Their chance for a future comes suddenly and unannounced. It begins with a resounding bang which echoes and bounces across the steep valley, and is followed by the immense ground-shaking chaos of a large earthquake, rolling on and on for more than 30 seconds. Bits of rocky mountainside are shaken loose and rocks and boulders begin to move, slowly at first but gathering momentum and material as they slide downhill.

The shaking stops but the mountainsides are still in motion, still falling. A steep-sided gully below the patch of mature trees has collapsed into itself, unzipping the hillside above. The interlocked mass of beech branches and trunks, roots and soil, is wet and heavy, and begins to sag towards the empty space below. Suddenly the soil and roots part company with the sheer rock beneath and the whole slope begins to slide. The bottom trees collapse like skittles into a giant heap, while those above begin to totter and sway, eventually splaying out in every direction.

When the earth and trees eventually stop falling, the valley looks a very different place. Huge scars of bare rock are interspersed with wide swathes of fallen trees. The next few times it rains the streams and river are stained brown with mud. But out of the destruction comes new life and opportunity. Just as these mature trees had their beginning more than 400 years ago on the backs of fallen trees knocked over in a storm, so their death will herald a new beginning for the waiting few who managed to survive the mayhem, and for the next generation of seeds to be blown from the surviving forest. Individuals die, but the forest is resilient, and on the slopes of these young, unstable mountains catastrophe, like rain, is a normal way of life.

Right: Near its upper altitudinal limits beech forest becomes a stunted goblin forest festooned in mosses and lichens.
Over page: Young silver beech seedlings on the dim forest floor wait in a state of suspended growth for light that will give them an opportunity to complete their race towards the canopy.

Earthquakes

With the enormous pressures and forces at work in the subduction zone between the Pacific and Australian plates, it's not surprising that many earthquakes occur along it as strain builds up and is occasionally released. Shallow earthquakes are a regular feature along the length of the subduction zone, but while deep earthquakes, which originate from depths greater than 40 kilometres, are common in Fiordland and from Marlborough northwards they are curiously infrequent along the Alpine Fault. Evidence from radiocarbon dating of plant material in landslides caused by earthquakes, and from growth-ring data of old trees, shows major ruptures of the Alpine Fault occur on average once every 100 to 300 years. The last big shakes on the Alpine fault have been dated to the years 1460, 1630 and 1717, the last one occurring between the visits of Abel Tasman and Captain Cook.

When they happen, these deep earthquakes are very strong; between Tasman and Cook's voyages some low-lying areas of Westland were dragged eight metres to the northeast. Over time successive large earthquakes have also raised the land on the eastern side of the fault relative to that on the west. It's possible to see evidence of these movements in rivers and streams on the West Coast, where once straight watercourses now dogleg in an S shape across the fault, and sizeable scarps separate the higher side of the stream on the eastern side from the lower western side.

While some geologists fear that the Alpine Fault is overdue for another large earthquake, others argue that rocks at depth may be absorbing much of the tension by gentle folding and flowing, and that perhaps deep earthquakes are not a common feature of the fault.

Landslides caused by floods or earthquakes may seem catastrophic initially, but in the long term they create a forest that is a mosaic of different-aged stands of trees. Landslide from Mount Hawkins into the Mahitahi River, Westland.

SHELTER IN THE ALPS

Millions of years of evolution have refined the ability of alpine plants and animals to cope with the freezing temperatures and fierce climate of the mountains. But for us humans the mountains are an alien environment; we evolved initially as creatures of the tropics, so the mountain world is not one for which we are naturally adapted. Survival comes from dressing for warmth, and having shelter from the elements.

Shelter in the alps

The task of making shelter is simplest in the bush, where it's possible to make temporary lean-to shelters from branches stacked against each other, and cut soft leaves and stems for mattresses. Arthur P. Harper, one of the founders of the New Zealand Alpine Club, worked with Charlie Douglas exploring valleys on the West Coast during the 1890s; by his reckoning:

. . . between October and March in the mountains, within 3000 feet of sea-level, it is really not necessary to carry canvas, unless, of course, one is fastidious as to shelter. It is always possible to build a good "whare" or "mai-mai" with bark stripped from the rata, totara or cedar . . . Of firewood there is an inexhaustable supply and a good variety to select from, that it is always possible to keep a fire burning, without any necessity to economise, a great consideration in bad weather.

Douglas' bush home was usually what he called a batwing tent, a small floorless tent erected beneath a flysheet suspended by cord between trees, which was angled so rain would run off, and high enough off the ground to allow Douglas to light a fire under it. He slept wrapped in a blanket.

The earliest back-country huts were probably built during the 1860s, when gold prospectors travelling across the mountain passes of the Southern Alps to the West Coast built simple timber-slab huts. Inveterate tramper Mark Pickering, who reckons he's stayed in over 900 of New Zealand's more than 1400 back-country huts, believes the oldest surviving one may be a stone hut on Mount Peel Station, in the headwaters of the Rangitata River. It was built during the mid to late 1860s as a boundary keeper's hut, at a time when men performed the job of fences.

Mountain huts don't normally last as long as this, as they are more usually built from less durable materials

During more than 40 years of mapping and exploring, explorer Charlie Douglas's usual habitation was his batwing tent, which consisted of a tent fly rigged over a small sleeping tent and fire. Photograph by Arthur Harper, above Franz Josef Glacier 1893–94.

such as timber framing and corrugated iron. Above the treeline there are even fewer raw materials from which to manufacture a building, and the elements are even more punishing, ensuring a short life for most high-altitude huts.

Tents have always offered vital portable shelter. Climbers Reverend William Spotswood Green, Emil Boss, Ulrich Kaufmann and an extra, unexpected visitor had as their base camp at the foot of Mount Cook a tent that was small but able to accommodate the four of them. They set it up in a manner that was far more sophisticated than most of the simple single-layer canvas tents available at the time, but they also knew they were dealing with an inhospitable alpine climate:

. . . *on a dry patch of stones we pitched our small duck tent, and pegging it down, pitched the larger tent on*

top of it. A stratum of air was thus inclosed [sic] between the double walls, which we calculated would add not a little to the snugness and dryness of our quarters . . . Though the large tent was but six feet high the two hammocks hung conveniently over one another, and left plenty of room for the two cork mattresses on the grounds; to add to the comfort of the ground beds Kaufmann cut a quantity of the long dry grass and placed it under the mattresses. Strong guy ropes were then made fast to the bushes around, to prevent our encampment being shaken in a storm, and a curtain of mosquito netting to keep out the flies made our home as comfortable as circumstances would permit.

By 1891 the government had constructed the first track to the Ball Glacier, and the first hut, Ball Hut, had been built.

Above: Joseph Kinsey and party in a tent camp on flats at the edge of beech forest. 1895.
Right: Chief guide at the Hermitage, Peter Graham (standing at right of photo, with ice axe), with a mountaineering party at the Hochstetter Bivouac. 1905.

No. 956. The Hochstetter Bivouac, 6,977ft.

As mountaineer and author Jim Wilson put it:

The latter was sometimes euphemistically described as a "two-roomed edifice", but was in fact a corrugated-iron shell with no floor, divided into "ladies'" and "gentlemen's" quarters by a curtain of canvas. No matter, it was a thousand times better in a bad storm than a flimsy tent.

Other huts quickly followed, based on the same design.

Every alpine hut has an epic story behind its construction. Many of the first alpine huts were built by mountain guides as an extra job fitted in at the beginning or end of their summer guiding season. The New Zealand Alpine Club, along with other clubs, also took an active role in funding and building huts. The builders have often had to live in snow caves or polar tents while building a hut, and bad weather was always a challenge, preventing work, blowing down partially erected framing and stripping cladding from the walls. Most huts were prefabricated as much as possible before the parts were carried to the site. In the twentieth century, fixed-wing planes eased the burden of carrying heavy loads to hut sites, while helicopters revolutionised alpine building.

In 1898, surveyor T. Noel Brodrick sited a new hut beneath the peak of Malte Brun, on a grassy terrace 150 metres above the Tasman Glacier. The Malte Brun Hut became a popular overnight destination for parties willing to make the eight-hour walk up the rough glacier. Although horses were used to carry loads over easy ground it was sheer hard work building the hut, as all the building materials — from nails to wood and corrugated iron —

Above: Interior of Ball Hut 1895. The hut was partitioned into men's and women's sleeping areas by a canvas curtain. Guides and porters carried all the food and climbing supplies for their clients from the Hermitage.
Left: The original Ball Hut was a popular destination for day and overnight parties. The Gifford tramping party were photographed outside the hut in January 1907.

had to be carried most of the way on people's backs. For this and future huts the load-bearers experimented with ways of easing the burden: travelling on skis and pulling sleds, and even using huskies from Admiral Byrd's 1929 Antarctic expedition to pull laden sleds.

Mueller Hut in Aoraki Mount Cook National Park has been rebuilt five times since 1915. In 1949 the original hut needed replacing, and technology came to the builders' aid; instead of men having to carry the timber up the steep mountainside on foot, it was air-dropped in by an Air Force Dakota plane. The packages were pushed out of the plane with a small parachute attached to slow their descent, and men then sledded the packages down to the hut, using the parachute as a brake and steering with an ice axe. All the packages were retrieved, and the hut was completed on schedule in 1950, but unfortunately before it was ever used it was destroyed by an avalanche. A temporary hut was built using material salvaged from the ruins before a new hut, the fourth, could be built. When the land under this hut began to slump as a result of receding glaciers, the hut was replaced with the current incarnation, delivered to the site ready to erect in 130 helicopter loads.

Many of the alpine huts throughout the alps have been the victims of natural disasters, sometimes tragically when people were in residence. Snow and ice avalanches, as well as rock avalanches and storms, have all taken their toll, while others have succumbed to the ongoing battering inflicted by high winds and low temperatures. Some huts, on the other hand, simply became too popular, and too small to cope with increased visitor numbers.

The availability of helicopters and improved engineering and building technology have been matched by increasingly ambitious building projects, so in a sense it hasn't become any easier to build mountain huts. In 2005 the 42-year-old Plateau Hut, above the Tasman Glacier in the Aoraki Mount Cook National Park, was replaced; the new hut is twice the size of its predecessor, and as the existing hut site was too small to accommodate a larger building, part of it had to be cantilevered out over a steeply sloping rock face. Sixty tonnes of building had to be helicoptered in in pieces, and in the absence of heavy machinery such as cranes, it was designed to be self-supporting as it was assembled. The challenge of building in the mountains is always the same: a hut must be able to withstand hurricane-force winds, and heavy rain and snow. Plateau Hut is bolted to solid rock with 66 one-metre-long high-strength bolts, held in place with very strong glue. Built in less than four months, Plateau Hut, like the hundreds of other Southern Alps tramping and climbing huts, large and small, will provide shelter in the mountains for generations of climbers to come.

By the standard of suburban houses, back-country huts may seem basic buildings, but they are a home away from home, and more importantly they allow us tropically adapted humans to survive our mountain experiences. They have also become an integral part of the experience of being in the New Zealand mountains, as tramper, author and hut connoisseur Mark Pickering eloquently describes:

There are huts that leak, huts that sweat, huts that smell

The original Mueller Hut was built on the slopes of Mount Sealy in 1915, and all the building materials had to be carried up to the site on people's backs. The hut remained in use until 1949, when it was replaced.

of mutton fat, huts that fly away, huts that aren't on any map, and huts that are in the wrong place. You find huts that have burnt down and are sadly missed; and some that are like warts on the landscape and you wish would burn down. But many huts sit so aptly on the land that you think they must have grown there, and these are cherished.

At the sophisticated end of the shelter scale, a hotel such as the Mount Cook Hermitage offers complete comfort in a mountain setting. But even as it gives shelter the Hermitage is fighting its own battle with the elements. In New Zealand's rigorous alpine environment buildings tend not to stand the test of time, even when they are top-class hotels.

The earliest buildings in the Mount Cook area were simple one-room station cottages. One of the first runholders to settle there was Edward Dark, the owner of Glentanner Station; for his first few months he lived under a rock on the shores of Lake Pukaki. The original homestead cottages were made of cob, a combination of beech logs plastered with clay and thatched with snow tussock, as was the very first Hermitage hotel built on the floor of the Hooker Valley in a sheltered site next to a scrub-covered hill called Foliage Hill. It was built in 1884 by manager Frank Huddleston for a company of South Canterbury businessmen and runholders who planned to provide accommodation for the growing number of visitors coming to see Mount Cook and its neighbours. Cob walls were thick and warm, but winter frosts proved too harsh for the original clay walls of the Hermitage, which had to be protected by an outer layer of corrugated iron. A wooden extension was later added to the original building, creating accommodation for up to 30 visitors at a time, and in 1895, after the original company went bankrupt, the

Above: Horse-drawn coach leaving the Hermitage Hotel. Photograph circa 1906–08.
Right: A car and a party of tourists carrying walking sticks in the driveway of the Hermitage Hotel in Mount Cook village. Photograph by Leslie Hinge, date unknown.

government agreed to buy the building and the business.

By the early 1900s the Hermitage had become a thriving business, and by 1913 work had already begun on a new, larger building when time ran out for the original building. Australian climber Freda du Faur was staying at the hotel at the time and wrote:

From the day of our return to the end of March it rained solidly — in fact, just to prove what it could do in that line it rained twenty-four inches in twenty hours, and we had a second flood. Fortunately the Easter crowd had departed, and there were only about twenty people in the hotel. The Muller River came down in full force, and instead of dividing as on the first occasion came straight into the hotel. In no time we were inundated. The annexe was awash, the drawing-room, front bedrooms and dining-room were ankle-deep in water, and everybody had to decamp to the back hall bedrooms and smoking room. During the night the annexe broke away from the main building and settled into the stream that had undermined it. In the morning by way of variety it snowed; the water receded and the house was inches deep in silt . . . The poor old Hermitage was a wreck, damaged beyond all hope of mending . . . The old happy carefree, home-like days spent in the rambling old cottage buildings were over.

The second Hermitage survived until 1957 when it was destroyed in a fire, but by the end of 1958 the third Hermitage was built, and remains the basis of today's large hotel.

Plants have evolved their alpine dress-sense over millions of years, and have had no need to follow the vagaries of fashion and design. Humans, on the other hand, have evolved

Above: A Hermitage Hotel luggage label.
Right: Mountains and glaciers have always been popular tourist destinations.

TRAVEL IN NEW ZEALAND

at the FRANZ JOSEF Glacier

A GLEAMING JEWEL in the MOUNTAIN SIDE

their mountain clothing over only a few hundred years, but in that time the rate of change has been extraordinary, moving from flax and feathers to thick cotton or wool and on to synthetic fabrics. The same principles apply to both plants and humans: the idea is to keep the wind and cold out, and trap warmth inside. Dressing for the mountains involves not just issues of warmth; clothes must also be able to stand the rigours of the New Zealand bush.

Maori travellers wove sturdy sandals from flax or cabbage tree leaves; depending on the terrain these needed replacing every day or two, but the raw materials were readily available and new sandals could be quickly woven. Flax or tussock stems could be quickly fashioned into gaiters for leg protection against spiky speargrass. Cloaks woven from flax and feathers, or fashioned from kuri, or Maori dog, skins provided protection from plants and the elements.

Some early European surveyors and explorers borrowed heavily from the Maori for ideas on how to dress when working in the bush, as surveyor and engineer Arthur Dudley Dobson wrote in his memoirs:

During the exploring days the clothes worn were the strongest procurable, moleskin trousers, very thick and heavy, either brown or white (moleskin is a thick twilled cotton material, and when wet it is almost waterproof and like soft leather), stout flannels, and a flannel shirt. When not actually working a blue serge shirt was worn over those in lieu of a coat, and a vest for state occasions. Strong water-tight boots and leggings to the knees, a soft felt hat, a strong leather belt round the waist, with a sheath-knife and a small pouch for a watch and money, completed the costume. When working in the bush, cutting lines, as survey hands, or when working on the claims as miners, trousers and a flannel shirt were all that were required.

The original Hermitage Hotel was built in 1884 by manager Frank Huddleston. The cob cottage sat in a sheltered site where the present-day White Hills camp ground is situated. Frank Huddleston painted this view from the position of the current Hermitage in 1886, showing Mount Cook in the background.

When working with the Maoris, we were so much in and out of the water, canoeing and travelling along the beaches, where there were so many creeks to cross, that we wore, during the day time, two flannel shirts — one, without sleeves, around the waist like a kilt, the other one as a shirt, and light rug over the shoulders, which acted as a coat, and as we were always carrying a swag of some sort, the ends over the shoulders eased the cutting of the swag straps. When working on the beaches and in the river-beds we wore on our feet Maori sandals. We carried all our loads in the Maori kawe, two long flat bands of plaited flax . . . Very heavy loads, up to 200 lbs, were carried in this fashion. I always carried a dry suit of clothes, tied up in oil-skins, and dressed as soon as I camped for the night.

George Mannering gave a brief list of necessary clothing for the alpine climber of the 1880s:

. . . woollen shirts and knickerbockers of warm tweed material are the best, and great comfort is to be found in a loose-fitting boating "sweater" worn over the waistcoat . . . The most necessary gear for ice and rock work is suitable boots, broad-soled and flat-heeled, shod well but not too thickly with heavy hobs, wrought nails being preferable to cast.

William Spotswood Green, attempting Mount Cook with Emil Boss and Ulrich Kaufmann in 1882, described how:

. . . as we might expect days of heavy rain and would have considerable difficulty in drying our clothes if once they got wet, we came to the conclusion that it would be safest to stick to our waterproof coats. Kaufmann and Boss, attired in these yellow oilskins, looked often more like North Sea fisherman than anything else. My large cape

Woollen shorts and knickerbockers, and brimmed hats, were standard dress for mountaineers in 1895. Puttees wrapped around the mens' calves provided protection for their shins and prevented stones slipping into their boots.

was loose enough to hang outside my knapsack and keep all beneath it dry.

Victorian women faced particular challenges in the mountains, as long skirts were not just awkward and cumbersome, but could be downright dangerous; in Europe in 1908, the first attempt by a woman to climb the Matterhorn had to be called off less than 100 metres below the summit when strong winds blew her billowing crinoline petticoats and skirt over her head. Australian climber Freda du Faur, climbing in the early 1900s, solved the problem of combining decency with practicality by wearing woollen knickerbockers underneath a skirt which she shortened to just above knee length. Other women climbers wore their long skirts, but while climbing pinned them up using safety pins provided by the mountain guides.

Wool remained the fibre of choice for mountaineering clothes for decades, with oatmeal-coloured longjohn underwear and the classic red- or blue-chequered Swanndri or bush shirt both becoming distinctive parts of the New Zealand outdoor wardrobe. From the 1970s onwards, synthetic fabrics such as fleece and pile began to offer a lightweight alternative to heavy wool, and revolutionised tramping and climbing clothing. As these polyester-based fabrics have become more sophisticated, there has also been a revival in the use of wool garments, which modern spinning and knitting techniques have made lighter and less scratchy than their predecessors.

There has been a similar evolution in rainwear, from Boss and Kaufmann's oilskins, via totally waterproof but unbreathable PVC and nylon, to today's breathable membrane fabrics such as Goretex.

Victorian women climbers were expected to wear the long cumbersome skirts that were the fashion of the day, but more daring women such as May Kinsey wore more practical shortened skirts over knickerbockers and puttees. This photo has the caption 'Old May in her den' 1895.

Kea are the world's only mountain parrot. Kea probably began to hone their skills in mountain living when the alps were first appearing five million years ago, and two million years of glaciations then allowed — or perhaps forced — them to perfect an alpine lifestyle.

Mountain parrot

A gentle snow has been falling steadily for a few hours, and among the gnarled, twisted trunks of the lichen-covered beech trees it is dim and quiet. About ten metres away up the slope the dwarfed trees give way to a thick tangle of low bushes and tall snow tussocks, their outlines softened beneath a comforter of accumulating snow. Some snow penetrates the sheltering umbrella of the tree canopy, dusting lumpy roots and mossy rocks with a light sprinkling of white, like icing sugar.

A dark shape hunches in the crook of a branch, sheltered by an awkwardly angled trunk. The few snowflakes that land on it soon melt into drops of water that sit, quivering slightly, on glossy khaki feathers, until in a sudden flurry the kea vigorously shakes himself and the drops fly off. Two black eyes snap open and, tilting his head to the side, the bird lifts one foot and vigorously scratches under his chin. The itch satisfied he returns the foot to the branch, and runs the edge of his large, curved bill cursorily down

his chest to smooth the feathers back into place. Ruffling his downy under-feathers for warmth he hunches his head and returns to his patient vigil.

Under a nearby tree, in a chamber formed between boulders and roots, his mate sits half asleep, her head resting on a pillow of dry moss and snow tussock stems, her body arched around three small eggs tucked well in against the bare skin of her brood patch. It is August, late winter, and even in the shelter of the nest cavity it is cold; the eggs demand her body warmth. She has been incubating the eggs for three and a half weeks, and by the sound of tiny pipping calls and movement within one of the eggs she knows it is close to hatching. Her eye flickers open, and she shifts her weight as she senses the eggshell cracking slightly.

Darkness settles over the mountains of Arthur's Pass, and some time during the night the snow stops falling. Clouds gradually clear and as stars appear in the moonless

In a sheltered underground nest a female kea (*Nestor notabilis*) incubates two eggs and a tiny chick which has been hatched only long enough for its white down to dry.

sky the temperature drops and the soft snow begins to harden with frost. Inside the nest a tiny chick is trying to kick its way clear of the last clinging piece of eggshell; its mother shifts her weight to one side and, chattering quietly, reaches down and one by one pulls all the pieces of broken shell away. The wet, pink-skinned chick lies exhausted from the marathon effort of breaking free, and the female gathers it in tightly to dry it against the heat of her body.

After several hours the chick stirs and cries, and the female wakes to feed it for the first time. The chick's wet down has dried to fluffy white, and its eyes are sealed shut as it tries to lift a head that seems too large for its skinny neck. The female opens her beak, which seems enormous next to the little chick, and scoops it under the chick's head, resting her upper mandible against the fleshy pad at the base of the chick's bill. Then she regurgitates a thin slurry of food from her crop, channelling it along her lower mandible directly into the chick's open beak. Sated with the warm meal the chick almost immediately falls asleep again, and the female rearranges it among the eggs before falling asleep herself.

In the half light of early morning a quiet *keargh* from outside the nest wakes her, and she carefully rises, pausing to stretch her legs and wings as she walks towards the nest entrance. On their usual branch nearby her mate is waiting for her, and she quickly joins him. He opens his bill as she urgently presses her open bill against it, and heaving slightly he regurgitates food for her. As soon as she has fed she returns to the nest, pausing only to drag the bits of eggshell out the nest entrance before she settles back on the chick and eggs.

Twice more that day the female is summoned outside by her mate to be fed; the chick feeds much more often than that, although at the moment its demands are small and it is easily satisfied. Late in the afternoon the second egg begins to pip and crack, and in the early hours of another freezing morning the female tucks a second damp body next to the fluffy puff of the first. Every hour she feeds first one then the other chick, holding their wobbly heads gently despite a bill that seems if as it could skewer them.

While she is busy with the babies, her mate is hard-pressed to find food for them all. The lingering southerly airstream has turned once soft snow in the alpine zone to solid ice, and he is having difficulty breaking through to find the sweet, shrivelled berries he knows lie underneath: white snowberries, orange *Coprosma* and red snow totara. He doesn't bother going too high as he knows his best chances of finding food lie in the thick scrub near the forest edge. He resorts to walking as he searches, trusting in the grip of his sharp claws and beak on the ice, his version of crampons and ice axe. He knows of reliable food sources, but for now they are too far away; he can't leave for more than a few hours at a time.

Over the next two days the final chick hatches. The brood of three is getting stronger and more demanding with each day, although their eyes are still closed. The adult pair have been through this many times before; this is the third time they have used this nesting cavity, and the male knows the surrounding territory intimately.

Finally the temperature warms, and the snow softens and melts a little, revealing easy food below. Each time the male approaches the nest now to call the female away to feed he hears a growing chorus from the ever-hungry chicks, but he never enters. Once, while he is away, a young female kea approaches; she sits on the ground outside for a while, then slowly enters the nest tunnel. The nesting female shows no animosity; the kea round here are well known to each other, and chances are she is the female's offspring from a previous year, still too young to breed. She stays a couple of minutes, and then leaves.

In early September a warm nor'west wind melts much of the low snow, but the hint of spring is tantalisingly brief, and by the time the first chick is opening her eyes for the first time another sou'wester has dumped new snow. The

Top right: Two tiny kea chicks, one a day old and the other just hours old share the nest with an as yet unhatched, egg.
Bottom right: The large fleshy wattle around a kea chick's bill provides a soft pad into which the female kea gently hooks her upper mandible during feeding, thus ensuring food is accurately delivered.

fresh snow brings eager skiers to the field at Craigieburn and, pushed to find food for the ever-demanding brood, the male flies there late one morning, a journey of more than 25 kilometres. He has timed his visit with lunchtime, when people are eating and their leftovers make easy kea pickings. He is not alone; other younger kea have been skifield regulars all winter. The rest linger after lunch, heading to the carpark to amuse themselves amongst the cars and ski racks, but the male returns directly to the nest. His quiet call fails to bring the female from the nest, and he realises why when she appears next to him on the feeding branch. She had been on her own brief foraging trip, and quickly heads to the nest to feed what she has collected to the chicks. He waits and she returns to be fed, but her absence from the nest indicates that from now on it will take both their efforts to feed the chicks.

The chicks have grown so much the female has difficulty fitting them beneath her at night, but their down has thickened and turned to grey, and is better able to keep them warm. During their mother's absences they huddle together, and when she returns it is to the sight of three yellow beaks bunched together like the bright centre of a grey fluffy flower, waving agitatedly as if in an unseen breeze. To begin with there was a big size difference between the first and last chicks hatched but the female has been favouring the smallest one, which has rapidly gained in size. The earliest alpine flowers have begun to bloom next to melting snow patches, and the chicks' diet now includes regurgitated petals and new leaves, as well as dried fruits and seeds from last summer, and an occasional assortment of sandwiches and chips from skifield lunches. For the first month it was always only the female who entered the nest to feed the chicks, but now the male ventures in for

Previous page: Kea are strong fliers, and have large home ranges. They have been known to travel up to 60 kilometres in a single day.
Left: Kea cope well walking on snow. They have long sharp claws that act like crampons, and on very steep or slippery slopes they may use their strong hooked beak as an ice axe for extra grip.

the first time, finally meeting the new family which has been the hidden centre of his world for so many weeks. He is larger than the female, and his upper bill is longer, but despite his daunting size the chicks eagerly take the food he offers. From now on both parents feed them regularly and often.

By late October the grey chicks are nearly the size of their mother. They are shuffling around the nest interior, playing and mouthing each other, and investigating the dishevelled remains of the plant material the female had carefully lined the nest with many months earlier. They have just begun to sprout their first pin feathers, which poke through the soft down like so many days' growth of unshaved stubble. The base of their bills, their nostrils and eye-rings are bright canary yellow, but will slowly darken over the next three years as they grow to maturity.

Outside the nest spring is at its peak; the forest has been full of song for the previous weeks as other birds announced their breeding territories and called to potential mates, but the song has quietened as breeding has got underway. Using their strong beaks as shovels and picks, the kea pair has been grubbing in soft soil in the alpine zone around the roots of *Dracophyllum* and speargrass plants in search of soft roots and burrowing grubs, to supplement the chicks' diet of leaves and flowers.

In mid-November the oldest chick ventures out as far as the nest entrance for the first time; she sits in a patch of late afternoon sun. Flags of yellow-green *Usnea*, or Aaron's beard lichen, festoon the goblin forest and wave gently in the light breeze. The sloping lichen- and moss-covered trunks of the beech trees are a textured painter's palette of greens, with hints of yellow, blue and grey. The chick's feathers are developing their own shades of green, from khaki through olive to almost emerald.

Young kea chicks grow very rapidly, and their white down turns grey before they start growing feathers. The female is responsible for feeding the chicks while they are small, while she, in turn, is fed by the male.

Over the next few days her siblings join her for increasing periods outside. Their father is now doing most of the feeding, and they beg him for food. He carefully obliges. He doesn't stay long as he must head off in search of more food, and before long the chicks are left on their own again. There are so many new objects to smell and taste and touch that they don't go far, and when they tire of exploration they return to the nest to nap. As their tails develop, and their feathers thicken and the last of the tattered remnants of baby down rub off, they begin to look more like adult kea, although the crowns of their heads are still a distinctive baby yellow. At the same time their co-ordination improves, and a friendly shove is less likely to send them accidentally reeling. Now when they roll onto their back they do it by choice as they lark and play with their nest mates. They begin to flex their wings, which sport lengthening flight feathers, and it's not long before they are eagerly practising flapping. The area in the vicinity of the nest has begun to look decidedly tatty from their constant investigations, and although they are still eager to return to the nest each night, it won't be long before their parents will lead them away.

They have much to learn, as the mountain environment is a very challenging one, even for a bird as smart, curious and dextrous as a parrot. We usually think of parrots as brightly coloured tropical birds, but New Zealand's parrots are sombre in colour, and the alpine zone is a very long way from the tropics. Kea have the distinction of being the only parrot in the world to live in high, snowy mountains; their close relatives the kaka are forest parrots, while the rare flightless kakapo moved between the forest and the low-alpine zone in the days before it became extinct on mainland New Zealand. Together kea, kaka and kakapo are an ancient group of parrots that dates back to the evolution of the parrot family as a whole; they may have been in New Zealand since it broke away from Gondwana. New Zealand's other forest parrots, the much smaller *Cyanoramphus* parakeets, are newcomers that arrived here from New Caledonia just half a million years ago.

Kea were once widespread through both the North and South islands, but seem to have disappeared from the North Island after the arrival of Maori, at the same time disappearing from the dry forests east of the alps. There used to be other mountain birds but the upland moa, the mountain goat of New Zealand native birds, is extinct, and once widespread takahe are now confined to Fiordland. Now it's only kea and a truly alpine bird, the diminutive rock wren, which live in the alpine zone year-round.

The little wren is as much part of the Southern Alps' unique identity as the big mountain parrot. These endearing, hyperactive birds, with their distinctive bobbing motion, long spindly legs and exceptionally long toes, seem unlikely residents of the alpine zone, but in every sense they are our truest mountain bird.

While waiting for mist to clear during their first attempt to climb Mount Cook in 1886, George Mannering and Charles Fox amused themselves:

. . . watching the antics of some queer little wrens. These birds are absurd-looking little creatures with long legs and longer toes, plump buff-coloured breasts, no tails, staring little eyes, and looking for all the world like boiled potatoes with their jackets on, set up on hairpins and let loose on the rocks.

Explorer Charlie Douglas wrote that they were:

. . . as a rule mountain birds are true troglodites, but sometimes they visit the low country . . . The largest wren is a funny bird to watch, hopping about a camp. He is continually on the move, wings and legs going all the time. If he ever sleeps except hopping I don't know, never having seen one quiet except on its nest.

A juvenile kea, identifiable by its bright yellow eye ring, nostrils and base of its bill, learns to use its bill to delicately squeeze the juices from a snowberry fruit.

Rock wrens weigh just 14 to 22 grams, and are found only in the mountains of the Southern Alps, Fiordland and northwest Nelson. Despite their diminutive size the almost tail-less rock wrens live year round in the low-alpine zone, making their home among the stable boulders and small bushes of old rock falls and on scrub-covered cliffs. As Douglas pointed out they spend much of their time underground, scuttling like feathered mice through the sheltered cracks and crevices of the rocks, and fossicking around inside bushes.

The rock wren is exceptional not just for its rare ability to live year-round in the alpine zone, but for its ancestry. It belongs to an ancient family of *Acanthisittidae* wrens, which are one of New Zealand's distinctive Gondwanan bird families, along with moa and wattle birds such as kokako. New Zealand's wrens are considered to be the most ancient surviving members of the *Passerine* group of

songbirds and, even more unusual among songbirds, three of the six species were flightless. Sadly, only two wren species survive today, the rock wren and its forest cousin the rifleman. The rock wren would have once shared its low-alpine home of tussock and scrub with the extinct long-billed wren, which was flightless and, at 30 grams, nearly twice the size of the rock wren. Rock wrens can fly, although their wings are small and rounded, and they seldom flit more than a few metres at a time, staying low to the ground as they do so.

Because of their remote alpine habitat, rock wrens were one of the last of New Zealand's native birds to be described. Julius Haast discovered them in 1866, and sent specimens to two prominent ornithologists who both recognised and described the bird as a new species.

Rock wrens have evolved particular strategies to cope with living in a cold environment which is snow-

Previous page: A young kea practises flying.
Right: Despite its diminutive size, the rock wren (*Xenicus gilviventris*) is a true mountain denizen, capable of surviving cold alpine winters.

covered for many months each year. They have become ground feeders that seldom fly, as flying involves opening air sacs and drawing in cold air which lowers a bird's core temperature. Rock wrens' legs are well back on their body, allowing them to keep their centre of gravity well forward as they scramble up and over boulders, and the exaggeratedly long rear and central toes on their large feet provide a wide, steady base. Rock wrens have a distinctive way of scrambling around, using both feet to hop, and never stepping or running. Their toes are very strong and dextrous, and can be used to pry lichens and mat plants apart, and to grab large prey such as centipedes or millipedes. Their toes are also capable of fine, almost finger-like picking, when gleaning along tussock shoots.

Most of the time rock wrens use their fine, short bill to search tangled vegetation, rocky cracks and crevices, spiderwebs and the ground for invertebrates as varied in size as mites, thrips, worms, crane flies, spiders, beetles, caterpillars, flies and moth larvae. Occasionally during the warmer summer months, when flying insects are common, rock wrens will hunt flying or jumping insects on the wing. In the middle of summer they spend time gleaning the surfaces of warm rocks for invertebrates, but during autumn and winter they concentrate their efforts in nooks and crannies where invertebrates are most likely to be sheltering or pupating. Adult insects have hard exoskeletons that are hard to digest, and as a result rock wrens have to regurgitate pellets of indigestible material several times a day.

Rock wrens are resourceful birds, and during the colder months when invertebrates are harder to find they will also eat sweet, energy-rich *Coprosma* berries, snow totara berries and snowberries, and even seeds. They have occasionally been seen sipping nectar from mountain flax flowers. When it's cold, wet or windy, rock wrens retreat among sheltering rocks and underneath bushes, where they can continue feeding protected from the bad weather. This is also where they spend much of the winter. No one knows how such tiny birds survive winter, when their low-alpine home is often snow-covered and temperatures are low; perhaps when it's very cold they go into a state of torpor, saving energy by lowering their body temperature and heart rate. But they are certainly active for much of the winter, and on sunny days it's not unusual to catch their almost inaudible high-pitched call and see them bobbing on a rock poking above the snow.

Rock wrens time their breeding to coincide with the greatest abundance of food. As soon as the snow begins to melt in spring, pairs begin to build their large, tightly woven nests in a sheltered place, such as in a crevice on a sunny cliff or tucked underneath a bush. Both the male and the female build the nest, which has walls as thick as six to eight centimetres made from matted and intertwined grass stems and mosses, which is so dense as to be waterproof. The nest is well lined with soft lichens and insulating feathers; rock wrens are such enthusiastic feather-gatherers that the fearless little birds will happily take feathers offered to them by passing trampers. Curious around people, rock wrens are fiercely territorial when it comes to other rock wrens, and will chase away neighbouring birds which intrude into their territory. The territory may be as small as a hectare or as large as ten hectares, depending on the quality of the habitat, the amount of plant cover and the richness of its food supply.

The female lays up to five tiny white eggs, which her mate helps her to incubate for nearly three weeks. The pair alternate sitting shifts of about 40 minutes with vigorous feeding bouts. Their nest is so well insulated that it's usually at least 15°C warmer inside than outside. By the time the naked, helpless chicks hatch, many invertebrates have also hatched or emerged from their winter diapause, and both parents work flat-out to find food for the chicks and themselves. Co-operation is the key to maximising the short productive season, and to ensuring the successful fledging of the one brood the pair produces each year. The male works hard to maintain a good pair bond with his mate,

Between spring and autumn the alpine zone offers a rich smorgasbord of flowers, leaves, fruits and invertebrates for alpine birds such as rock wrens and kea to feed on. Yellow-flowered snow marguerites (*Dolichoglottis lyallii*) in flower next to an alpine waterfall.

continually courtship-feeding her with the choicest berries and energy-rich invertebrates, even while he's busy collecting food for the rest of the family. The chicks are fed fat-rich, soft-bodied insect larvae, and their parents feed them until they fledge when they are three and a half weeks old.

The fledglings are quickly independent and feeding themselves within a week of leaving the nest, although they stay in a family group with their parents for a month or so, until they moult for the first time. By the time they are three months old, nearly two thirds of the fledglings have already found a mate and established their own territory, ready to breed early the following spring, before they are even a year old. For little birds to survive in the harsh alpine world, speed and good timing are very much of the essence.

Unfortunately global warming and increasing predation pressure by rats and stoats in the alpine zone threaten the rock wren's future. Who knows how much longer we have to enjoy the subtle company of this ancient bird which survived New Zealand's turbulent geological past to create a niche for itself on the high slopes of our young mountains.

Having begun breeding during the short, cold days of winter, the kea pair is ready to lead the chicks away from the nest in early December, during the mild, generous months of summer. The family stay together for several months, exploring the intricacies and vastness of their Arthur's Pass world. In a short time the juveniles are introduced to the sombre beech forest, the rich tangle of low-alpine shrubs that separates forest from alpine grassland, the nooks and crannies among the stable jumbles of boulders on the fellfields, the bare scree slopes which fan out below steep gullies and bluffs, and the snow patches that cling to the high, bare, rocky peaks. For the first six weeks out of the nest their father continues to feed them full time. Then, as they slowly begin to gather food for themselves, he feeds them less and less, although they still beg for food when they are hungry. They adopt a distinctive crouch when they want food: they lower their body and head towards the ground, hold their wings close to their body, and fluff out their feathers. They face their parent in quiet persistence; if he moves away, they move too.

Like small children, kea fledglings learn by doing — and by putting everything in their mouth. In this way they discover that their beak is a versatile tool which can be forceful and destructive, or delicate and precise. They are clumsy and unco-ordinated at first, and completely undiscriminating about what they try to eat: anything and everything is touched, mauled and often destroyed. Gradually they learn to feed themselves, digging through moss and in the soil around plant roots looking for caterpillars, beetles, moths and grubs, and they discover the lipid-rich fruits of snow totara, and sweet, juicy snowberries. They slowly become experienced in the art of searching, excavating and demolishing, using their feet to hold and brace objects, and manipulating their mobile tongue to hold or rub objects against the hard palate of their upper bill. The young kea will need to remember all this, to be able to recognise places even when they are buried under snow, to know exactly where good food sources lie.

The kea family is always on the move. After feeding for perhaps half an hour, the parents suddenly announce their departure with loud calling, and the family takes to the air in a dazzle of flashing orange underwings. In just a few minutes they can be several kilometres away, feeding in a completely different environment. One day the parents lead the youngsters to a hut for their first introduction to humans. To the birds, the humans' behaviour is perplexingly contradictory; at first the people encourage the birds to come close, enticing them with food, and then when the birds become bold enough to start investigating the clothes and boots strewn around on the ground they begin to shout and chase the birds away. It is the youngsters' first lesson in how to behave around people, how to look for opportunity while remaining wary and ready to escape.

Once they have left the nest, young keas are fed by their father. They solicit food from him with a distinctive hunched begging posture.

Kea didn't used to temper their boldness with caution; in his account of exploring the headwaters of the Rakaia River in 1860, author and runholder Samuel Butler wrote:

To the unscientific it is a rather dirty looking bird, with some bright red feathers under its wings. It is very tame, sits still to be petted, and screams like a real parrot. Two attended us on our ascent after leaving the bush. We threw many stones at them, and it was not their fault that they escaped unhurt.

Many New Zealand birds used to be that tame and fearless, although only weka were as inquisitive as kea. But the resourcefulness which has been their chief asset has also often got them into trouble. Writing in 1883, climber William Spotswood Green described the conflict that already existed between kea and early sheep farmers:

Southerland [the shepherd on Birch Hill Station] was early astir and away up the mountain-side with his gun to try and shoot some keas, which we could hear every morning and evening screaming about a thousand feet above us. These parrots are the great enemies of the shepherds, as since sheep have been introduced into the colony they have developed a taste for kidney fat, and pitching on the backs of the poor unresisting animals hold on to the wool with their claws while with their powerful, curved bills they eat through the flesh till they reach the wished-for delicacy. At first I was inclined to doubt this story, but its truth has been established by such unimpeachable authority that it must be accepted as fact.

The kea saw opportunity in the sheep; the farmers saw menace in the kea, and for more than a hundred years they waged war on the mountain parrots, sanctioned by the government, which paid a generous bounty for each kea beak. At least 150,000 kea were killed, and that doesn't include the many birds which went into the cooking pot to make 'parrot soup' for hungry explorers and climbers such as Green.

Nobody knows how many kea are left today; the commonly quoted figure of 5000 is based on little evidence. Kea have a highly visible presence in the mountains, and have been known to fly as far as 60 kilometres, between Arthur's Pass and the Mount Hutt skifield, so it's possible their actual numbers are even lower than the estimate. Two American researchers who studied kea at Arthur's Pass for three years suggest total kea numbers may be as low as 2000.

This new generation of kea, at least, has official protection, conferred as recently as 1986. The only conflict in the young birds' lives at the moment is play fighting, an activity for which they seem to have an endless capacity. Each day they rough-and-tumble with one another, jumping, somersaulting, kicking and biting in mock battles that test their agility, sharpen their reflexes, and provide hours of entertainment.

The kea family doesn't have exclusive rights to its mountain domain; they share it with other families, whom they meet from time to time. The young kea are very interested in the other young birds and begin to form play groups, leaving the adults to sit to one side. As summer wears on, the adult pair begins to spend more time apart from the youngsters, who are increasingly independent. The parents begin to spend more time foraging on their own, making the most of the abundant food before another winter and another breeding season.

By autumn the young kea are spending most of their time in a large gang of other youngsters, led by several older males whose role seems to vary between babysitter and ringleader. Their wanderings take them from mountain top down to the Arthur's Pass village, from skifields still closed for the season back to the rich berry harvest of the alpine zone. On rainy days they retreat into the beech forest or shelter under rock overhangs; on windy days they ride the thermals and updrafts rising among the rocky

Juvenile kea spend lots of time playing and fighting with one another. Vigorous flapping during play strengthens their flight muscles and improves their co-ordination, as well as establishing social hierarchies.

The inquisitive kea

Explorer Charlie Douglas often encountered the kea, which he said:

. . . frequents the mountain ranges perching like a miniature condor on dizzy precipices. Unlike the Kakas who have a dozen different cries the Kea has just one, weird Key-a-key-a, hence its name. Sounding like the wail of a lost spirit the cry is rather a startling sensation while climbing a dangerous precipice, suggesting a possible corpse lying a thousand feet below, with the kea standing on the head picking out the eyes . . . The moment they see a man coming into their haunts they flock around and follow him, as if they were afraid he was going to steal some of their property . . . They will often alight on a gun barrel or a stick if held out to them. Many a time in the mountains I have had to get up in the early morning to save the tent fly from being torn to pieces by the Keas.

In a scene reminiscent of the ice ages, a family of kea forage above the Dart Glacier.

bluffs, learning to manoeuvre and dance in mid-air and accomplishing the art of landing on a sixpence.

During the first storm of winter they experience snow for the first time, and are intrigued by the way it disappears when they try to catch it. As the snow settles deeper, and food becomes harder to find, they follow the older birds to the Craigieburn skifield where they settle in for the winter. Well fed by the rubbish and leftovers they don't need to forage much for natural food, and instead turn their abundant energy to testing cars and buildings to destruction. When bad weather closes the skifield and leftovers are scarce the kea gang returns to the bushline to forage.

Their first birthday passes; by now the young birds' lower bills, eye-rings and nostrils are fading to a pale yellow, and their feathers are dull and worn, as they have not yet moulted for the first time. The skifield closes and the birds leave with the skiers, back to remoter parts of the mountains where the first alpine flowers push bravely through the melting snow. Summer passes in a blur of feeding, exploring, playing and sleeping in the sun. There is a strong but fluid hierarchy of dominance in the gang, and a kea's day is a succession of aggressive encounters with various members of the group. Subtle nuances in the way each bird fluffs or flattens its head feathers indicate its mood and intention. The juveniles use aggression to supplement their poor feeding skills; they have turned their baby begging crouch into a ritualised hunch that resembles a Japanese bow, often accompanying it with screaming. If they approach a feeding adult male and position themselves in the hunch, the male is more than twice as likely to tolerate them feeding nearby or let them take his food than if they had just approached him normally. The hunch allows them to behave aggressively, yet mask their intentions with a submissive child-like pose; it is an effective technique.

The juvenile birds spend many hours playing with each other. Scientists have observed that the structure, intensity and frequency of their play is unique among birds, and more akin to primates. Play is a rough-and-tumble melée of jumping and flapping at each other, rolling over, biting, locking bills, pushing with their feet and generally wrestling with one another. Like human children young kea also enjoy playing with 'toys', maybe a rock, stick or flower, and will entertain themselves for hours at a time.

Not all kea interactions are boisterous; again like primates, kea preen and groom each other, especially around the head. It's a pleasurable sociable activity, and birds actively solicit each other for preening.

One day the kea siblings are feeding near their old nest site when they come across their parents, accompanied by three newly fledged chicks who seem a little overwhelmed by the chaos and enthusiasm of the gang. Yet by the end of summer they have joined its ranks, tagging along at 'kea school'. Four of the oldest birds have quietly slipped away from the group, forming pair bonds with females who had remained mostly outside of the group; this winter they will breed for the first time, needing to call on their new-found skills to find food for their families.

By the time she is three years old the oldest youngster has lost most of her childish yellow eye-ring and nostrils, and sports the dark grey bill of a mature female. She is now a sub-adult and has been spending more and more time with an older male who joined the group last winter after his mate died. They seek out one another's company, sitting next to each other and gently preening the other's head and neck. When enthusiastic play-fights break out between the younger members of the gang they are as likely to move away from the group as to join in. The young female's two brothers are both having an awkward kea adolescence. They hang back from the gang, unwilling to play, and older birds are increasingly aggressive towards them. They are slower to mature than their sister, and it will be another two or even three years before they begin to breed.

This year the gang is having no difficulty finding food. Both the beech trees in the forest and the snow tussocks in the alpine zone are fruiting and seeding. The kea spend many hours among the canopy of the beech trees, carefully using their bills as forceps to pick the small nuts and crushing them between their tongue and the hard roof of their mouth. Later in the season they move into the alpine zone, stripping the plentiful seeds from the waving wheat-like tussock stalks.

By the end of summer the young female and her mate have left the group completely, and are exploring an area of forest, hopping awkwardly over mossy boulders as they look around trees and search under rocks for a space that could make a good nest. Eventually the female finds the perfect spot, which opens out into a dry cavity at the end of a narrow metre-long tunnel. This has been a kea nest before, but it's long abandoned.

Before snow covers the alpine grassland the female must gather bedding for the nest. She brings beak-loads of snow tussock stems and pulls soft, dry moss and papery lichens off nearby beech trunks, piling it all into the cavity which now smells sweetly of straw. Her job is complete well before the first big snowfall, but the pair are in no hurry to mate; they must wait until later, timing the hatching of their chicks with the following spring. They turn their attention to a detailed exploration of the surrounding forest and shrubland, ensuring they'll know the best places to search for food when they have chicks to feed. There is a lot of snow this winter, and food takes a lot of finding; there is a strong temptation to join the younger birds at the skifield, but they resist . . . most of the time.

It's mid-September before the female lays her first clutch of two small eggs, just half the size of hens' eggs. Her mate has experience in his role of feeding his mate but she is guided only by instinct, keeping the eggs warm, turning them regularly, not lingering outside when her mate calls her off to feed. When the first chick hatches she automatically knows how to lift its little head, and feed it just the right amount.

When she and her mate lead their boisterous twosome up the mountain in the middle of summer they join a dynasty of mountain parrots. The chicks soon meet their grandparents, and by the end of summer have joined a noisy band of cousins whose energetic play is a hallmark of their intelligence and the resourcefulness which enables them to adapt to an alpine lifestyle, and whose noisy screeches mark these mountains as distinctly New Zealand.

On first meeting, kea may seem very un-parrot-like with their drab green feathers, but their gaudy underwings make a dazzling display.

Epilogue

Mr Explorer Douglas' birds

Charlie Douglas led an extraordinary life. From 1867 onwards he spent 40 years exploring and mapping the remote and rugged valleys, glaciers and mountains of South Westland, often with just a dog for company. He knew the western Southern Alps from Hokitika in the north to Jackson Bay in the south more intimately than anyone has ever known any part of them, and in 1897 he was awarded the Gill Memorial by the Royal Geographical Society 'for his persistent exploration during twenty-one years of the difficult region of forest and gorges on the western slopes of the New Zealand Alps.'

Born in 1840, he emigrated to New Zealand from his native Scotland in 1862 and five years later fetched up on the West Coast. He never left, dying in Hokitika in 1916, seven years after the second of two strokes left him paralysed and unable to speak. He was the black sheep in a well-to-do family of painters and bankers, and although he began a career in banking he didn't care about money or material possessions and gave them away to travel to the far side of the world. He never trained as a surveyor or geologist, but after 20 or so years filing unofficial reports on his explorations of unmapped country his friends Chief Surveyor Gerhard Mueller and geodetic surveyor G.J. (George John) Roberts finally persuaded him to join the survey department on the West Coast. His official designation was Explorer. He was given a prismatic compass, a survey chain, map-drawing tools and a wage of eight shillings a day, which kept him in food, sketching materials and pipe tobacco, and he was a diligent report and letter writer.

Mr Explorer Douglas, as he became known, was practical and resourceful, tolerant of discomfort and able to live off the land. He was a thoughtful, solitary man, an original thinker, and an astute observer of nature. His observations on the creatures he encountered and whose company he enjoyed give us a remarkable insight into a mountain world which has changed greatly since his time:

The Weka prowled around the tent, annexing anything portable, and the Kiwi made night hideous with its piercing shriek, the Blue Duck crossed over to whistle a welcome. The KaKa swore and the Kea skirled, Pigeons, Tuis, Saddlebacks and Thrushes (piopio) hopped about unmolested. The chorus of the bellbird was heard in the dawning & all were tame and inquisitive, but now all this is altered. The Digger with his Dogs, Cats, rats, Ferrets and Guns have nearly exterminated the Birds in the lower reaches of the southern rivers . . . But the Flats of the Copland put a fellow in mind of old days; it was full of birds all tame and inquisitive as of old.

This was a New Zealand in which native birds that are now extinct or very rare were astonishingly common and tame, and it was easy to catch kakapo, blue duck, kea and weka for the cooking pot. However, Douglas was greatly concerned at the rapid disappearance of many birds, and fretted about the effect of introduced animals.

At one time the Kakapo swarmed in that beech country from the sea beach to near the snow line, and in two instances I have caught them on a snowfield, as if they were trying to cross the Divide . . . To know what it was like to be in a good kakapo country before the advent

Previous page: When they are less than a year old juvenile kea become independent from their parents, and spend the next couple of years belonging to large gangs of roving youngsters and sub-adults.

of the ferret and stoat, one had to go to the flats of the Landsborough or the Thomas Range. The birds used to be in dozens round the camp, screeching and yelling like a lot of demons, and at times it was impossible to sleep for the noise. The dog had to be tied up or matters would have been worse. It would have been killing and fetching all night long. But alas this is a thing of the past; when last up the Landsborough there wasn't a bird to be found unless by going high along the spurs.

The Southern Alps today are much poorer than when Charlie Douglas began exploring and recording his observations — and we are all much poorer as a result. While some species, such as the piopio and kakapo, are either extinct or confined to safe offshore islands, many other birds have survived, but in ever dwindling numbers. Blue duck, yellowhead, orange-fronted parakeet, kaka and many others cling on in parts of the Southern Alps, but their long-term survival depends on the development of effective long-term control measures against rats, stoats and possums, among others. Unfortunately the mast seeding of both beech trees and snow tussocks benefit introduced predators as much as they do native birds and invertebrates; every time there is a mast seeding year predator numbers surge, and bird numbers fall as a result. Poisoning and trapping is buying some time, but it's expensive and labour intensive, and deals with populations only in a few key areas.

Much of the Southern Alps area is now protected in national parks, reserves and wilderness areas. The first national park to be gazetted in the alps was Arthur's Pass in 1929, inspired by the conservation vision and efforts of botanist Leonard Cockayne, and supported by such luminaries as mountaineer Dr Ebenezer Teichelmann. The first reserves at Mount Cook were set aside in the 1880s, 'to conserve for all time a place whose beauties would not be easy to exaggerate, and will undoubtedly be one of the attractions of the globe.' However, the area wasn't gazetted as a national park until 1953, a year after the passing of a comprehensive National Parks Act which finally articulated the commitment to conservation of the government of the time. Nelson Lakes National Park followed soon after, in 1956, and in 1961 the parks were joined by what is now known as Westland Tai Poutini National Park, the nucleus of which was the scenic reserves gazetted at various times since 1911 to protect various lakes and glaciers. Mount Aspiring National Park was created in 1964.

Significant areas such as the Landsborough Wilderness Area, Lewis Pass and Craigieburn Forest Park lie outside the national parks system, but are protected and managed by the Department of Conservation. In 1990, the Te Wahipounamu South West New Zealand World Heritage Area was declared, encompassing the area from Arthur's Pass to Fiordland, in recognition of this area's outstanding scenic and natural values.

Who knows what the future holds for the glaciers, plants and animals of New Zealand's mountains. Global warming definitely poses a significant and immediate threat, largely from the speed at which it is progressing; but then again, the world is also thought to be nearing the end of a warm interglacial period, and interglacials are generally followed by glaciations.

The Southern Alps Ka Tiritiri o te Moana has always been an environment of change and destruction, and the mountain world of forests and alpine gardens that we see today has been around for less than 10,000 years. The only certainty is that while their glaciers and inhabitants may come and go, these young mountains have a long tumultuous life ahead of them, but they won't be around forever.

Appendix 1

The highest peaks

People have a fascination with the height of mountains. In Britain, for instance, the 284 highest peaks in the Scottish Highlands, which are all taller than 3000 feet (900 metres), are known as the Munros, and despite their relative lack of height, attempting to climb every Munro is a popular goal. A Marilyn, on the other hand, is any hill in the British Isles which has at least 150 metres of relative height; the name is a pun on Marilyn Monroe (or Munro).

New Zealand's highest peaks don't have a collective name as such, but in the days of imperial measurements the mountains that were 10,000 feet (3048 metres) or taller were known as the Ten Thousand Footers. The first person to climb all of them was Andrew Anderson, who climbed his last one in 1950. The modern metric equivalents are the 3000 metre peaks, of which Mount Aspiring is the only one lying outside the central alps.

Aoraki, Mount Cook high peak **3754 m**, middle peak **3717 m**, low peak **3593 m**
Mount Tasman **3497 m**
Mount Dampier **3440 m**
Mount Vancouver **3309 m**
Silberhorn **3300 m**
Mount Hicks **3198 m**
Malte Brun **3198 m**
Mount Lendenfeld **3194 m**
Mount Graham **3184 m**
Mount Torres **3160 m**
Mount Sefton north peak **3150 m**, middle peak **3138 m**, south peak **3048 m**
Mount Teichelmann **3144 m**
Mount Haast east peak **3114 m**, middle peak **3099 m**, west peak **3065 m**
Elie de Beaumont east peak **3109 m**, west peak **3054 m**
La Perouse south peak **3078 m**, north peak **3060 m**
Mount Douglas **3077 m**
Mount Haidinger south peak **3070 m**, north peak **3061 m**
Mount Magellan **3049 m**
Mount Malaspina **3042 m**
Minarets east peak **3040 m**, west peak **3031 m**
Mount Aspiring **3033 m**
Mount Hamilton **3025 m**
Mount Dixon **3004 m**
Glacier Peak **3002 m**

(source: *New Zealand Wilderness* magazine January 2002)

Previous page: Winter wraps the alpine gardens of the Southern Alps in a blanket of snow. Looking across Lake Leeb to Mount Aspiring partly obscured in cloud in the distance.

Appendix 2

A mountain lexicon

The word 'mountain' comes from the Latin *mont*, and from that common root many languages share recognisable words. New Zealanders often refer to their mountains in an affectionate diminutive as 'the hills', and 'the tops' are the mountain slopes above the treeline.

The Latin root *oro* means to do with mountains; therefore orogeny with their creation, and orographic to do with their geography.

Snow has its own language; light, dry snow which falls as large, fluffy flakes is *powder*, while wet, heavy snow quickly melts. *Graupel* is precipitation formed when freezing fog condenses on a snowflake, and forms a ball of *rime ice*. On cold, clear nights, water vapour moving up through the snow freezes as *hoar crystals*. *Corn* is coarse, wet, granular snow, created by alternate freezing and thawing, which makes for good spring skiing. *Skins* enable skiers to move across sloping snow. In the past, animal skins were laid along the bottom of skis with the nap of the fur laid so the ski could slide forward but friction prevented it running backwards. Climbing skins for skis are now made with artificial 'fur', and are glued to the base of the ski.

In its first year fallen snow is known as *névé* (see also below), and *firn* is snow that has lain for more than a year and has become granular ice. A mass of snow sliding down a sleep slope is an *avalanche*, shortened to *avo* or *slide*. *Sastrugi* are small, irregular ridges of snow formed by the wind, which lie parallel to the wind's direction. The *nival zone* on a mountainside is the highest part of a mountain, where snow lies year round.

In search of someone to blame for bad weather, New Zealand trampers and climbers refer to a weather god known as *Hughie* or *Huey*. *Mare's tails*, or high, thin cirrus clouds, are the first indicator of a change in the weather, while *hogsbacks* or *lenticular clouds* are lens-shaped clouds associated often with northwesterly winds; the clouds are the tops of wind waves which indicate high winds. *Crud* is awful weather in general, and *murk* and *whiteouts* are a result of low cloud and very poor visibility. John Pascoe wrote that a blizzard is 'the inside of a duck'.

Glaciers have a complex scientific terminology. The *névé* or accumulation basin is the area at the head of the glacier where snow and ice accumulate. A glacier also has a *trunk*, or *body*, and a *snout* or *terminus*. A *crevasse*, or *slot*, is a crack in the surface of the glacier caused by tension and stretching in the ice. A *bergschrund*, often shortened to *schrund*, is a particular kind of often large crevasse which forms when the névé at the head of the glacier pulls away the steep, rocky headwall.

When a glacier moves over a steep drop it forms a jumbled *icefall*, and irregular ice blocks or pinnacles called *seracs* often form. *Ablation* is the loss of glacial ice by melting and evaporation, and the *equilibrium line* or *end-of-summer line* is where the glacier's annual gains (new snow) and losses (ablation) are equal.

Rocky debris caught up in or on a glacier is *till*, and once it is pushed out to the sides it forms *moraine*, literally stone walls. *Lateral moraines* form alongside the glacier, *medial moraines* form on top of it when another glacier joins the main flow, and the *terminal moraine* is a wall of debris delivered by a glacier that accumulates at the terminus. *Rock flour* is fine silt produced by a glacier as it grinds boulders and bedrock beneath it; it washes out into rivers and lakes downstream of the glacier, and gives them a distinctive milky appearance, like that of Lake Pukaki.

A *moulin* or *kettle hole* is a sinkhole on a glacier's surface down which meltwater and rainwater swirl on their way down to join subterranean watercourses flowing through or beneath the glacier.

Acknowledgements

A high, steep-sided 'armchair' basin scoured out of the mountainside glacial action is a *cirque*, and if it still contains a glacier this is referred to as a *cirque glacier*. A *hanging glacier* perches on a steep mountainside. A *valley glacier* tends to occupy a large valley, and a *compound glacier* like the Tasman Glacier is made of various tributary glaciers which feed into it. A sharp ridge formed between two cirques is an *arête*; Mount Aspiring's steep ridges are classic arêtes, and the peak itself is a glacial *horn* caused by a number of glaciers cutting back to a common point.

Tramping has its own vocabulary; even the word *tramping* is a unique New Zealand word for hiking or bush-walking. A *pit* is a sleeping bag, and a *pit day* is a rest day, often spent in the sleeping bag. A *billy* or *billycan* is used for cooking and boiling water for a *brew*, or hot drink, and *scroggin* or *scrog* is a mix of nuts, dried fruit and chocolate. A *long drop* is a pit toilet, *cairns* are stacks of rocks used for marking routes, and a *fly* is a piece of light nylon cloth that can be suspended between trees to make a shelter from the rain.

I would like to thank the scientists who gave freely of their time and knowledge while I was researching this book, some of whom also graciously cast their expert eyes over finished chapters: Professor Alan Mark, Dr Simon Cox, Dr Trevor Chinn, Brian Patrick, Dr Ian Turnbull and Ian McLellan. I have also drawn heavily on a wide body of published scientific literature, and Professor Dave Kelly and his many colleagues deserve a special mention for their prolific publishing on tussock and beech. I have endeavoured to be as factually accurate as possible, however any mistakes or errors in interpretation remain my responsibility.

This book has benefited from previous work experiences in and around the Alps, and I would like to thank Dr Rod Hay for providing me with an early opportunity to research rock wrens; Mike Meads for time spent searching for alpine giant weta; Dr Colin O'Donnell for the opportunity to survey forest birds in 'Charlie Douglas country' in South Westland; Rod Morris for formative and enjoyable times filming kea; Scott Nicol for a brief exploration of the world of ice on the Dart Glacier; and the staff of Mount Aspiring National Park and Fiordland National Park who opened my eyes to the wonderful worlds of those parks.

I have come to this book enriched by many rambles and tramps in the alps, and a few memorable climbs and ski trips; thanks to the many friends whose company have made those trips such a pleasure, especially Fraser Goldsmith, Garry Nixon, Alicia Warren and Laurence Fearnley. Thanks also to Wiz and the team from Queenstown Rafting who made the Landsborough River rafting trip so much fun.

An enormous thanks to Jo Ogier, whose wonderful art work enhances this book even more than I imagined it might. And a heartfelt tribute to the exceptional publishing team at Random House, whose belief and hard work have helped create a book that is as monumental as the mountains themselves: Jenny Hellen, Sarah Ell and Nic McCloy.

Author's note on other writings

I am not the first person to write about the Southern Alps; I follow in a fine tradition of authors who each have their own distinctive voice. Sadly, there are no written records of early Maori experiences in the mountains; we can only speculate on their physical travels between coasts, and we cannot begin to imagine how they felt. The earliest European explorers and surveyors kept diaries and sent letters which record their experiences, but even so we lack much of a written record from other people around at the time, such as gold-diggers and early shepherds.

Scientists and officials kept meticulous notebooks and records, and began to publish their findings in reports, newspaper articles and books. Early mountaineers were keen to share their successes and failures in print, and the first tourists wrote of their travels with crusading zeal, encouraging others to follow. From the 1930s onwards mountaineer John Pascoe began to write frequent, eloquent books about his own experiences and those of early explorers. Every decade or so the baton of alpine writing and photography has passed to a new bearer, and Philip Temple, Andy Dennis, Craig Potton, Neville Peat, Rob Brown, Shaun Barnett and Pat Barrett have all been part of this group, contributing a wide range of national park handbooks, road guides, tramping books and various photographic books.

There are an ever-increasing number of biographies and autobiographies on people from Haast to Hillary, and Teichelmann to Thomson, and several collections offer a smorgasbord of historic accounts. Graham Langton has a passion for sharing the history of mountaineering, and the *New Zealand Alpine Journal* annually offers a collection of articles about personal climbing experiences. *New Zealand Geographic* magazine provides a steady stream of natural history and history stories relating to the alps.

Classic scientific works such as Hugh Wilson's field guide to the plants of Mount Cook, and *New Zealand Alpine Plants* by Alan Mark and Nancy Adams are both practical guides as well as works of great botanical art. There is a growing number of new photographic identification guides for plants, animals, fungi and more, and popular science books such as Glen Coates' *The Rise and Fall of the Southern Alps* brings up-to-date information out of the pages of scientific journals.

For those who wish to leave their armchair and head for the mountains we can thank the trampers and climbers who have patiently compiled route guides both above and below the snowline; Geoff Spearpoint's and Robin McNeil's latest updates of the venerable Moir's guidebooks offer a lifetime of possibilities for exploration in the alps, and Mark Pickering, Sven Brabyn and others also offer enticing guides to possibilities for adventure in the mountains.

Some people record their mountain impressions and experiences in pictures rather than words, using paintings, prints or photographs to capture and interpret the alpine world, and many of these are held in museums and galleries, as well as private collections. And let us not forget the skills of the mapmakers who create practical works of art that enable us to find and lose ourselves in the wilderness. To all these people, we owe a debt of gratitude, for their records and insights help make our understanding of the mountain world much richer.

Bibliography

Books

Alack, Frank, *Guide Aspiring*, Oswald-Sealy, Auckland, 1962.

Beckett, T. Naylor, *The Mountains of Erewhon*, A.H. & A.W. Reed, Wellington, 1978.

Bishop, Nic, *Natural History of New Zealand*, Hodder & Stoughton, Auckland, 1992.

Brailsford, Barry, *Greenstone Trails: the Maori search for pounamu*, A.H. & A.W. Reed, Wellington, 1984.

Burrows, Colin (ed), *Handbook to the Arthur's Pass National Park*, Arthur's Pass National Park Board, 1974.

Burrows, Colin, *Julius Haast in the Southern Alps*, Canterbury University Press, Christchurch, 2005.

Coates, Glen, *The Rise and Fall of the Southern Alps*, Canterbury University Press, Christchurch, 2002.

Crowe, Andrew, *Which New Zealand Insect?*, Penguin Books, Auckland, 2002.

Cockayne, Leonard, *New Zealand Plants and their Story* (4th edition, ed. E.J. Godley), Government Printer, Wellington, 1967.

Darby, John; Fordyce, R. Ewan; Mark, Alan; Probert, Keith and Townsend, Colin (eds.), *The Natural History of Southern New Zealand*, University of Otago Press, Dunedin, 2003.

Dawson, Bee, *Lady Travellers: the tourists of early New Zealand*, Penguin Books, Auckland, 2001.

Dawson, John and Lucas, Rob, *Nature Guide to the New Zealand Forest*, Godwit, Auckland, 2000.

Dennis, Andy and Potton, Craig, *The Alpine World of Mount Cook National Park*, Cobb/Horwood Publications, Auckland, 1984.

Department of Conservation (author Craig Potton), *From Mountains to Sea: the story of Westland National Park*, Cobb/Harwood Publications, 1990.

Diamond, Judy and Bond, Alan B., Kea, *Bird of Paradox: the evolution and behaviour of a New Zealand parrot*, University of California Press, Berkeley & Los Angeles, 1999.

Dobson, Arthur Dudley, *Reminiscences of Arthur Dudley Dobson, engineer 1841–1930*, Whitcombe & Tombs, Auckland, 1930.

Du Faur, Freda, *The Conquest of Mount Cook and Other Climbs: an account of four seasons' mountaineering on the Southern Alps of New Zealand*, George Allan & Unwin, London (1st edition) 1915; Capper Press edition, Christchurch, 1977.

Ell, Gordon and Ell, Sarah (eds.), *Great Journeys in Old New Zealand: travel and exploration in a new land*, Bush Press, Auckland, 1995.

Gibbs, George, *Ghosts of Gondwana: the history of life in New Zealand*, Craig Potton Publishing, Nelson, 2006.

Green, William Spotswood, *The High Alps of New Zealand: or a trip to the glaciers of the Antipodes with an ascent of Mount Cook*, Macmillan & Co., London, 1883; Capper Press edition, Christchurch, 1976.

Hall-Jones, John, *John Turnbull Thomson: first Surveyor-General of New Zealand*, John McIndoe, Dunedin, 1992.

Heather, Barrie and Robertson, Hugh, *Field Guide to the Birds of New Zealand*, Viking/Penguin, Auckland, 1996.

Holm, Janet, *Caught Mapping: the life and times of New Zealand's early surveyors*, Hazard Press, Christchurch, 2005.

Host, Emily, *Thomas Brunner*, Nikau Press, Nelson, 2006.

Hunter, Grant, *Coast to Coast: who was first?*, Fifth Camp, Christchurch, 2007.

King, Carolyn M. (ed), *The Handbook of New Zealand Mammals*, Oxford University Press, Melbourne, 2007.

Lands & Survey Department (editor Jane Pearson, principal writer Andy Dennis), *The Story of Mount Cook National Park*, Cobb/Horwood Publications, Auckland, 1986.

Langton, Graham, *Mr Explorer Douglas: John Pascoe's New Zealand classic*, Canterbury University Press, Christchurch, 2000.

Langton, Graham, *Armchair Mountaineering: a bibliography of New Zealand mountaineering*, New Zealand Alpine Club, Christchurch, 2006.

Maclean, Chris, *John Pascoe*, Craig Potton Publishing and The Whitcombe Press, 2003.

Mark, Alan and Adams, Nancy, *New Zealand Alpine Plants*, Godwit, Auckland, 1995.

Mannering, George Edward, *With Axe and Rope in the New Zealand Alps*, Longmans Green & Co, London, 1891.

McKerrow, Bob, *Ebenezer Teichelmann: Pioneer New Zealand mountaineer, explorer, surgeon, photographer and conservationist — cutting across continents*, Tara-India Research Press, New Delhi, 2005.

Metcalf, Lawrie, *A Photographic Guide to Alpine Plants of New Zealand*, New Holland, Auckland, 2006.

Molloy, Les and Smith, Roger, *Landforms: the shaping of New Zealand*, Craig Potton Publishing, Nelson, 2002.

Moore, Betty and Langton, Graham, *My Mountain Calls: Jane Thomson and her mountain adventures*, Betty Langton & Graham Langton, Waitati, 1999.

Moreland, A. Maud, *Through South Westland: a journey to the Haast and Mount Aspiring New Zealand*, Witherby & Co., London, 1911.

Nathan, Simon, *Harold Wellman: a man who moved New Zealand*, Victoria University Press, Wellington, 2005.

Nelson Lakes National Park (author Craig Potton), *The Story of Nelson Lakes National Park*, Department of Lands and Survey & Cobb/Horwood Publications, 1984.

Ogden, John; Stewart, Glenn and Allen, Robert, 'Ecology of New Zealand Nothofagus Forests' in Veblen, Thomas et al (eds.), *The Ecology and Biogeography of Nothofagus Forests*, Yale University Press, New Haven & London, 1996.

Parkinson, Brian, *New Zealand Alpine Flora and Fauna*, Reed Publishing, Auckland, 2001.

Pascoe, John, *Unclimbed New Zealand: alpine travel in the Canterbury and Westland Ranges, Southern Alps*, George Allan & Unwin Ltd, London, 1939.

Pascoe, John, 'The Mountains of New Zealand' in *The Mountain World 1968/9*, George Allen & Unwin Ltd, London & Rand McNally & Co, Chicago, 1970.

Pascoe, John, *Exploration New Zealand*, A.H. & A.W. Reed, Wellington, 1971.

Peat, Neville, *Land Aspiring: the story of Mount Aspiring National Park*, Craig Potton Publishing, Nelson, 1994.

Peat, Neville and Patrick, Brian, *Wild Rivers: discovering the natural history of the central South Island*, University of Otago Press, Dunedin, 2001.

Pickering, Mark, *A Tramper's Journey: stories from the back country of New Zealand*, Craig Potton Publishing, Nelson, 2004.

Bibliography

Articles

Potton, Craig, *The Southern Alps*, Craig Potton Publishing, Nelson, 2005.

Powell, Paul, *Men Aspiring*, A.H & A.W. Reed, Wellington, 1967.

Ralph, David, *From Tussocks to Tourists: the story of the central Canterbury High Country*, Canterbury University Press, Christchurch, 2007.

Ridley, Geoff and Horne, Don, *A Photographic Guide to Mushrooms and Other Fungi of New Zealand*, New Holland, Auckland, 2006.

Temple, Philip, *Mantle of the Skies: the Southern Alps of New Zealand*, Whitcombe & Tombs, Christchurch, 1971.

Temple, Philip, *New Zealand Explorers: great journeys of discovery*, Whitcoulls Publishers, Christchurch, 1985.

Tennyson, Alan and Martinson, Paul, *Extinct Birds of New Zealand*, Te Papa Press, Wellington, 2006.

Turner, Samuel, *The Conquest of the New Zealand Alps*, Fisher Unwin Ltd, London, 1922.

Vance, William, *High Endeavour: the story of the Mackenzie Country*, A.H & A.W. Reed, Wellington, 1980 (revised edition).

Wardle, John, *The New Zealand Beeches: ecology, utilisation and management*, New Zealand Forest Service, 1984.

Wilson, Hugh, *Wild Plants of Mount Cook National Park*, Whitcoulls Ltd, Christchurch, 1978.

Wilson, Jim, *Aorangi: the story of Mount Cook*, Whitcombe & Tombs, Christchurch, 1968.

New Zealand Geographic magazine publishes many articles on New Zealand's weather, explorers, and places and species related to the mountains.

New Zealand Wilderness magazine publishes articles on tramping and outdoor activities in New Zealand, including many that touch on the Southern Alps. Various issues between 2000 and 2003 contained a series of historical biographies of explorers and mountaineers by Graham Langton.

New Zealand Alpine Journal is published annually, and *The Climber* four times a year by the New Zealand Alpine Club; it contains many articles on climbing and issues related to the Southern Alps.

Bibliography

Selected scientific papers

Chinn, T.J., 'New Zealand glacier responses to climate change of the past century', *New Zealand Journal of Geology and Geophysics*, 39: 415–28, 1996.

Craw, Dave, 'A river runs through it: river capture in South Island alpine valleys', *New Zealand Alpine Journal*, 56: 118–21, 2004.

Fitzharris, Blair; Lawson, Wendy and Owens, Ian, 'Research on glaciers and snow in New Zealand', *Progress in Physical Geography* 23(4): 469–500, 1999.

Fitzsimons, S.J. and Veit, H., 'Geology and Geomorphology of the European Alps and the Southern Alps of New Zealand – a comparison', *Mountain Research and Development*, 21(4): 340–9.

Heath, S., 'Rock wrens in the Southern Alps of New Zealand', in *Flora and Fauna of Alpine Australasia: ages and origins* ed. Barlow, B.A., CSIRO, Melbourne, 277–88, 1986.

Henderson, R.D., 'The Southern Alps Experiment: or why is the West Coast as wet as the West Coast is?', *New Zealand Alpine Journal*, 106–9, 1998.

Henderson, R.D., Extreme rainfalls in the Southern Alps of New Zealand', *Journal of Hydrology (NZ)* 38(2): 309–30, 1999.

Hochstein, M.P.; Claridge, D.; Henrys, S.A.; Pyne, A.; Nobes, D.C. and Leary, S.F., 'Downwasting of the Tasman Glacier, South Island, New Zealand: changes in the terminus region between 1971 and 1993', *New Zealand Journal of Geology and Geophysics*, 38: 1–16, 1995.

Kelly, Dave; Harrison, A.L.; Lee, W.G.; Payton, I.J.; Wilson, P. R. and Schauber, E.M., 'Predator satiation and extreme mast seeding in 11 species of *Chionochloa* (Poaceae)', Oikos 90: 477–88, 2000.

Kirkbride, M.P., 'Relationships between temperature and ablation on the Tasman Glacier, Mount Cook National Park, New Zealand', *New Zealand Journal of Geology and Geophysics*, 38: 17–27, 1995.

Kirkbride, M.P., 'Ice flow vectors on the debris-mantled Tasman Glacier, 1957–1986', *Geografisika Annaler* 77A, 147–57, 1995.

Mark, A.F., 'The environment and growth rate of narrow-leaved snow tussock, *Chionochloa rigida*, in Otago', *New Zealand Journal of Botany*, 3: 73–103, 1965.

Mark, A.F., 'Flowering, seeding, and seedling establishment of narrow-leaved snow tussock, *Chionchloa rigida*', *New Zealand Journal of Botany*, 3: 180–95, 1965.

Mark, A.F., Indigenous grasslands of New Zealand' in *'Ecosystems of the World 8B Natural Grasslands – Eastern Hemisphere and résumé*' ed. R.T. Coupland, Elsevier, 361–410, 1993.

Mark, A.F. and Dickinson, K.J.M., 'New Zealand Alpine Ecosystems' in *'Ecosystems of the World 3 Polar and Alpine Tundra*' ed. F.E. Wielgolaski, Elsevier, 311–45, 1997.

Mark, A.F.; Dickinson, K.J.M. and Hofstede R.G.M., 'Alpine vegetation, plant distribution, life forms and environments in a perhumid New Zealand region: oceanic and tropical high mountain affinities', *Arctic, Antarctic and Alpine Research* 32(3): 240–54, 2000.

McKone, M.J.; Kelly, D.; Harrison, A.L.; Sullivan, J.J. and Cone, A.J., 'Biology of insects that feed in the inflorescences of *Chionochloa* (Poaceae) in New Zealand and their relevance to mast seeding', *New Zealand Journal of Zoology*, 28:89–101, 2001.

Morales, C.F.; Hill, M.G. and Walker, A.K., 'Life history of the sooty beech scale (*Ultracoelostoma assimile*) (Maskell), (Hemiptera: Margarodidae) in New

Bibliography

Websites

Zealand *Nothofagus* forests', *New Zealand Entomologist* 11: 24–37, 1988.

Pawson, E. and Hans-Rudolf E., 'History and (Re)discovery of the European and New Zealand Alps until 1900', *Mountain Research and Development*, 21(4): 350–58, 2001.

Rees, Mark; Kelly, Dave and Bjørnstad, Ottar N., 'Snow Tussocks, Chaos, and the Evolution of Mast Seeding', *The American Naturalist*, 160(1): 44–59, July 2002.

Sturman, A. and Wanner, H., 'A comparative review of the weather and climate of the Southern Alps of New Zealand and the European Alps', *Mountain Research and Development*, 21(4): 359–69.

Thomas, W.H and Broady, P.A., 'Distribution of coloured snow and associated algal genera in New Zealand', *New Zealand Journal of Botany*, 35: 113–7, 1997.

Tisch, Phillip A. and Kelly, Dave, 'Can wind pollination provide a selective benefit to mast seeding in *Chionochloa macra* (Poaceae) at Mt Hutt, New Zealand?', *New Zealand Journal of Botany*, 36: 637–43, 1998.

Winkworth, R.C.; Wagstaff, S.J.; Glenny, D. and Lockhart P.J., 'Evolution of the New Zealand mountain flora: Origins, diversification and dispersal', *Organisms, Diversity & Evolution*, 5: 237–47, 2005.

New Zealand Dictionary of Biography www.dnzb.govt.nz
New Zealand History Online www.nzhistory.net.nz
Te Ara Encyclopaedia of New Zealand www.teara.govt.nz
Department of Conservation www.doc.govt.nz

Image credits

Alexander Turnbull Library
4–5 (A.E. Birch Collection), 43, 74, 77, 79, 80–1, 84–85, 88–89, 113 (A.E. Birch Collection), 122–3, 136, 139 (Making New Zealand Collection), 140–1 (Joseph Kinsey Collection), 143 (Burton Bros Collection), 144 (John Pascoe Collection), 147, 149 (Joseph Kinsey Collection), 150 (Joseph Kinsey Collection), 153 (Joseph Kinsey Collection), 154 (Michael Collett Collection), 193, 200, 203, 204, 207, 208 (Mildred Mueller Collection), 210, 212, 215, 217, 250 (A.E. Birch Collection), 253, 254 (Joseph Kinsey Collection), 255 (A.E. Birch Collection), 256 (A.C. Gifford Collection), 257 (Joseph Kinsey Collection), 259 (A.C. Gifford Collection), 260 (Michael Collett Collection), 261 (Leslie Hinge Collection), 262 (courtesy of The Hermitage Hotel), 263, 264, 267 (H Brusewitz Collection), 268 (Joseph Kinsey Collection)

Trevor Chinn
70

Arno Gasteiger
3, 8–9, 10, 13, 19, 20–1, 26–7, 37, 44, 52, 65, 90, 101, 116–7, 121, 124, 126–7, 134–5, 156, 159, 170–1, 198–9, 218, 224, 246–7, 270, 276, 284–5

Hedgehog House
39 (Jim Harding), 51 (Ian Whitehouse), 57 (Pascal Niklaus), 58 (Colin Monteath), 73 (Peter Morath), 97 (Dave MacLeod), 103 (Colin Monteath), 107 (Pete Taw), 119 (Auscape, Tui De Roy), 132 (Colin Monteath), 165 (Colin Monteath), 166 (Nick Groves), 195 (Gordon Roberts)

Jo Ogier
1, 22, 28, 42, 94, 98, 108, 133, 142, 173, 191, 212, 238, 269, 280

Rod Morris
40, 47, 63, 163, 175t, 175b, 177t, 177b, 178 all, 181, 182t, 182b, 187, 189, 190, 196, 233, 235, 237, 241, 273, 275, 278, 281, 282, 290, 292, 294, 297

NASA
25 (Jacques Descloitres, MODIS Land Rapid Response Team, NASA/GSFC)

Natural Sciences Image Library
31 (Harley Betts), 34 (G.R. 'Dick' Roberts), 67 (G.R. 'Dick' Roberts), 68l (Landcare Research), 68r (Pauline Syrett), 93 (G.R. 'Dick' Roberts), 104 (G.R. 'Dick' Roberts), 169 (Harley Betts), 172 (Pauline Syrett), 184 (Peter E. Smith), 194 (Peter E. Smith), 221 (Harley Betts), 223 (Peter E. Smith), 227 (Peter E. Smith), 231 (Peter E. Smith), 239 (Angus McIntosh), 243 (Peter E. Smith), 245 (G.R. 'Dick' Roberts), 287 (Landcare Research)

Rob Suisted/Nature's Pic Images
16, 33, 48, 55, 110–1, 129, 131, 161, 196, 229, 248, 289

Index

Page numbers in **bold** indicate illustrations.